*The Mailbox*® 1999–2000 Kindergarten Yearbook

Founding Editor in Chief: Margaret Michel
Senior Editor: Angie Kutzer
Associate Editor: Michele M. Dare
Executive Director, Magazine Publishing: Katharine P. S. Brower
Editorial Administrative Director: Stephen Levy
Curriculum Director: Karen P. Shelton
Contributing Editors: Cindy K. Daoust, Sherri Lynn Kuntz, Michele M. Stoffel Menzel, Jan Trautman, Allison E. Ward
Copy Editors: Karen Brewer Grossman,  Karen L. Huffman, Tracy Johnson, Debbie Shoffner, Gina Sutphin
Staff Artists: Pam Crane, Nick Greenwood, Rebecca Saunders (SENIOR ARTISTS); Cathy Spangler Bruce, Theresa Lewis Goode, Clevell Harris, Susan Hodnett, Sheila Krill, Rob Mayworth, Kimberly Richard, Greg D. Rieves, Barry Slate, Donna K. Teal
Cover Artist: Lois Axeman
Typesetters: Lynette Maxwell, Mark Rainey
Editorial Assistants: Terrie Head, Melissa B. Montanez, Karen White, Jan E. Witcher
Educational Consultant: Nancy Johnson
Library: Dorothy C. McKinney (ASSISTANT)

ISBN 1-56234-379-3
ISSN 1088-5552

The Education Center, Inc.
P.O. Box 9753
Greensboro, NC 27429-0753

Look for *The Mailbox*® 2000–2001 Kindergarten Yearbook in the summer of 2001. The Education Center, Inc., is the publisher of *The Mailbox*®, *Teacher's Helper*®, *The Mailbox*® BOOKBAG®, and *Learning*® magazines, as well as other fine products. Look for these wherever quality teacher materials are sold, or call 1-800-714-7991.

# Contents

**Thematic Units/Specials (cont.)**

# BULLETIN BOARDS & DISPLAYS

# Bulletin Boards & Displays.......................

It's time to shape up for kindergarten! In advance, use construction paper cutouts to title a board as shown. Then cut out a supply of simple paper dolls from skin tones of construction paper. Also cut out a large, colorful geometric shape for each child. Have each child choose a paper doll and a shape. Write (or have him write) his name on the shape; then invite him to use art supplies to decorate the paper doll to resemble himself. Help each child mount his completed doll and shape on the board. During a group time, have each child use a pointer to show the class his name and his project. Then encourage the whole class to say the name of that shape together.

Holly Schlobohm—Gr. K, Westfield "Y" Children's Center, Westfield, NJ

Teamwork is the secret ingredient that creates *and* solves this puzzle! To prepare, cut a large sheet of white poster board into as many pieces as you have children. Label each piece with the name of a different student. Then give each child her piece of the puzzle and invite her to decorate it as she likes. Ask each child to place her decorated piece on a large, flat surface in your puzzle center. During center times, encourage children to put the puzzle together—once, twice, or many times! Then mount the completed puzzle on a poster board frame.

Becky Krapf—Gr. K
Richard Mann Elementary School
Walworth, NY

# Jack-o'-Lantern, Jack-o'-Lantern, You Are Such a Pretty Sight!

Light the Halloween mood in your classroom with this glowing display. Mount a string of holiday lights on a board. Then invite each child to use art supplies to create a jack-o'-lantern, instructing her to cut out a place for her jack-o'-lantern's nose. Then display each project on the board, poking a lightbulb through the nose. Add a title and some construction paper leaves; then set your room aglow!

Kari Murray—Gr. K, Lincoln School, West Allis, WI

# Turkey Dressing

These tricky turkeys will tickle your students' imaginations! For each child, duplicate the turkey pattern (page 14) on tagboard. Have each child team up with his family (at home) to disguise his turkey in hopes of avoiding the turkey's Thanksgiving Day demise. Display each completed turkey; then invite children to guess the identity of each turkey-disguise designer.

Lisa Lucas—Gr. K
Saints Peter and Paul School
Garfield Heights, OH

# We're Falling For You!

Your classroom will glisten and glimmer with this unique fall tree. To begin, ask children to paint or color a large supply of cardboard tubes brown. Arrange the tubes on a wall to resemble a tree. Title the display as shown. Then invite each child to paint a sheet of paper with colored glitter glue. When the glue is dry, have her cut out a large leaf shape from the paper. Then use a permanent marker to write her name on the leaf. Tape the glittery leaves to the tree for a sparkling fall display! (Tip: Be sure to clean your paintbrushes well after this activity!)

Sheila Crawford—Five-Year-Olds
Kids Kampus
Huntington, IN

Judi Lesnansky
New Hope Academy
Youngstown, OH

Santa Claus is coming to town *and to your classroom!* First determine the width that you'd like your display to be. Then cut two sheets of red bulletin board paper accordingly. Also cut an equal length of tan and white bulletin board paper. Trim a scalloped border around the white sheet to resemble Santa's beard. Glue the beard to the bottom of the tan sheet (the face). Then trim one of the red sheets to resemble Santa's hat. Glue the hat to the top of the face. Use construction paper scraps, along with cotton balls or fiberfill, to create details for Santa's hat and face. Finally, glue the remaining red sheet of paper below the beard to resemble Santa's body. If desired, add black construction paper legs to complete this jolly old elf. Display your students' holiday-related work on Santa's spacious belly.

Michelle Wilson—Gr. K
Park Springs Elementary School
Coral Springs, FL

Ride on in to a happy new year! Cut out a large bus from yellow paper. Mount the bus on a wall; then use construction paper, paint, and aluminum foil to add details to the bus. Have each child decorate a construction paper cutout to resemble himself. Mount these projects in the windows of the bus. Top off the display with hand cutouts, party hats and horns, streamers, and a title.

Pam Ingram and Sandy
   Ingram—Gr. K
Davenport School
Lenoir, NC

What a wonderful winter scene! Mount several tree and post cutouts on a background as shown. Use colored paper to decorate milk cartons to resemble birdhouses. Then glue a birdhouse to the top of each post. Accent the scene with tufts of cotton, real popcorn strings, and colorful ring-shaped cereal. Invite each child to use craft supplies to create a bird to add to the scene. Winter is here!

Pam Ingram and Sandy Ingram—Gr. K

H-e-e-e-re's February—from *A* to *Z!* To get started, take a look at the quilt-block suggestions below (and substitute your own ideas as desired). Then have each child use a variety of art supplies to create a different block of this phonetic February display. If you have fewer than 26 children in your class, ask for volunteers to work on more than one block. Finish off the quilt with a signature block, signed by each child who contributed to the project. From hearts to history, it's fabulous February!

A – America
B – Black History Month
C – chocolates
D – dental health
E – eagle
F – father of our country
G – Groundhog Day
H – Honest Abe
I – I love you!
J – just 28 days
K – key to my heart
L – log cabin
M – mittens
N – north wind blowing

O – Old Glory
P – penny
Q – quarter
R – roses
S – Statue of Liberty
T – tell the truth
U – U.S. mail
V – valentine
W – White House
X – "X-tra" candy
Y – Yes, I'll be your valentine!
Z – ZOOM! goes February, the short month!

Taryn Way—Gr. K
Los Molinos Elementary School
Los Molinos, CA

# Friendship Makes the World Go Round!

Sara is a gud sengr.

Jamie shrz.

Edie is chrful.

Ben is nice.

I like Patrick.

Mark is a good helper.

Tal is fast at runen.

Josh is a good redr.

Elizabeth is gud at sokr.

Pam is rely good at art.

Bo is good at math.

Jeff is a gd hlpr.

To create this display, post a construction paper earth and the title. Have each child craft a person from skin-toned construction paper. Mount all the craft people around the earth. From a basket of class names, have each child choose a classmate's name. Ask each child to write one good trait about the person he chose. Then have him cut out and glue his writing to a heart cutout. Mount the hearts around the earth.

adapted from an idea by Traci Schaffert, Hillcrest School, Morristown, NJ

Let's go fly a kite! In advance, take a photo of each child posing as if she were flying a kite. Mount each photo on a background as shown. Invite each child to use art supplies to create a colorful kite. Then help her staple a length of yarn to the back of the kite. Glue the loose end of the yarn to the child's photo; then staple the kite to the board. Whoosh—off it goes!

Leah Taylor—Gr. K, Maranatha Chapel, San Diego, CA

Have students brainstorm different springtime animals—such as birds, lambs, or frogs—and then name something each of the animals might see in spring. (For example, a frog might see a lily pad.) Invite each child to make a springtime animal and its corresponding object. Then arrange the animals and objects on a display along with captions similar to the ones shown. It sure looks a lot like spring!

Felice Kestenbaum—Gr. K, Goosehill Primary, Cold Spring Harbor, NY

To create this display, cover the bottom half of a blue background with white paper. Sponge-paint the white paper brown to resemble dirt; then use your finger to draw worm tunnels in the wet paint. Mount paper grass above the dirt. Have each child make a worm by sliding Cheerios® onto a pipe cleaner, then bending each end to hold the cereal in place. Mount the worms on the board and add cutout butterflies and flowers as desired.

Pam Ingram & Sandy Ingram—Gr. K, Davenport School, Lenoir, NC

Are you one of those teachers who just can't resist that Kodak® moment? Here's a display idea for all those precious photos. Cut off a sheet of bulletin board paper sized to fit a board. Invite children to paint the bottoms of each other's feet and then walk on the paper. When the paint is dry, cover the board with the decorated paper, add a title, and mount the photos as desired. Ah, memories!

AnnaLisa R. Damminger—Gr. K
Mullica Hill, NJ

Teachers and students alike chill out with this end-of-the-year display. Post a large Popsicle® cutout (divided into small sections) on a wall or board; then add the title. At the end of each day, invite children to discuss ways that they noticed their classmates being cool. Perhaps one student helped another. Or maybe a certain child was particularly patient in a difficult circumstance. After a child shares, invite the "cool" child to color in one section of the Popsicle. When the whole Popsicle is colored in, have *real* Popsicles for everyone!

Judi Lesnansky
New Hope Academy
Youngstown, OH

# Turkey Pattern
Use with the bulletin board on page 7.

# ARTS & CRAFTS FOR LITTLE HANDS

## Shapely Clowns

Bring in these clowns to reinforce shapes and body parts! Put your children's silly clown creations on a bulletin board parade; then encourage each child to identify the clowns' shapes and body parts. It's the greatest display on earth!

**You will need:**

a class supply of white construction paper
a variety of large colorful sheets of construction paper
one 11" circle tracer
large basic shape tracers
scissors
glue
yarn
bingo markers
assorted markers
1 craft knife (for adult use only)
1 small inflated balloon per child (optional)
masking tape (if the balloon is used)

**Teacher preparation for each child:**

1. Trace and cut out an 11-inch, white construction paper circle.
2. Trace a large basic shape on colorful construction paper.
   (If abilities permit, have your students do these steps for themselves.)

To make a clown, give a child a white construction paper circle for the clown's head. Then invite him to cut out a large (pretraced) shape and glue it to his clown's head to resemble a funny body. Next, help him trace his hands and feet onto colorful construction paper, cut them out, and then glue them to the clown's body. Finally, encourage the child to use the art supplies to create facial features and a hat, and to decorate his clown's costume. If you'd like to add a balloon nose, use the craft knife to cut a small X in the center of the nose area. Insert the knotted end of a small inflated balloon; then tape it to the back of the clown's head. Start clowning around!

Carolyn Schroeder and Mary Jones—Gr. K
South Terrace Elementary, Carlton, MN

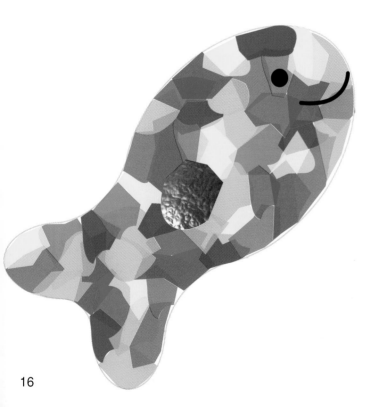

## Shimmering Sharing

These colorful reminders about the importance of sharing are a real catch for your classroom windows! In advance, use an enlarged copy of the fish pattern on page 32 to make several tagboard tracers. Then read aloud *The Rainbow Fish* by Marcus Pfister (North-South Books Inc.), a uniquely illustrated book about friendship and sharing. Afterward, invite each child to trace a fish pattern onto clear Con-Tact® covering and then cut it out. Instruct the child to remove (and discard) the paper backing. Then have her press a small piece of aluminum foil onto her fish to resemble a shiny scale. Next, have each child tear a piece of colorful tissue paper to resemble fish scales. Then encourage the child to share her tissue paper scales with other students, and vice versa, so that everyone has a variety of colors. Then have the child arrange her colorful collection of scales on her fish until it is completely covered. Have the child use a permanent marker to draw an eye and mouth on her fish. Use clear tape to mount these fish onto your classroom windows for shimmering sharing reminders.

Teresa Shankle, Hospitots Preschool, Johnson City, TN

16

## Fingerpainted Football Jerseys

Touchdown! These child-made jerseys are sure to score big with your students! For each child, cut out a large football jersey shape from fingerpaint paper. Then use masking tape to spell each child's first or last name on a different jersey. Also tape a number of the child's choice to the jersey. To complete her jersey, have a child fingerpaint her cutout completely, covering the tape too. When the paint is dry, help each child carefully peel off the tape to reveal her name and jersey number. A winning lineup of these personalized jerseys boosts kindergarten spirit!

Angelina Vargo—Gr. K
Hansel and Gretel Early Learning Center
Harrisburg, PA

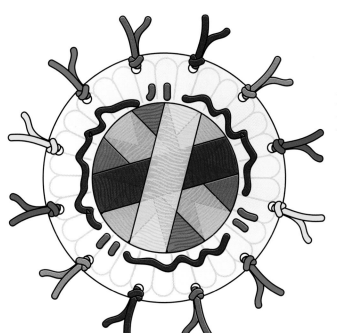

## Fiesta Favors

These colorful crafts add festive flair to your celebrations for National Hispanic Heritage Month (September 15–October 15). To make one, first cut out the center of a nine-inch paper plate. Repeat with a second plate; then discard the cutouts. Cut several different colors of crepe paper streamers into 7 1/2-inch lengths. On the front of one plate, squeeze a thin line of glue along the rim, then crisscross the streamers over the opening until it is completely covered. Glue the back of the second plate on top of the first one to frame the streamers. When the glue is dry, use markers to decorate the rim. Punch holes around the rim; then loop short lengths of colorful yarn through each hole. Wave these festive favors in a parade or classroom celebration. Olé!

Mary E. Maurer, Children's Corner Daycare, Durant, OK

## A Burst of Balloons

Add a bunch of color to your classroom with these pretty projects! To prepare, cut a balloon shape from copy paper for each child. Tape aluminum foil to the edges of a warming tray; then set the tray on low heat. When the tray has warmed, place a balloon cutout on the tray. For padding, layer newspaper on either side of the balloon. With adult supervision, invite a child to color the balloon cutout, pressing down heavily. When the crayon wax has melted, remove the balloon and let it cool on a flat surface. To complete the balloon, tape a string to the back of it. Mount these colorful balloons in a bunch that bursts with a welcome display of eye-catching color.

adapted from an idea by Maribeth Foster
Head Start
Longview, WA

### Pizza Pizzazz

Did you know that October is National Pizza Month? Well, it is! So spice up your art activities with this personal pizza project. In advance, cut out a cardboard or tagboard pizza slice for each child. To make one slice of pizza, paint red pizza "sauce" on the slice. While the paint is still wet, sprinkle on dried oregano, and then lightly press on shredded tissue paper to resemble cheese. When the paint is dry, glue on your choice of creative toppings (see the illustration for ideas). If desired, glue each personal pizza piece onto a different paper plate. Then display all the plates on a red-and-white checked background titled "Pizza Pizzazz!" Mmmm—it's positively pizza!

Janeen Danielsen
Dike Discovery Center, Dike, IA

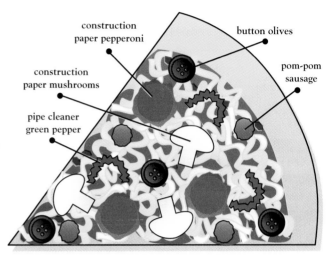

construction paper pepperoni
button olives
construction paper mushrooms
pom-pom sausage
pipe cleaner green pepper

### The Cornfield Crew

Scare up a field of creativity with these cute cornfield characters! In advance, gather a large supply of fabric scraps. Also collect a paper towel tube and a paper lunch bag for each child. To make one scarecrow, stuff the bag with crumpled newspaper; then tie the top closed. Using markers, draw facial features on the bag. Next, cut out scarecrow clothing from the fabric scraps and glue them onto the paper towel tube. (If desired, make simple tracers for children to use to make the scarecrow clothing.) Then use craft glue to attach the bag as shown. Use assorted art supplies—such as buttons, bandanas, raffia, and construction paper—to add the desired finishing touches. These scarecrow creations look right at home mounted among a field of construction paper cornstalks.

Sheila Crawford—Five-Year-Olds
Kids Kampus, Huntington, IN

### Patch o' Pumpkins

Perch a puffy pumpkin in the pumpkin patch! To make one, trace and cut out two same-sized pumpkins from sturdy art paper. Sponge-paint one side of one pumpkin with orange paint. (If abilities permit, provide red and yellow paint and have youngsters mix the colors together to create many different shades of orange to use in their work.) Arrange crumpled tissue paper, newspaper, or plastic grocery bags on the unpainted pumpkin. Then position the painted one over the crumpled material and staple or glue the edges together. Next glue on a construction paper stem and a large green pumpkin leaf. Then spiral-cut a green circle to resemble a vine and glue it to the back of the pumpkin. Perch these pretty pumpkins in your classroom patch. Just perfect!

Lori Hamernik—Gr. K
Prairie Farm Elementary, Prairie Farm, WI

## Nighttime Neighbors

'Tis the season for these nightly neighbors to grace the rafters of your classroom! In advance, photocopy the wing patterns (page 28) onto tagboard; then cut them out to make tracers. To make one bat project, glue two 2" pom-poms to the center of a 9" tagboard moon. Then trace two wing patterns onto construction paper and cut them out. Fold each wing (as shown); then glue just the inside part of each wing next to the body. Add the finishing features by gluing on construction paper ears, two wiggly eyes, and two pipe cleaner legs. Display these beautiful bats high along a classroom wall or hallway.

Sheila Neupauer—Gr. K, Ellwood City Children's Center, Ellwood City, PA

Fold here.

## Holiday Magnets

Patterning practice adds the decorative flair to these versatile holiday magnets. To make one, paint one side of a large craft stick. When the paint is dry, create a festive pattern by arranging plastic confetti pieces. Glue each piece of the pattern onto the craft stick. Then attach a length of magnetic tape to the back of the stick. These magnets make great little gifts or seasonal decorations.

Lori Marie Turk—Pre-K and Gr. K
Most Precious Blood School, Walden, NY

## An Elegant Table

These pretty place settings serve up big helpings of left and right practice as well as patterning and creativity. In advance, cut a large supply of colorful, one-inch construction paper squares. To make a placemat, glue a pattern of colored squares around the perimeter of a large sheet of construction paper. Next draw or paint your favorite holiday foods on a white paper plate. Glue the plate to the center of the placemat. Fold and staple a napkin on the left side of the plate. Finally, glue a paper or plastic knife and spoon on the right side of the plate, and a fork on the left. Display each child's project on a board titled "A Holiday Table for [number of students in your class]."

Karen Saner—Grs. K–1
Burns Elementary, Burns, KS

### Knock, Knock

Who's there? A festive, child-made doorknob hanger that's just right for holiday gift giving.

**You will need:**
one 14" length of wide ribbon for each child
one 14" length of narrow ribbon for each child
dried apple slices
cinnamon sticks
pre-tied (if necessary) red, green, and white bows
scissors
craft glue

To make a doorknob hanger, cut an upside-down *V* out of one end of the wide ribbon. To make a hanging loop, fold the straight end of that ribbon over the narrow ribbon as shown. Then glue the wide ribbon in place. Next arrange and glue on apple slices, cinnamon sticks, and bows. When the glue is dry, encourage youngsters to choose recipients for their beautiful banners.

Anne M. Cromwell-Gapp—Gr. K
Connecticut Valley Child Care Center
Claremont, NH

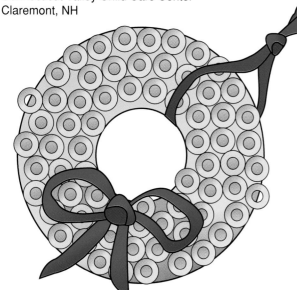

### Cheery Cheerios®!

Check out these cheerful child-made Cheerios® wreaths! Give each child a tagboard wreath cutout. Then have her glue Cheerios to the front and back of her wreath. When the glue is dry, invite each child to paint her wreath to reflect the holiday or occasion she desires. (For example, a child might paint her wreath blue and gold to celebrate Hanukkah; red and green for Christmas; or even your school colors to celebrate school spirit.) When the paint is dry, use craft glue to attach a pre-tied bow. Then tie a length of colorful yarn through the middle hole to make a hanger. Invite your youngsters to use their wreaths to deck the halls and walls of your school.

Lori E. Walter—Gr. K, Roosevelt School, Lodi, NJ

### What's Your Name, Deer?

Hang onto this versatile reindeer necklace idea! You can adapt it to make holiday nametags, magnets, ornaments, and more! To make a necklace, have a child use a fine-tipped marker to write his name and draw a reindeer face—minus the nose—on a wooden craft spoon. Then instruct him to lay the handle of the spoon across the middle of a pipe cleaner (as shown). Have him bend the pipe cleaner around the spoon to create the beginnings of antlers. Next have him cut a pipe cleaner in half and twist those short pieces onto the antlers. Then instruct each child to glue on a pom-pom nose. Finally, help each child hot-glue the middle of a gold cord length to the back of the spoon.

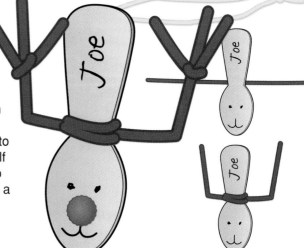

Joe Appleton—Gr. K, Hillandale School, Durham, NC

## Marvelous Mazao

*Habari gani?* (What's the news?) *Umoja!* (Unity!) If you're celebrating this first principle of Kwanzaa, try your hands at making a *mazao*—a straw basket of fruit—which is the traditional symbol for this principle. To begin, cut out a basket shape from butcher paper. If desired, use a marker to add details to the basket; then glue it to a construction paper background. Next use a variety of halved and whole fruits and vegetables and colorful paints to make prints on a sheet of art paper. When the paint is dry, cut out each print and glue it "in" the straw basket. Display each child's marvelous mazao during the seven days of Kwanzaa.

adapted from an idea by Carmen Carpenter
Highland Preschool
Raleigh, NC

## Blowing in the Wind

Perk up those wintry windy days with these snowman windsocks. For each child, duplicate the snowman pattern (page 29) on white construction paper. Provide craft glue and a variety of craft supplies, such as fabric scraps, buttons, pipe cleaners, and crayons. To make a snowman windsock, cut out the pattern. Use the craft supplies to decorate the middle of the white portion to resemble a snowman. After the glue dries, cut along the white dotted lines on the pattern. (Do not cut past the dotted lines!) Then form the snowman's hat and body into a cylinder and staple it closed. Gently pull out the cut sections to resemble the brim of the snowman's hat. Add desired details such as a fabric scarf and pipe cleaner arms (poked in). Glue crepe paper streamers to the bottom of the snowman. Finally, make a hanger by punching a hole in each side of the hat and attaching a length of yarn. Display these wintry little fellows where they might catch a current of air every now and then.

Sharon Johnson—Gr. K, Guardino Elementary, Clayton, NY

## It's a Whiteout!

Your children will have creative fun designing their own versions of this project! In advance, photocopy the polar bear pattern on page 28. Then use the pattern to make stencils, tracers, and sponge cutouts. (If available, you could also use bear-shaped cookie cutters.) Provide wiggle eyes, black markers, and a supply of white craft items, such as paint, doily scraps, beads, buttons, sequins, and packing pieces. Give each child a sheet of blue construction paper. Then invite her to use the supplies to create an all-white blizzard scene. (Instruct her to leave a little space on the bottom of her paper.) Then, when the scene is dry, have each child write about her scene on the bottom of the page. Why, couldn't you tell? It's a skating polar bear eating popcorn in a snowstorm!

adapted from an idea by Rita Beiswenger
Crescent Avenue Weekday School
Fort Wayne, IN

# Arts & Crafts
## for Little Hands

### Heart Art

Roll out your art cart and get ready to make these wonderful works of "heart"! In advance, make a heart frame by cutting out a heart shape from a 9" x 9" construction paper square. Set the frame aside. Next pour a nickel-sized dollop of clear corn syrup near each corner of a 9" x 9" tagboard square. Choose a color or two of food coloring; then add a few drops to the corn syrup. Fingerpaint with the colored corn syrup until the tagboard is covered with a *very thin* layer of syrup. While the syrup is still wet, position the frame on top of it. If desired, sprinkle the wet syrup with glitter, sequins, or other small craft items. When the syrup is *completely* dry, display these lovely masterpieces with the title "Art From the Heart."

Tip: Save the heart cutouts (from the frame) to use for other art projects, seasonal manipulatives, or notepaper.

Lola M. Smith, Hilliard, OH

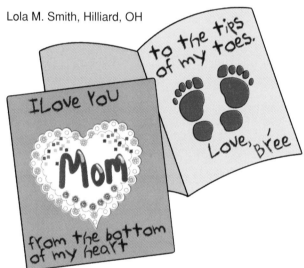

### All My Love!

Whether it's for Valentine's Day or just any ol' day, this card gets right down to the heart *and toes* of the matter! To create one card, fold a large sheet of construction paper in half. Then open the card and make a set of footprints on the right side. While the footprint paint is drying, decorate a doily heart with art supplies, such as glitter, puffy paint, and sequins. Label the heart with the recipient's name; then glue it to the front center of the card. Finish by writing the greeting (as shown) on the card. There—ready for a *very* special delivery!

Cheri Beckwith—Eagle River, AK

### Top o' the Rainbow

Along with March comes leprechauns, rainbows, and shamrocks! So blend these seasonal symbols to create a collection of eye-catching windsocks. To make a windsock, enlarge the hat pattern (page 31) 150 percent and then photocopy it two times onto green construction paper. Cut out the hats and decorate them as desired. Then apply glue just around the side edges of the back of one hat. Press the hats together, leaving the top and bottom edges unglued. When the glue is dry, bend a 3" x 10" strip of tagboard to form a cylinder and then staple it together. Gently slide the cylinder into the hat, creating a rounded, 3-D look. Next glue each of six colorful streamers to the inside bottom of the hat. Attach a shamrock cutout to the bottom of each streamer. Punch a hole in each side of the top of the hat; then tie a length of yarn to the holes. Suspend these windy wonders in an area of your classroom that is likely to receive a gentle breeze every now and then.

glue

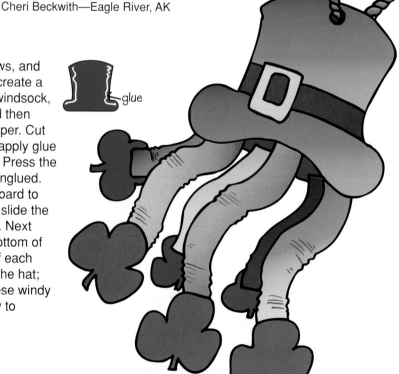

22   D. Hautala, Washington Elementary School, Ely, MN

## My Own Little Abacus

Here's an abacus that's just right for little hands to make and use. To make one abacus, you'll need a copy of the abacus label (page 30), a Styrofoam® brick, ten 12-inch lengths of medium weight wire, and 55 small beads. To begin, color the abacus label and then glue it to the brick as shown. If necessary for your students, use a permanent marker to mark dots on the brick to indicate exactly where each wire should be inserted. Next insert one end of a wire near the numeral 1. Slide one bead onto that wire; then insert the loose end into the other side of the brick. Continue in the same manner, adding the appropriate number of beads on each wire. Encourage children to use these projects for counting, adding, and subtracting activities. Busy little hands!

Jenny Hulsberg, Hendricks Day School, Jacksonville, FL

## A Merry Carousel

These festive projects take a little time, but the results are well worth it! Are you ready to ride?

**For each child, you will need:**
copies of the carousel ponies on page 30
  (or you can make your own ponies)
two 7" paper plates
two 7" to 10" circular doilies (plain or child decorated)
10 pipe cleaners (assorted colors)
five 1" sections of toilet paper tubes
hole puncher
glue
scissors
crayons

1. Color the carousel ponies. Cut out the colored ponies and set them aside.
2. Stack the two plates; then punch five equidistant holes through both thicknesses (as shown).
3. To make a carousel pole, twist two pipe cleaners together; then poke one end of the twisted pair through a hole in one paper plate. Spread apart the pipe cleaner tips to keep the plate from sliding off. Repeat this process for each of the five holes in that plate.
4. Glue one pony to each toilet paper ring; then slip each ring over a different carousel pole.
5. To add the top canopy, slide the free end of each pole through a hole in the second paper plate and spread apart the pipe cleaner ends.
6. Glue a doily to the top and bottom plates as shown.

Display these very merry carousels on a classroom counter. Or poke a hole in the center of the top plate; insert and knot a length of curling ribbon to make a hanger; then suspend each project from the ceiling.

adapted from an idea by Tracey Jean Quezada—Gr. K
Presentation of Mary Academy, Hudson, NH

*Step 2*

*Step 3*

*Step 4*

23

# Arts & Crafts
## for Little Hands

## Fabulous Flower Carts

What's the scoop on spring? Laundry scoop flower carts! To prepare, collect a class supply of clean laundry scoops. Poke a hole in opposite sides of each one as shown. Next cut out two sturdy cardboard wheels for each scoop.

To make one flower cart, have a child use a marker to draw lines on each wheel as shown. Then help him use a brad to attach each wheel to a hole in the scoop. Have the child place a small block of Styrofoam® in the scoop and then cover the Styrofoam with Easter grass. Next have him cut out small construction paper flowers and glue each one onto a toothpick. If desired, invite the child to squeeze a dot of green glue in the center of each flower. When the glue is dry, have the child gently insert each toothpick into the Styrofoam. Now that's a crafty cart!

Faye Barker and Debbie Monk—Gr. K
Bethesda Elementary
Durham, NC

## Ducky Little Baskets

Get your ducks in a row with these nifty Easter baskets. To prepare, collect a class supply of gallon-sized yellow milk jugs. (If possible, check with a local dairy for donations.) Cut the top half of each jug as shown. Provide each student with a jug. Have her glue on construction paper eyes, wings, and a beak. (If desired, glue on some yellow craft feathers, too.) Fill the basket with Easter grass, chocolate eggs, and other yummy treats. Or invite the child to use her basket on your class egg hunt. Quack, quack! Easter's on its way!

Connie Ellington—Gr. K
County Line Elementary
Winder, GA

## Picket Fences and Flowers

This idea has your budding artists painting a picket masterpiece! To prepare, make several picket fence stencils by gluing together craft sticks as shown. When the glue is dry, place the stencils at a center along with the following: small sponges, flower-shaped sponges, large sheets of white construction paper, and shallow pans of green, pink, yellow, and purple paint.

To make a picket painting, have a child place fence stencils across the bottom half of his paper. Direct him to dip a small sponge into green paint and stencil around and through the fence. Next have the child use flower-shaped sponges to make pink, yellow, and purple flower prints above the fence. When the paint is dry, invite the child to add a yarn stem and construction paper leaves to each flower. Lovely!

Susan DeRiso
Barrington, RI

24

## Potted Present

Make a mother's day with this unique gift! Have each child sponge-paint a small clay pot. Then help her fill a resealable plastic bag with soil. Place the bag inside the pot along with a packet of flower seeds. Next wrap clear cellophane around the pot and tie it with a ribbon. What a bloomin' good idea!

Sheryl Spears—Gr. K
Idalia School
Wray, CO

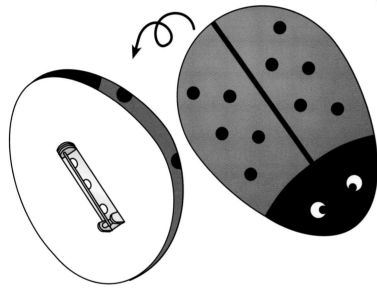

## Lovely Ladybug Pins

Pins are in! To make one ladybug pin, fill a plastic spoon with plaster of paris. Before the plaster sets completely, gently push in a pin backing. Allow the plaster to dry overnight; then pop it out of the spoon. Use sandpaper to file any rough edges. Then paint the rounded side of the plaster to resemble a ladybug. When the paint is dry, set it with acrylic spray; then glue on wiggle eyes. If desired, encourage each child to give his ladybug to a special lady in his life.

Wendy Rapson—Gr. K
Kids in Action
Hingham, MA

## Beautiful Butterflies

Spring into spring with these beautiful butterflies. To prepare, enlarge the butterfly pattern (page 31) 150 percent and then photocopy it to make a class supply. Stock an area with the following items: butterfly cutouts, a shallow pan of water, spring-type clothespins, and crumpled tissue paper squares in a variety of colors.

To make a butterfly, have each child use a clothespin to hold a piece of tissue paper as shown. Direct him to lightly dip the paper into the water and then press the paper onto a butterfly. The tissue paper's color will bleed onto the butterfly. (Some types of tissue paper will not bleed as much as others. Be sure to test the tissue paper first.) Encourage the child to use this procedure to paint his butterfly a variety of colors. When the paper is dry, instruct the child to cut out his butterfly. Display these masterpieces in your room or in a hallway and invite visitors to flutter by the butterflies!

Jean Gomes—Special Education, K–2, M. Carey School, Waverly, IA

# Arts & Crafts
## for Little Hands

### Let's Celebrate!

No matter what the celebration, these easy-to-make party hats are a perfect fit. To prepare, gather an assortment of craft items, glue, a stapler, and a hole puncher. Each child will also need a nine-inch paper plate, two 20-inch pieces of yarn, and a large pom-pom. Cut out one-fourth of each plate, as shown. Next, overlap and staple together the cut edges of the plate to form a cone-shaped hat. Have each child decorate her hat. Then punch a hole on each side of the hat and help the child tie a piece of yarn to each hole. To finish the hat, invite the child to glue the large pom-pom to its point.

Lin Attaya—Gr. K
Hodge Elementary School
Denton, TX

### Sunglasses Pouch

Sunglasses rarely come with their own cases, so why not have your students create these pouches as gifts? Duplicate the sunglasses greeting (page 32) onto colored tagboard for each child. Each child also needs a seven-inch square of craft foam, access to a hole puncher, two pipe cleaners, fabric paints, glue, and sequins. To make a pouch, fold the foam square in half. Through both thicknesses, punch holes that are approximately an inch apart along one end and the open side as shown. Use pipe cleaners to lace up the pouch. If there is leftover pipe cleaner, simply lace it back through to add reinforcement. Finish the pouch with a little decoration. Direct each child to cut out a sunglasses greeting, sign his name, and slide it into the pouch. Here comes the sun!

Tonya House—Pre-K
Anna's Little Red Schoolhouse
Bowling Green, KY

### Artsy Alligators

These tongue-depressor alligators are sure to make little ones open up and say "Aah!" Gather the materials listed below and then help each child follow the directions. Use the finished gators as counters, nonstandard units of measurement, or as figures for the habitats created in "Get Swamped!" on page 201.

**Materials needed:**
— two large craft sticks (per child)
— two 5" green pipe cleaners (per child)
— craft glue
— uncooked rice
— green tempera paint
— paintbrush
— two 7 mm wiggle eyes (per child)

**Directions:**
1. Wrap and twist the pipe cleaner pieces around one of the craft sticks to form legs as shown.

2. Glue the two craft sticks together to form the alligator's body.
3. Spread glue on the top side of the body. Cover the glue with a layer of rice. Then squirt glue along the open edges between the sticks and fill in the gaps with rice.
4. When the glue is dry, paint the whole alligator green, except for the rice between the sticks on one end. (This will represent the alligator's teeth.)
5. When the paint is dry, glue on wiggle eyes.

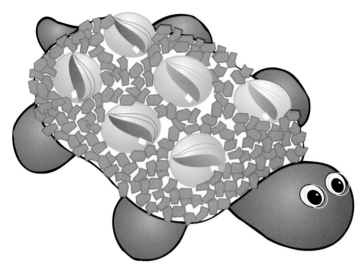

## Tactile Turtles

Creating these turtles is a good way to use leftover craft supplies. Provide each child with a handful of Crayola® Model Magic® modeling compound. Challenge him to create a turtle. Then get out your remaining beads, aquarium gravel, tile pieces, buttons, or some pebbles from outdoors. Invite each child to use the materials to give his turtle's shell some texture. (Craft glue may need to be applied to some items before pushing them into the shell.) Allow the glue and modeling compound to dry. Then, if desired, use tempera paint or markers to color the turtle's head, feet, and tail. Finish the turtle by gluing on two wiggle eyes. These turtles are truly one of a kind!

Christine Guanipa—Gr. K
Covenant School
Arlington, MA

## Father's Day Fun

Help youngsters show that their pops are tops with these interactive cards. Ahead of time, make several tagboard tracers of the fish pattern on page 32. Then gather the materials needed (see list) and assist as youngsters complete the directions below. Dads will love using the removable fishing pole to "fish" for a compliment. What fishy fun!

**Materials needed:**
— 1 sheet of 12" x 18" blue construction paper (per child)
— one 4" square of white construction paper (per child)
— colored construction paper
— markers
— 2 craft sticks (per child)
— 5 metal paper clips (per child)
— 8" length of yarn or string (per child)
— small magnet (per child)
— 1 Velcro® dot (per child)
— scissors
— glue

**Directions:**
1. Cut a wavy line across one of the longer sides of the blue paper to resemble water. Then fold the wavy edge up approximately two inches. Glue the sides to form a pocket.
2. Draw a picture of your father or other male friend on the white paper. Cut out the figure.
3. Cut out boat hull and sail shapes from construction paper. Use the shapes and a craft stick to create a sailboat as shown. Glue the boat, with the man inside, to the left side of the paper.
4. Attach one side of the Velcro dot near the man's hand. Attach the other piece of Velcro to one end of the second craft stick. Tie the string and magnet onto the other end of the craft stick to resemble a fishing pole. Stick the fishing pole onto the man's hand.
5. Trace and cut out five fish from colored construction paper. Then attach a paper clip to the end of each fish.
6. Write "Happy Father's Day!" on the boat's sail. Next, write "My [dad] is..." along the water. Then label each fish with a different descriptive word.
7. Insert the fish into the pocket so that the paper clips are pointing upward.
8. If desired, use construction paper to complete the scene by adding a sun, clouds, and birds.

Seema Gersten and Marni Mellor
Harkham Hillel Hebrew Academy
Beverly Hills, CA

27

## Bat Wing Patterns
Use with "Nighttime Neighbors"
on page 19.

## Polar Bear Patterns
Use with "It's a Whiteout!" on page 21.

Use with "Blowing in the Wind" on page 21.

# Carousel Pony Patterns
Use with "A Merry Carousel" on page 23.

## Abacus Label Pattern
Use with "My Own Little Abacus" on page 23.

| 1 | 2 | 3 | 4 | 5 | 6 | 7 | 8 | 9 | 10 |
|---|---|---|---|---|---|---|---|---|---|

## My Abacus

# Carousel Pony Patterns
Use with "A Merry Carousel" on page 23.

## Abacus Label Pattern
Use with "My Own Little Abacus" on page 23.

| 1 | 2 | 3 | 4 | 5 | 6 | 7 | 8 | 9 | 10 |

# My Abacus

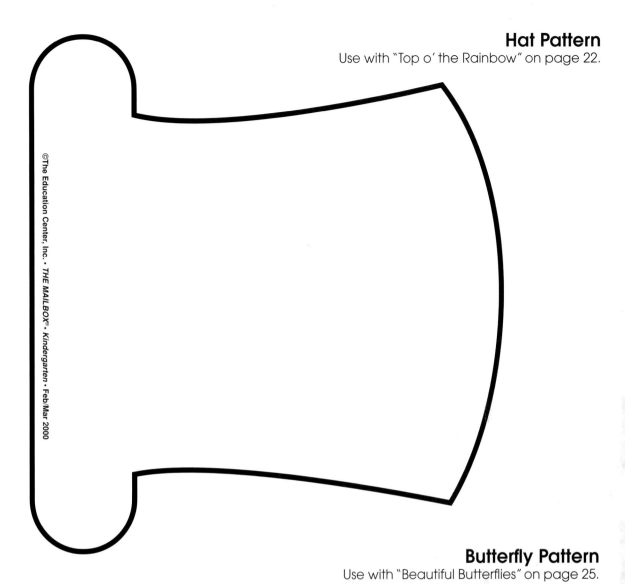

## Butterfly Pattern
Use with "Beautiful Butterflies" on page 25.

## Sunglasses Greeting
Use with "Sunglasses Pouch" on page 26.

You brighten my life!

Love,

©2000 • The Education Center, Inc.

You brighten my life!

Love,

©2000 • The Education Center, Inc.

## Fish Pattern
Use with "Shimmering Sharing" on page 16 and "Father's Day Fun" on page 27.

# LEARNING CENTERS

# Learning Centers

## This Little Piggy…

Little ones will get a kick out of this play dough center idea that reinforces number recognition. Draw six toeless feet on tagboard. Program each foot with a different numeral from 0 to 5. Laminate the feet; then cut them out. Invite your youngsters to create play dough toes, and place them on each foot according to the numeral on the cutout. If desired, give your youngsters extra guidance by adding dots to each foot as shown. For added variation, program a right set and a left set of feet in the same manner. Challenge students to find a pair of feet with matching numbers and then to add the correct number of toes to each foot. Now that's how you keep 'em on their toes!

Lisa Nelson, Horizons School—Home Study, Concord, CA

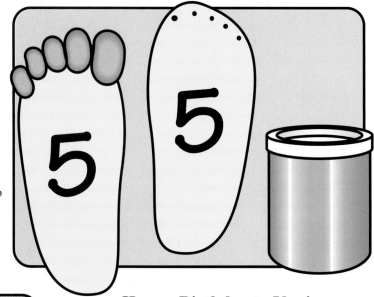

## Happy Birthday to You!

Your dramatic-play area is sure to be a hit when you set it up with a birthday party theme. Stock the center with party hats, cups, plates, and empty gift-wrapped boxes. Provide tape and streamers for youngsters to decorate the area; then add pencils and invitations for your little ones to invite guests. If desired, make a pretend cake for the center with a block of floral foam or packing foam. Glue lace onto the foam or use squeezable fabric paint to resemble icing. As a final touch, include a Pin the Tail on the Donkey game in the area. Happy birthday, everyone!

Tacy Howell—Gr. K, Montair Elementary, Danville, CA

## Matchmakers

Sharpen your students' visual discrimination skills with this unique idea. Laminate two identical posters or two identical sheets of fabric or wrapping paper with interesting pictures or designs. Mount one poster or sheet on a metal surface. From the second poster or sheet, cut out different pictures or designs. Attach a strip of magnetic tape to the back of each cutout picture. Place the cutouts in a plastic resealable bag; then set them with the poster. Challenge students to match the pieces in the bag with the pieces on the poster. Before long, you will hear excited little voices chirping, "I found it!"

Emily Porter—Gr. K, Garth Elementary, Georgetown, KY

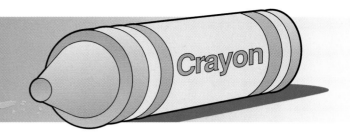

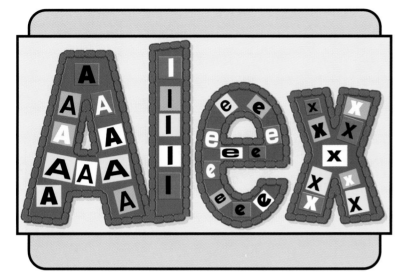

## Names in Newsprint

This center idea is just off the press to help students recognize the letters in their names. On a sentence strip or piece of tagboard, use a colored marker to write a child's name in big block letters. Place the name cards in a center along with old newspapers and magazines. Then direct each student to search through the provided materials to find the letters in her name. Have her cut out the letters and glue them on her name card as shown. To add tactile clues, glue yarn around each letter. Show off these newsworthy names by mounting each child's name card and photograph on a bulletin board.

Tracey Quezada—Gr. K, Varnum School, Lowell, MA

## Button, Button…

Who's got the button? Here's a fun center idea that reinforces color recognition and also introduces the concept of varying shades of color. Stock your center with a variety of colorful buttons and laminated paint-chip samples. (Paint-chip samples are available free of charge at any paint or home-improvement store.) Invite students to sort the buttons by color and then match them to the colors on the samples. Color skills are "buttoning up" with this activity!

Brenda S. Beard—Gr. K
Greenbrier Elementary
Greenbrier, TN

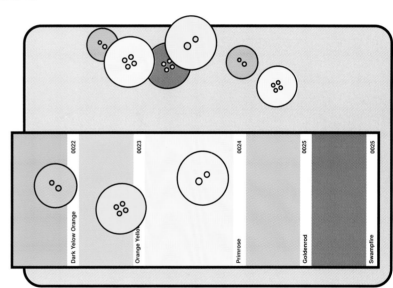

## Let Their Fingers Do the Walking

Memorizing phone numbers is fun with this hands-on center! In advance, write each child's name and phone number on a sentence strip or piece of tagboard. Attach magnetic tape to the back of each card; then place the cards in a center along with a tub of magnetic numbers, a cookie sheet, and old telephones. Invite each visitor in this center to place her card on the cookie sheet, and arrange the matching magnetic numbers on the card. Afterwards, have her practice dialing her phone number on one of the provided telephones.

Karen Bryant, Miller Elementary, Warner Robins, GA

### "Bat-rrr" Up!

Here's a measurement activity your youngsters will go batty over. For each child, make a construction paper copy of the bat measuring tape on page 42. Also make a class supply of the recording sheet on page 43. Place these items in a center along with some scissors, glue, and a supply of small wiggle eyes. Help each child cut and glue the pieces of the measuring tape where indicated. Next invite her to glue two wiggle eyes onto each bat. Challenge the child to use her bat tape to measure each object in your classroom that is pictured on the recording sheet. Have her write the results on her paper. Your youngsters will really "measure up" with this idea!

Sherry Fenton—Gr. K, Petroglyph Elementary, Albuquerque, NM

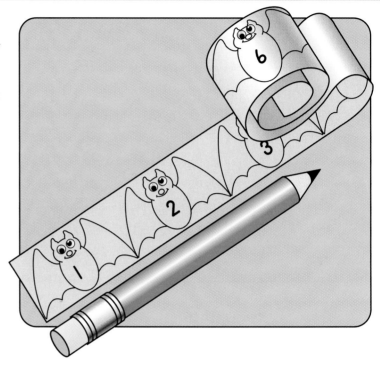

### Memories!

Light the corners of your youngsters' minds with this unique game. Place several seasonal items at a center—such as an acorn, an apple, a leaf, a small pumpkin, and a cob of Indian corn. Invite pairs of students to visit the center and view the objects for several seconds. Then have one of the students cover up the items with a towel or small blanket while the other child attempts to recall each item from memory. As a variation, have one child close her eyes while the other child removes an item from the table. Then have the first child open her eyes and guess which object is missing. What a smart idea!

Sue Lein—Gr. K, St. Pius X Grade School, Wauwatosa, WI

### Leafy Names

What's more fun than jumping in a pile of fresh fall leaves? Writing your name with leaves! For each child, pencil her name in the middle of a sheet of poster board. Place the poster boards in your art center along with a collection of colorful leaves and acorns. Invite each student to find her poster board, and then glue pieces of the fall foliage onto the letters and the background (similar to illustration shown). When all the projects are finished, mount them on a wall or bulletin board to create a "fall-bulous" display!

Shannon Garms, Garland, TX

## Christmas Treehouse

Delight your little elves with this Christmas tree playhouse. To prepare, paint a large tree shape on each side of a refrigerator box. After the paint dries, cut off the top and bottom box flaps; then cut out a door (in the back of the box) and small, round windows (on each of the remaining sides). If desired, cut slits in the box's corners; then hang garland so it appears to drape around the trees. Cut out simple ornaments from construction paper, laminate them, and attach a small piece of hook-side Velcro® to the back of each one. Attach small pieces of loop-side Velcro® to the trees. Stock the inside of the box with pillows, Christmas books, empty boxes, gift-wrapping supplies, and simple elf costumes (such as red and green felt hats). Invite each child in this center to decorate the tree and then enjoy some "tree-mendous" dramatic play inside.

Diann M. Kroos, SRI/St. Elizabeth Child Development Center, Lincoln, NE

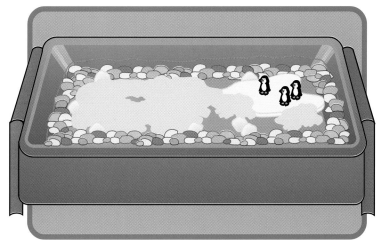

## Ice Is Nice!

This cool discovery center is sure to make a splash with your students! Fill a water table with crushed ice and large blocks of ice to simulate the Antarctic region. Line the edges of the table with rocks to resemble the rocky coastline. Add small penguin figurines. Encourage students at this center to explore the cold water, slush, and ice with the help of a few penguin friends. If desired, have students sprinkle salt onto the ice and observe the results. (Salt melts the ice.) Have warm water and plenty of towels on hand for cleanup afterward.

Sherri Wolf, Beverley Hills Preschool, Alexandria, VA

## What a Pair!

These artistic mittens will strengthen students' hand-eye coordination skills while brightening your winter classroom. In advance, cut out pairs of large mittens from various colors of bulletin board paper. Place the mittens in the art center near an easel stocked with white tempera paint. Invite two students to visit the center and choose a pair of mittens. Next have each child take a turn painting a design onto her mitten, and helping her partner copy it. When the mittens are completely decorated and the paint is dry, connect them with yarn. Then tape the matching mittens to a wall for a cheerful display. What a marvelous cooperative learning experience!

Julia Mashburn—Gr. K, Black's Mill Elementary, Dawsonville, GA

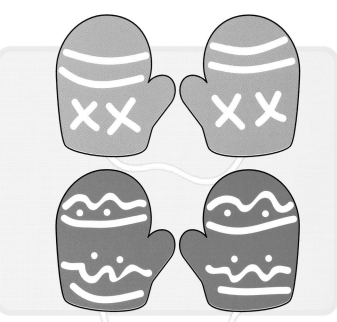

# Learning Centers

## Half 'n' Half

If your young mathematicians are ready for some fraction fun, create this math center activity with the help of your die-cutting machine. Die-cut several pairs of symmetrical shapes from construction paper. Cut one of each pair exactly in half. Make a cut in the other shape from each pair, but make sure it creates two unequal pieces. Glue each cut shape to a large index card, leaving a small gap between the pieces. Then use two of the cards to make the headers as shown. Laminate all the cards and then place them in your math center.

When a child visits this center, he sets out the headers, then sorts the shapes cut in half from those not cut in half. Remind youngsters to look for shapes that have two *equal* parts to help them sort the "halves" from the "halve-nots"!

Kaye Sowell—Gr. K, Pelahatchie Elementary School, Brandon, MS

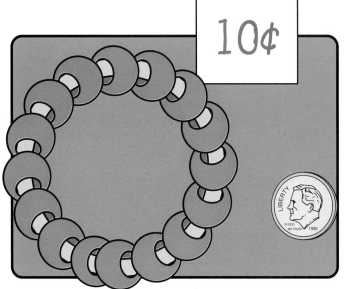

## Baubles and Bangles

Invite little ones to stop and shop at a jewelry store set up in your dramatic-play area. Collect old costume jewelry (skip the pins for safety's sake), gloves, scarves, and small gift boxes. You might even include some jewelry your students make from beads, pasta, or Styrofoam® peanuts! Create signs showing prices for various items. Have some children run the store, arranging the jewelry in attractive displays and selling jewelry and accessories. Others can role-play customers, purchasing items to wear throughout center time or to give to classmates (to be returned to the center later). Provide customers with real coins in wallets and handbags and make sure the clerks have some coins for making change. Students will be practicing their money skills while they expand their imaginations!

Lynda Bogdahn—Gr. K, Mountain Way School, Morris Plains, NJ

## Sequencing Slices

This prop for your reading area delivers an opportunity for youngsters to retell a favorite circle story, such as *If You Give a Mouse a Cookie* by Laura Joffe Numeroff (HarperCollins Children's Books). Simply cut a piece of felt to fit in the bottom of a clean pizza box (donated from a local pizzeria). Glue the felt in place. Then cut a pizza-sized circle from tagboard. Cut the pizza into equal slices and illustrate one event from the story on each slice. Laminate the slices; then attach the hook side of a piece of self-adhesive Velcro® to the back of each one. Place the slices in the box, along with the book they illustrate, and label the box with the story title. Place the box in your reading area. Invite youngsters to read the book and then assemble the pizza to follow the story's sequence.

Cindi Zsittnik, Surrey Child Care Center, Hagerstown, MD

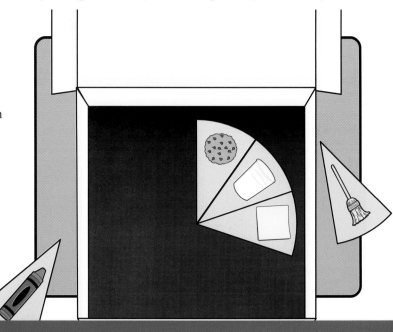

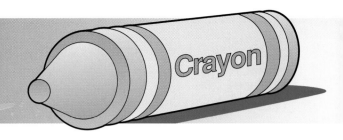

## Valentines for Sale!

If you have been shopping around for a fun, unique way to reinforce money concepts, stop right here! This clever center idea has youngsters identifying coins and coin values, and also makes use of old Valentine's Day cards. To prepare, make a mat by gluing several Valentine's Day cards onto a large sheet of construction paper. Then label each card with a price that students can match using pennies. (If desired, make additional mats for students to use with nickels and dimes.) After placing a basket of corresponding coins near each mat, invite your little sweethearts to examine the different valentines and then place the correct number of coins on each card. What a lovely idea!

Lyn Edwards—Gr. K
Oakwood Elementary
Kalamazoo, MI

## Terrific Hieroglyphics

The Egyptians did it. Now your youngsters can too! Have each student make his own *glyph,* a picture that represents information. To prepare, create a chart with sentences similar to the one shown. Cut a supply of small squares from purple and pink construction paper. Place the squares in a center along with some crayons, glue, and a supply of gold, silver, and blue foil stars. Then give each child a white heart cutout. Review the chart with your little ones; then encourage each child to decorate her heart by following the directions. Display the completed glyphs beside the chart and invite visitors to use the chart and guess which child created each glyph. When sending the glyphs home, be sure to include a copy of the chart to help parents crack the code. Your youngsters will have so much fun with this ancient form of communication, they will want to make a glyph for every season!

Valerie Jewell—Gr. K
Chattahoochee Elementary
Duluth, GA

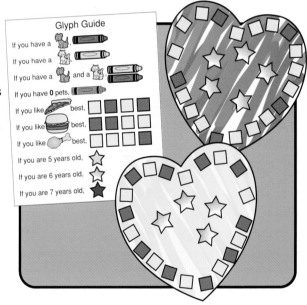

## In Like a Lion, Out Like a Lamb

When the March winds begin to blow, set up this seasonal game to help reinforce a variety of math skills such as number recognition and one-to-one correspondence. To prepare, cut out and program several construction paper lions and lambs similar to the ones shown. Place them at a center along with yellow pom-poms for lions and white cotton balls for lambs. To play, students each choose a lion or lamb cutout. The first player rolls a die and reads the number. He then uses cotton balls to cover that many circles on his cutout. The game continues until all players have covered all of the circles on their animal.

Sandi Bolze—Gr. K
Verne W. Critz Primary
E. Patchogue, NY

# Learning Centers

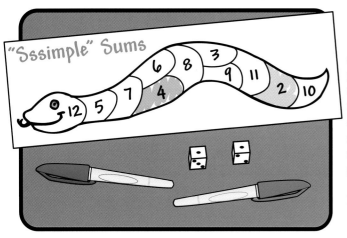

## "Sssimple" Sums

Slither into spring with this simple addition game. To prepare, use a permanent marker to draw a snake shape on a piece of laminated poster board. Then draw random lines on the snake to make 11 sections. Write a different number from 2 to 12 on each section. Place the gameboard, two dice, and overhead projection markers at the center. To play the game, each child rolls the dice and counts the number of dots that appear. Then he finds the matching number on the snake and colors that section. When all sections are colored, simply wipe the snake clean for another round of play. "Sssssuper!"

Kyle Welby—Gr. K, Epstein Hebrew Academy, St. Louis, MO

## Five Little Easter Eggs

Create some "egg-citement" with this bookmaking idea that reinforces color words, number words, and introduces simple subtraction. In advance, write the poem (at right) on two sheets of copy paper that have been divided into thirds as shown. Then copy one set per child. Have each child cut his booklet on the lines to make six pages. Next help the child stack his pages in order, staple them along the left edge, and write his name on the cover. Place all the booklets at a center along with different-colored construction paper, scissors, and glue. Tell your youngsters that they will complete one page per day.

To make a booklet page, fold in the right edge of the page two inches to create a flap. Read the first number word in the verse on the page. Cut out the corresponding number of colored egg shapes, arrange them in a row, and glue them below the verse—making sure the last egg fits under the flap. Write the color word of the last egg in the blank within the poem text. Complete each page in this manner. Finally, cut out five different-colored eggs and glue them to the cover of the book. Have students practice reading their booklets before sending them home for families to enjoy.

Natalie Haislip, Lawrenceburg Public School, Lawrenceburg, TN

| Five Little Easter Eggs | Three little Easter eggs,<br>Before I knew,<br>Sister ate the _____ one;<br>Then there were two.<br><br>3 |
|---|---|
| Five little Easter eggs<br>For all to adore.<br>Mother ate the _____ one;<br>Then there were four.<br><br>1 | Two little Easter eggs,<br>Oh, what fun!<br>Brother ate the _____ one;<br>Then there was one.<br><br>4 |
| Four little Easter eggs,<br>Two and two, you see.<br>Daddy ate the _____ one;<br>Then there were three.<br><br>2 | One little Easter egg,<br>See me run!<br>I ate the last one;<br>Then there were none!<br><br>5 |

Four little Easter eggs,
Two and two, you see.
Daddy ate the _pink_ one;
Then there were three.

2

Three little Easter eggs,
Before I knew,
Sister ate the _yellow_ one;
Then there were two.

3

## To the Moon!

Your youngsters will be taken "a-weigh" with this weight-comparison math center! In advance, collect ten different-sized "moon rocks" and write a different number from one to ten on the bottom of each one. Place the rocks at a center along with a balance scale, crayons, a supply of people counters (astronauts if possible), and graphs similar to the one shown. First ask each child to sequence the rocks. Then have her place the first rock on one side of the scale and add astronauts to the other side until they balance. Help the child graph the number of astronauts it takes to equal the rock. Encourage the child to continue weighing and graphing with the remaining rocks. When finished, ask the child to determine which "moon rock" is the lightest and which one is the heaviest. Mission accomplished!

Rachel Meseke Castro, Juneau Elementary, Juneau, WI

## Spin and Graph

Little ones will be spinning their way to graphing skills with this fun independent activity. To prepare, make a supply of the graphing sheet on page 44. Create a spinner by cutting a five-inch circle from tagboard. Divide the circle into five sections and glue a different shell (cut from one copy of the graphing sheet) onto each section. Add a metal spinner mechanism to the circle's center. (Or simply attach the shell cutouts to an existing spinner with five sections.) Place the graphing sheets, the spinner, crayons, and a timer in your math center.

To use this center, a child sets the timer for a specified amount of time, such as five minutes. She spins and then colors in a matching shell on her graphing sheet. She continues to spin and color until the timer goes off. Then she examines her graph to see which shell she had the *most* and the *fewest* of and if she had an *equal* number of any shells. Have her share her findings with you so you can assess her grasp of graphing.

Linda Havens—Gr. K, Parkwood-Upjohn Elementary, Kalamazoo, MI

Five Little Monkeys Ride Bikes

Nick

## The Scoop on Patterning

The weather's just right for some cool ice-cream math! To prepare this center activity, draw a large ice-cream cone on a 12" x 18" sheet of construction paper. Then cut some scoops of ice cream (sized to fit the cone) from various colors of construction paper. Make patterning cards by drawing ice-cream cones with various scoop color patterns on index cards. Laminate the cone, the scoops, and the patterning cards for durability. Then slip the scoops and cards into a two-pocket folder for easy storage. A child at this center chooses a patterning card, then creates the matching pattern with the large scoops and cone. Before you know it, little ones will have patterning practice licked!

Lisa Mascheri—Exceptional Education, Midway Elementary, Sanford, FL

## Order-Form Fun

What can you do with old book order forms from student book clubs? Use them in your literacy center! Invite youngsters to try any of these tasks with a book order form:
— Look for and circle a particular letter.
— Look for and circle sight words.
— Look for and circle matching words (or prices).
— Circle every book you have read or listened to.
— Locate your favorite book. Copy the title onto a sheet of paper and add an illustration.

Melissa Merritt—Gr. K, East End Elementary, Humboldt, TN

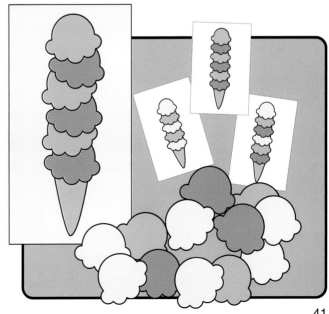

# Bat Measuring Tape

Use with " `Bat-rrr' Up!" on page 36.

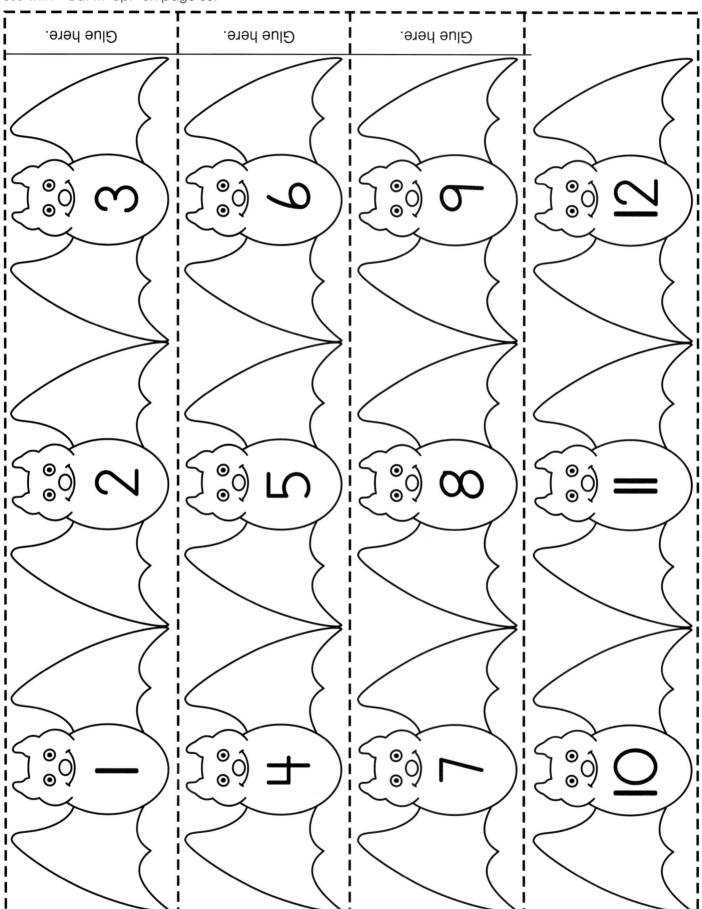

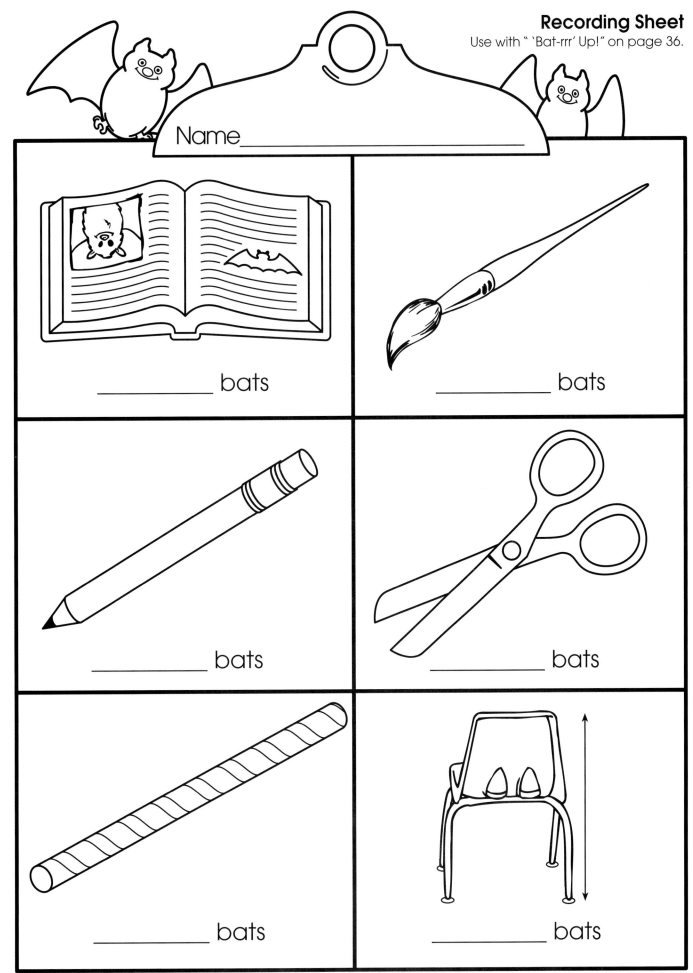

Name_____

_____ bats

_____ bats

_____ bats

_____ bats

_____ bats

_____ bats

Name _____

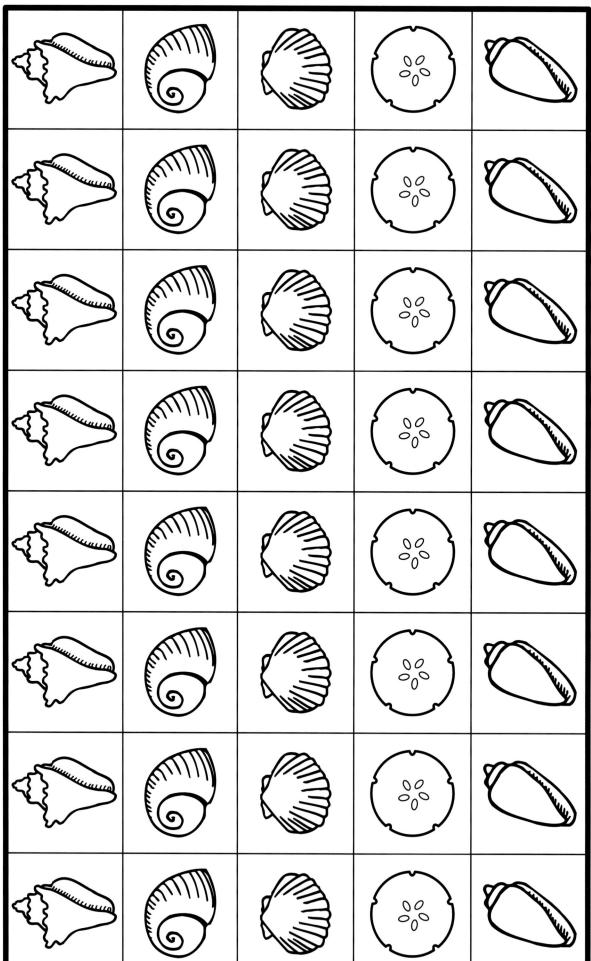

©The Education Center, Inc. • *THE MAILBOX®* • *Kindergarten* • June/July 2000

**Note to the teacher:** Use this page with "Spin and Graph" on page 41.

# LITERATURE UNITS

# Heigh-Ho, Heigh-Ho, It's Off to Work We Go!

Here's a collection of work-related books and activities designed to give your youngsters on-the-job training about their future career options. These hardworking ideas offer big payoffs when it comes to increasing your students' career savvy as well as their curricular skills. And the fringe benefits are priceless—student pride in the work they do!

*by Mackie Rhodes*

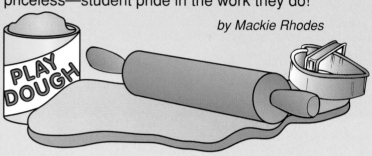

## Daddies at Work
## Mommies at Work
By Eve Merriam
Illustrated by Eugenie Fernandes
Published by Aladdin Paperbacks, 1989

*Daddies and mommies everywhere perform many labors of love for their children. But what else do daddies and mommies do? With simple, sensitive text and gentle illustrations, these books introduce youngsters to the world of work outside the home. These particular selections might also spark children's curiosity about their own parents' jobs.*

After reading and discussing these books, create a class collage to help children focus their attention on what parents or other adults might do at their jobs. To begin, provide a supply of blank paper and old magazines. Ask each child to cut out a picture of a person at work or of job-related tools. Then have her write (or dictate) about her picture. Next, help her glue the writing and the picture on a length of butcher paper titled "Everybody's Working." When each child has contributed to the collage, display it along a classroom wall and use it to reference various jobs during your career studies and to prompt dramatic play ideas. Look—everybody's working!

## I Am Me!
By Alexa Brandenberg
Published by Red Wagon Books, 1996

*What will you do when you grow up? In this book, nine young children aspire to careers that involve doing what they already like to do as children. Simple text and multicultural illustrations inspire readers to dream of all the possibilities!*

This book—along with natural curiosity—makes a perfect springboard for career explorations! To begin, add simple props and costumes to your existing centers to transform them into different job locations. For example, make your housekeeping area a restaurant by adding menus, notepads, and pencils. Turn your block area into a fire station by providing fire helmets, hoses (made from wrapping paper tubes with silver-tinsel water), and red and orange tissue paper flames taped to block buildings. Transform your writing area into a post office by supplying a cardboard mailbox, stamps, envelopes, paper, and mailbags. Convert your art area into a bakery by adding play dough, cookie cutters, rolling pins, trays, chef hats, and aprons. Encourage children to visit these centers and pretend to be the workers and the customers. During group times, invite children to share what types of playing or jobs they like. Lots of food for thought here!

She grows flowers.

## Mom Goes to Work

By Libby Gleeson
Illustrated by Penny Azar
Published by Scholastic Inc., 1992

*A group of children stay busy at school while their moms work at their respective jobs. Parallel pictorials depict the simultaneous activities of children and their working parents—and cleverly convey the message that children have jobs, too!*

After sharing this book, use the following home-school connection activity to expand students' career awareness and their understanding of the work done by their parents and other adults in their lives.

> **For each child, you'll need:**
> 1 copy of the poem on page 49
> 1 sheet of construction paper
> 2 half-sheets of construction paper
> 2 lengths of thick yarn
> art supplies for decorating
> access to a stapler
> glue

Instruct each child to make a job bag by folding the whole sheet of construction paper in half. Have each child glue the poem to one side of her bag. Then help her staple along the sides of the bag, leaving the top open. Next, have each child glue yarn handles on the bag and decorate it as she likes.

When the job bags are finished, have each child make two job cards by folding her half-sheets of construction paper. Have her store one of the folded job cards in her bag and then reopen the remaining one. On the open card, invite her to illustrate and write about (dictate) a job that she is responsible for at home or at school. Then instruct the child to refold the job card and slide it into her job bag. Invite each child to take her bag home and share her job card with a family member or friend. Encourage each child to ask her partner at home to use the blank job card to illustrate and write about his own job. As the job bags come back to school, invite each child to share both job cards with the group; then mount her bag and cards on a board titled "Jobs in the Bag!"

## Jobs People Do

By Christopher Maynard
Published by Dorling Kindersley Publishing, Inc.; 1997

*This treasury of careers provides a first-person description of each featured occupation along with a photo of a child modeling related career gear. Additional photos and smaller text offer more details if interest dictates. It's a career wish book that will send imaginations soaring!*

Integrate career awareness, listening skills, and lots of creativity with this idea. After sharing the book, ask each child to think of an occupation that he finds interesting. Encourage him to bring items from home and to use classroom art supplies to make related gear. Photograph each child in his outfit; then mount each photo on tagboard. Next, divide the photos into groups of five and add a cassette tape to each set. Color-code each piece of each different set. Then have each child record a first-person description of his career choice on the appropriate tape, leaving a pause between each narration. Label the back of each photo according to the order in which it is recorded on the tape. Store each photo-tape set in a separate zippered plastic bag; then place all the sets in your listening center. To do this activity, have a child choose a set, listen to the tape, and then sequence the pictures to correspond to the recorded descriptions. And what, may I ask, do *you* do?

I dig up dinosaur bones and put them together.

## What You Do Is Easy, What I Do Is Hard
By Jake Wold & Illustrated by Anna Dewdney
Published by Greenwillow Books, 1996

| That's easy! | That's hard! |
| --- | --- |
| 5 | 15 |

*A boastful squirrel claims that he accomplishes the hardest jobs of all...until he is challenged to trade places with a bee, a robin, a spider, and an ant! Sweetly comical illustrations will have youngsters giggling as they ponder the strengths and weaknesses of each character—and themselves!*

After sharing this story, guide children to summarize that each person has different skills and abilities that might make her better suited to some jobs than to others. Then invite youngsters to explore the variety of strengths and weaknesses among themselves—and sneak in a little math practice, too! To prepare, draw a two-column graph on the board. Label one column "That's Easy!" and the other "That's Hard!" Call out a skill such as, "Snap your fingers" or, "Hop on one foot"; then invite youngsters to try it. (It's helpful and fun to include a skill or two that you, the teacher, have difficulty doing—perhaps whistling or push-ups?) After each activity, have each child (and you!) attach a sticky note in the column that corresponds to her reaction to the given skill. Afterward, determine how many children thought that skill was easy and how many thought it was hard. Repeat the process as desired; then encourage children to talk about the variety of their strengths and weaknesses.

## Guess Who?
By Margaret Miller
Published by Greenwillow Books, 1994

*Who enjoys a guessing game that sparks interactive enthusiasm about jobs? Every reader of this Margaret Miller creation, of course! It's irresistible!*

After sharing this story, your youngsters will be ready for this game version of *Guess Who?* In advance, photocopy, color, and laminate the job cards on pages 50 and 51; then cut them apart. Choose a small group of students and give each of those students a different job card. Have the group stand in front of the class. In turn, encourage each child to prompt the rest of the class to guess who (what occupation) is pictured on his card. Instruct children to use clues that begin with *who,* such as "Who gives a dog a checkup?" or "Who serves food at a restaurant?" After all the workers have been guessed, give a different group of children new job cards; then play another round. Guess who is having lots of learning fun?

"Who serves food at a restaurant?"

"Who gives a dog a checkup?"

## Grandmother's Alphabet
By Eve Shaw
Published by Pfeifer-Hamilton Publishers, 1997

*Grandma can be anything—and so can I! Beautiful illustrations and sensitive text offer an extensive alphabetical list of occupations suitable for any grandmother, grandchild, or anyone in between.*

Reinforce career awareness and beginning sounds with this job-related idea. After sharing the book, invite each child to draw a picture of himself doing a job. When each child shares his illustration, guide the class to determine the beginning sound of the job represented. Then invite the artist to use a marker to label his illustration with that letter. Use a metal ring to bind all the pictures together in alphabetical order behind a title page. Throughout your career studies, encourage each child to add illustrations to the class-made book as he discovers additional jobs that interest him. In between *A* and *Z,* there's a very special job for me!

# More Work-Related Literature

### I Love You, Mom
By Iris Hiskey Arno
Illustrated by Joan Holub
Published by WhistleStop®, 1997

*In this special tribute, children boast about their talented and hardworking moms!*

### Mr. Griggs' Work
By Cynthia Rylant
Illustrated by Julie Downing
Published by Orchard Books, 1989

*Old Mr. Griggs loves his job at the post office! This man's steadfast devotion makes for a refreshing tale and a lesson in taking satisfaction and pride in our own work.*

### My Great-Aunt Arizona
By Gloria Houston
Illustrated by Susan Condie Lamb
Published by HarperCollins Publishers, 1992

*Arizona loved to read and dream about the faraway places that she would one day visit—but life's circumstances kept her close to home. Eventually Arizona became the teacher at her old one-room school—and she taught there for 57 years! Those touched by her life carry her in their minds wherever they go.*

### Pig Pig Gets a Job
By David McPhail
Published by Dutton Children's Books, 1990

*When Pig Pig announces that he wants to buy something, his mother surprises him by suggesting that he get a job. Together the two come up with an imaginative, practical way to help Pig Pig earn money and to take pride in his job.*

During a class discussion about occupations, I asked one little girl what her daddy did for a living. She proudly replied, "My daddy is a souvenir!" Rather puzzled, I checked her file and discovered that her father was a *civil engineer!*

*Leslie O'Donnell—Gr. K, Sedalia Park School
Marietta, Georgia*

### A Sign
By George Ella Lyon
Illustrated by Chris K. Soentpiet
Published by Orchard Books, 1998

*A young girl's fascination with the jobs of a neon sign maker, a tightrope walker, and an astronaut inspire dreams about her own future. As an adult, she explores how her dreams shaped her career as a writer and the author of this book.*

### Work
By Ann Morris
Published by Lothrop, Lee & Shepard Books; 1998

*Ann Morris' camera takes readers on a photographic journey around the world to observe all kinds of people doing all kinds of work. Vivid pictures and an informational index ignite interest in a variety of world cultures.*

### Worksong
By Gary Paulsen
Illustrated by Ruth Wright Paulsen
Published by Harcourt Brace & Company, 1997

*With lyrical text and rich paintings, this song of praise celebrates the everyday jobs of people all over the world.*

Order books on-line.
www.themailbox.com

## Job Poem
Use with *Mom Goes to Work* on page 47.

### Jobs
Mommies and daddies
And grandparents, too,
Are people with jobs—
With jobs that they do.

Aunts and uncles
And neighbors, it's true,
Are people with jobs—
With jobs that they do.

Boys and girls
Have jobs that they do.
I have a job—
How about YOU?

# Job Cards

Use with *Guess Who?* on page 48.

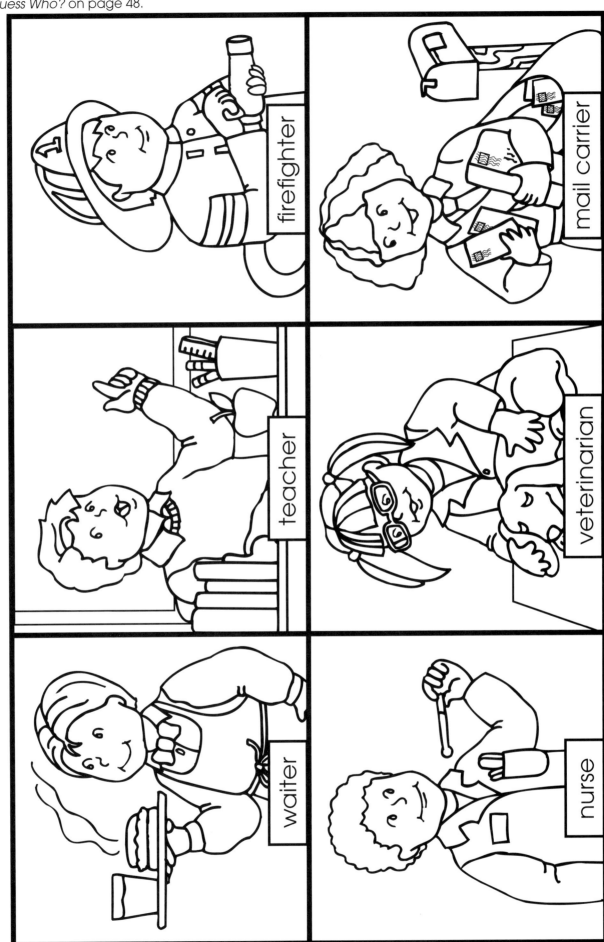

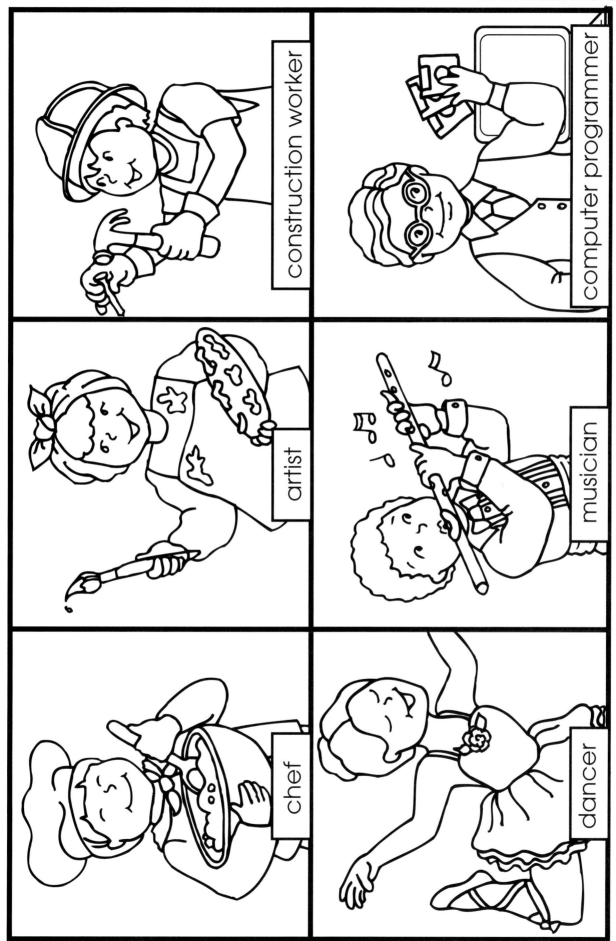

construction worker

computer programmer

artist

musician

chef

dancer

# Could You Repeat That, Please?

Share this delightful collection of books with repetitive texts with your class. Then follow up subsequent readings with the related extension ideas found here. Don't be surprised to hear youngsters ask for these selections again and again and again!

*by Mackie Rhodes*

## The Doorbell Rang
### By Pat Hutchins
### Published by Greenwillow Books, 1986

*A generous family is happy to share its cookies with unexpected guests. But when the portions are reduced to one cookie per person and the doorbell rings again, the family faces a dilemma. The surprise on the other side of the door will delight readers just as much as it does the characters in the book.*

Youngsters will be glad to share the fun and flavor of this math activity. After reading the story, divide your class into several small groups. Give each group a cup of Cookie-Crisp® cereal. Have members work cooperatively to distribute the cereal pieces evenly among the group. If desired, repeat the activity with a different amount of cereal. However, before the cereal is divided up this time, challenge youngsters to estimate the number of cereal pieces each group member will receive.

Got milk? Extend this activity into liquid form by giving each child a clear plastic cup and each group a carton of milk. Can the groups cooperatively quench *everyone's* thirst?

*(For more cookie-related learning, see page 235.)*

## To Market, To Market
### By Anne Miranda
### Illustrated by Janet Stevens
### Published by Harcourt Brace & Company, 1997

*Rhyming text, sprinkled with repetitive refrains, and hilarious illustrations capture the comical chaos of a shopper's day at the market. Readers will enjoy adventuring with this colorful character as she experiences the ups and downs of preparing for mealtime.*

Rhyming skills are in the bag with this small-group activity. To prepare, collect small toy animals (or pictures) with names that are easy to use in rhyming—for example, *pig, goat,* and *fish*. Hide each animal in a separate paper bag. Share the story and then play this guessing game. Give each child in the group a bag. In turn, have her peek into her bag to secretly identify the animal. Then have the child recite the chant below, completing the second line with a real or nonsense word that rhymes with her animal. Challenge the other students to use the clue to guess which animal is in the bag.

To market, to market,
   jiggity jag!
It rhymes with [boat].
   What's in my bag?

## Jump, Frog, Jump!

By Robert Kalan
Illustrated by Byron Barton
Published by Greenwillow Books, 1981

*A little frog jumps into and out of danger until he is finally trapped in a basket by three boys. How does the frog get away? Readers will jump with delight at the surprise ending!*

Hop to some letter or numeral recognition skills with this lily pad game. To prepare, cut out a supply of construction paper lily pads and laminate them. Label each lily pad with a different letter or numeral. During another reading of the story, have your students shout the "Jump, frog, jump!" refrain at the appropriate times. Afterwards, scatter the lily pads in an open area in the classroom. To play, have students hop around the lily pads on your signal "Jump, frogs, jump!" Then call out "Stop, frogs, stop!" and instruct each child to stop on a lily pad. Have her, in turn, identify the symbol on her lily pad.

If desired, extend this game to reinforce sequencing skills. Simply group the lily pads into sequenced sets of four or five; then position each group of pads close together on the floor. On your signal "Jump, frog, jump!" have a child jump in sequence on the lily pads in one of the groups and "ribbet" the name of each letter or numeral.

## I Went Walking

By Sue Williams
Illustrated by Julie Vivas
Published by Gulliver Books, 1989

*Simple, rhythmic text takes a young boy on a colorful walking adventure in which he encounters an assortment of farm animals. With a touch of humor, the vibrant paintings depict the warm affection between the child and his newfound friends.*

Reinforce classification skills with these child-made big books. To begin, share *I Went Walking* with your class and point out that the animals in the story are *farm* animals. Then ask students to name animals that might be found in other settings, such as a zoo, a jungle, a swamp, or even a pet store. Divide your class into several small groups. Assign each group a different environment. Have each child illustrate an animal that he might see while visiting that environment. Write his dictation about his animal following the text pattern "I saw a _____ looking at me." For each group, cut two tagboard covers that are twice as big as the pages. Program the inside of the front cover with "I went walking." and the inside of the back cover with "What did you see?" as shown. Then title the front cover with the name of the environment. Use metal rings to bind the book—with the student pages between the covers at the bottom. Invite each group to read its book to the class, and then place the books in your reading area for more enjoyment.

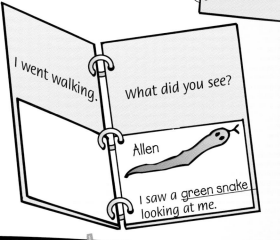

# Henny Penny

By Paul Galdone
Published by Clarion Books, 1968

*In this classic tale, an acorn drops on Henny Penny's head, and the alarmed hen sets out to warn the king that the sky is falling. Along the way she picks up a parade of friends who want to tag along. The bunch soon encounters the clever Foxy Loxy, who shows them a shortcut that leads right into his den and onto his dinner table!*

Foxy Loxy is quite a trickster in this story. After reading the book, invite youngsters to play this action-packed game in which the hen gets the chance to outfox—or at least outrun—the fox. To play, have students sit in a circle and designate them as foxes. Choose a child to be the hen and give her an acorn. Direct the hen to circle the foxes while singing the verse below. In the last line, have the hen name a seated fox—adding a rhyming ending to the fox's name to match the story characters' names—and then drop the acorn into that fox's lap. Just as in the Duck, Duck, Goose game, direct the fox to chase the hen around the circle. If the hen reaches safety (the empty spot in the circle), she joins the circle of foxes. But if she is caught, the hen sits in the fox's den (the middle of the circle) during the next round of play. Now invite the fox to become the hen, and continue the game until each fox has had a turn.

*(sung to the tune of "London Bridge")*

Oh, the sky is falling down, falling down, falling down.
Oh, the sky is falling down, [Jannah Lannah]!

# The Very Busy Spider

By Eric Carle
Published by Philomel Books, 1985

*A diligent spider continues to spin her web in spite of tempting invitations to play from her farm animal friends. As evening comes, her work is finally done. But when an admiring owl wants to know who built the web, the spider is too busy sleeping to take credit for her beautiful web.*

Here's a multisensory activity that will keep youngsters very busy retelling this tender tale. To prepare, duplicate the spider patterns (page 57) onto construction paper to make a class supply. Cut out each spider and the circle as indicated. For each child, collect an individual photo (or a photocopy of one). Provide students with sandpaper that can be cut into seven- to ten-inch strips.

After reading the story, invite each child to get very busy creating her own spiderweb. To make one, cut out four sandpaper strips. On a sheet of construction paper, arrange and glue on the strips to resemble a fence. Use thin lines of colored glue to create a spiderweb between the fence posts. While the glue dries, color the spider. Then tape the photo to the back of the spider so that the face can be seen through the opening. Finally, staple the spider to the web. Display the completed projects along with the title "Our Very Busy Spiders." If desired, place some toy farm animals nearby so that youngsters can visit the display and tell their own hands-on versions of this popular story.

Tiffany

## Cassie

Silly Cassie came to school.
She thought eating pizza
backwards was cool!

## Silly Sally

By Audrey Wood
Published by Harcourt Brace Jovanovich,
Publishers; 1992

*Silly Sally has quite an interesting way to travel—walking backwards, upside down! As she goes to town in her unique way, Sally meets a number of characters who join her silliness as they dance, leap, and sing. But when sleep overcomes the bunch, will they make it to town? The humorous ending will tickle readers of all ages!*

Celebrate Silly Sally in your classroom by doing everything backwards for a day. For each child, duplicate and send home the parent note (page 57) explaining the day. Welcome students into your classroom on Backwards Day by saying "Good-bye!" Start the day off with your closing song. Throughout the day, call students by their last names first. Have your rest time *before* lunch. Arrange to have pizza for lunch and then encourage students to eat it crust first. During circle time, sing the alphabet song backwards, starting with *Z*. And don't forget to walk backwards wherever you go!

At the end of the day, have each child draw her favorite part of Backwards Day. On her drawing, write "Silly [child's name] came to school. [She] thought [name of activity] backwards was cool!" Compile the drawings in a class book. Share the book with the group; then send students home with a hug and a "Good morning!"

## Frogs Jump: A Counting Book

By Alan Brooks
Illustrated by Steven Kellogg
Published by Scholastic Inc., 1996

*Ducks diving off a diving board and snakes water-sliding? This lively counting book will send imaginations soaring as groups of animals, from 1 to 12, appear from a magical hat. While the text is sensible—monkeys do indeed swing—the whimsical illustrations create the book's fun and frenzied tone (here they swing golf clubs!). Youngsters will definitely want to hear this story at least 12 times!*

Double the learning *and* the fun with this activity that reinforces counting and number recognition skills. To prepare, label a separate sentence strip with each number sentence from the book. After reading the story and discussing its absurdities, encourage students to interact with the story using the sentence strips. To do this, hold up each sentence strip in sequence. Ask students to chorally read the sentence, clap the corresponding number of times, and then pantomime the action. Afterward, place the sentence strips in a center for student partners to sequence, read, and act out together—"any way they want!"

Vvroom!

11 Eleven pigs squeal.

**Today is ...**

**Come and eat it up!**

| Monday string beans | Tuesday spaghetti | Wednesday zooop | Thursday roast beef | Friday fresh fish | Saturday chicken | Sunday ice cream |

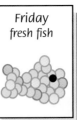

# Today Is Monday

### By Eric Carle
### Published by Philomel Books, 1993

*Based on the popular children's song, this story highlights a different food for each day of the week. And when Sunday arrives, all the foods are brought to the table for the world's children to enjoy together. Come and eat it up!*

After you read (and sing) the story, youngsters will eagerly make this reference chart to use with the book. To begin, divide your students into seven groups. Give each group a sheet of chart paper labeled with a different day of the week and its corresponding food item (according to the book). Then instruct the group to cooperatively illustrate its chart with the labeled food. Display the completed charts in sequence. Add a sentence strip labeled "Today is…" to the left of the display and a sentence strip with "Come and eat it up!" to the right. Then as your class sings the song, turn to the appropriate page in the book while a volunteer points to the corresponding phrase, day, or food name on the reference chart. For each new verse, invite a different student to use the chart to lead the singing.

# It Looked Like Spilt Milk

### By Charles G. Shaw
### Published by HarperCollins Publishers, Inc.; 1947

*The large white shape in this book sometimes looks like spilt milk. And at other times it looks like a rabbit, a birthday cake, or even an angel. But the shape is really none of these things. In simple art and repetitive text, this story illustrates the interesting and ever changing nature of a cloud.*

Read this story to your class on a partly cloudy day. After the reading, have youngsters observe the sky and discuss the clouds' shapes. Then create this fanciful display. Have each child use a white paint pen to trace a template of his choice (or draw his own shape) onto blue bulletin board paper. Then direct him to paint the shape white. After the paint dries, use the paint pen to label the shape.

Display the pictures on a matching blue background. In large white lettering, title the top left of the display "It looked like . . ." Then label the bottom right of the display "But it was just a cloud in the sky!"

It looked like ...
a bear
the letter W
a fish
a tree
a flower
But it was just a cloud in the sky!

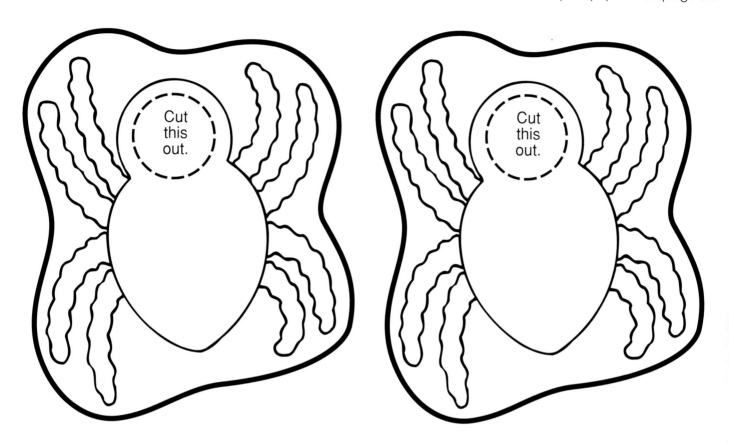

Cut this out.

Cut this out.

# It's Backwards Day!

Dear Parent,

We've just read the story *Silly Sally* by Audrey Wood. It was so much fun watching Sally walk backwards that we're going to try doing things backwards all day long! On _____, please send your child to school
(date)
with his/her clothes on backwards to set the stage for a day of fun. Come join us!

Thank you,

# Bundle Up!

Brrr. It's cold-weather season! So bundle up your class with this literature unit on winter clothing. Youngsters are sure to warm up to these cool cross-curricular ideas and activities.

*ideas contributed by Mackie Rhodes*

## *"Charlie Needs a Cloak"*
By Tomie dePaola
Published by Aladdin Paperbacks, 1988

*From spring through fall, Charlie shears the sheep, spins the wool, and sews the pieces of cloth together to make a beautiful red cloak for the winter. Simple text and amusing characters help illustrate the process of making wool clothing.*

Your youngsters will be spinning with excitement when they use this activity to make some yarn! After reading the story, review how Charlie straightened, spun, and then dyed the wool for his cloak. Next give each child several puffs of wool (cotton balls) and instruct her to gently unroll and straighten out the puffs. Have the child wet her hands slightly and then roll the wool between her palms to create strands. Next place several drops of food coloring in a small amount of water and invite the child to use the water to dye her yarn. Squeeze the liquid from the yarn; then set it aside to dry. While the yarn is drying, give each child a construction paper cutout of the figure on page 164 (enlarged). Direct her to draw winter clothing on the figure and then color the face to look like her own. When the yarn is dry, have the child glue it onto her figure's clothing. What cool wool!

## *Warm As Wool*
By Scott Russell Sanders
Illustrated by Helen Cogancherry
Published by Simon & Schuster, 1998

*When her family moved to the Ohio wilderness, Betsy Ward came ready to make warm new clothes for her children. She had a spinning wheel, a loom, and a secret stash of coins to buy sheep. But where would she find the sheep? This true-to-life story about the hardships, strength, and determination of one family will make readers feel as warm as wool.*

Counting skills are in the bag with this sheepish game. In advance, fill a supply of plastic resealable bags with wool (cotton balls). After sharing this tender tale, assign one child in a small group the role of wool-gatherer and give him a basket and three large tagboard coins. Instruct the wool-gatherer to close his eyes and then give each remaining child, or sheep, a random number of bags. Have each sheep quietly count her bags and then hide them behind her back. To play, the wool-gatherer opens his eyes and asks a sheep, "Little sheep, little sheep, have you any wool?" The sheep replies, "Yes, sir. Yes, sir, [two] bags full." The wool-gatherer offers the sheep a coin. Then the sheep counts each bag as she puts it into the basket. After buying wool from three sheep, the wool-gatherer counts his total number of bags and reports his results. To play again, appoint another wool-gatherer; then repeat the game in the same fashion. Not a "baaaaa-d" idea!

## Mrs. Toggle's Zipper
By Robin Pulver
Illustrated by R. W. Alley
Published by Aladdin Paperbacks, 1993

*Mrs. Toggle has a big problem. She's trapped inside her coat with a stuck zipper! And, worse yet, the "thingamajig" is missing. Even the efforts of her class, the school nurse, and the principal can't pull her out of her awful predicament. But the custodian offers a simple solution and soon all are happily going about their usual school routines.*

Zip up some cooperative teamwork with this coat relay. To begin, discuss how Mrs. Toggle's students and colleagues worked together to free her from her coat. Then divide your class into two or more teams. Position half of each team at opposite ends of an open area. Give the first player of each team a zippered jacket. At the start signal, the first player puts on the jacket, zips it, and then races to her team at the opposite end of the playing area. She unzips the jacket, removes it, and then helps the next player don and zip the jacket. That player then races to the next teammate and repeats the process. After each team completes the relay, unzip a bag of cool treats to distribute to your youngsters.

## The Jacket I Wear in the Snow
By Shirley Neitzel
Illustrated by Nancy Winslow Parker
Published by Mulberry Books, 1994

*A young girl, bundled up for a day in the snow, takes a teary-eyed tumble into her snowman. In response to her cries, the girl's mother begins the unbundling process. This rhythmic rebus story is layered with a humorous review of a child's winter wear.*

Help your youngsters dress for success with this activity! Pack a suitcase with adult-sized winter clothing similar to that in the story. After sharing the story, invite a small group of students to examine the winter wear in the suitcase. Next set a timer for approximately one minute. (Or adjust the time to students' abilities.) At the start signal, challenge a child to put on the winter clothing over his own before the timer rings. After each child has had a turn, discuss their dressing discoveries. For example, your youngsters may discover that putting shoes on before pants makes dressing difficult. When your class is familiar with this activity, put the suitcase in the dramatic-play area to prompt lots of wintry role-playing.

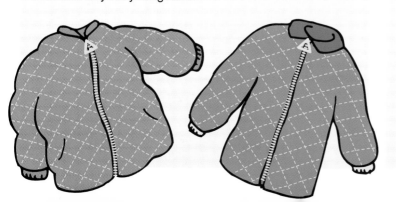

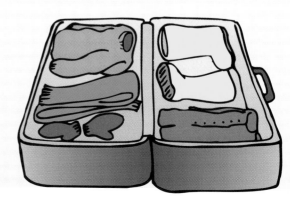

## The Mitten: A Ukrainian Folktale
By Jan Brett
Published by The Putnam Publishing Group, 1989

*One by one, a group of woodland animals discovers Nicki's lost mitten. Finding it warm and cozy, each animal squeezes into the mitten until it swells with furry, feathery, creatures. Then the mouse tickles the bear's nose, causing a sneeze to erupt and scatter the animals everywhere—just in time for Nicki to find his mitten!*

## The Hat
By Jan Brett
Published by The Putnam Publishing Group, 1997

*When the wind blows Lisa's stocking off the clothesline, it finds a home on curious Hedgie's head. Inspired by Hedgie's unusual hat, inquisitive farm animals then set out to find hats of their own.*

Look carefully at the illustrations in this book! After each of Hedgie's encounters with a farm animal, an article of clothing mysteriously disappears from the clothesline. After sharing this story with your youngsters, review the illustrations to help them discover what happens to each item of clothing. Then invite them to play this visual memory game. To begin, hang a variety of winter clothes on a clothesline. Have students view the clothes; then hold a sheet in front of the clothes and remove one item. Lower the sheet, and then ask students to identify the missing item. For an added challenge, hang sets of similar clothing, such as all mittens. Repeat the game as student interest dictates.

Share this delightful story; then stretch youngsters' imaginations as they make their own innovative booklets titled "The Sock." To prepare, photocopy the sock patterns on page 64. Next enlarge the smaller sock 110% and duplicate the pattern again. Then enlarge the pattern 120% and make a third copy. Duplicate these four different-sized pages for each child.

To make one booklet, cut out each of the socks to create four sock pages. Make a cover by tracing the largest sock pattern onto construction paper. Cut on the resulting outline, and then write the title on the cutout. Have each child sequence his pages by size and then place them behind the cover. Staple the booklet together along the left side; then have the child follow the directions below to complete his booklet. Encourage your youngsters to read their booklets to each other before taking them home.

**Page 1:** Draw a small animal. Write (or dictate) the name of the animal in the blank.

**Page 2:** Draw a medium-sized animal and the small animal from page 1. Write (or dictate) the name of the medium-sized animal in the blank.

**Page 3:** Draw a large animal, the medium-sized animal, and the small animal. Write (or dictate) the name of the large animal in the blank.

**Page 4:** Draw a picture of yourself, the large animal, the medium-sized animal, and the small animal.

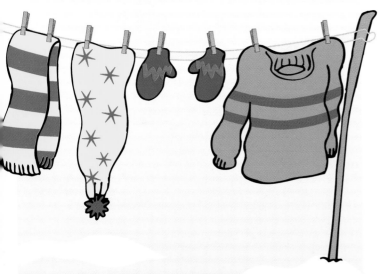

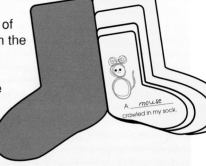

## The Mitten Tree

By Candace Christiansen
Illustrated by Elaine Greenstein
Published by Fulcrum Publishing, 1997

*Old Sarah watches the children at the morning bus stop, cherishing memories of her own children at that age. When she spies a little boy with no mittens, she knits a pair and hangs them on the blue spruce tree for him. Each morning thereafter, she secretly adorns the tree with her hand-knit mittens. In return for her generosity, a mysterious friend begins to leave baskets of yarn on Sarah's doorstep.*

After reading this heartwarming tale, reinforce youngsters' visual-discrimination skills with this class mitten tree. To make mittens for your tree, have each child drip different colors of paint onto white construction paper. Help her fold the paper in half and then unfold it so that the paint forms two matching designs. When the paint is dry, refold the paper and draw a mitten outline on the back. Have the child cut on the outline through both thicknesses to create two matching mittens. Laminate the mittens; then punch a hole at the bottom of each one. Mount a large paper pine tree on a bulletin board; then use a pushpin to hang one mitten from each pair on the tree. Place the remaining mittens in a basket near the tree and invite youngsters to match pairs by hanging each mitten's mate on the pushpin. Now that's a hands-on activity!

## Runaway Mittens

By Jean Rogers
Illustrated by Rie Munoz
Published by William Morrow & Company, Inc.; 1988

*Every time Pica needs his mittens, he discovers that they have run away again. His sister, Etta, jokingly suggests that he needs special glasses for finding his runaway mittens. But on one especially cold and stormy night, Pica's mittens are found right where they need to be—keeping a litter of newborn pups warm!*

Communication skills will be up and running with this fun center game. Place a red mitten in your dramatic-play area; then invite a pair of children to the area. Have the first child close his eyes while the second child hides the mitten. After the mitten is hidden, the first child opens his eyes and begins to look for it. The second child leads his partner to the mitten by giving clues or directions. When he finds the mitten, the children switch roles and play again.

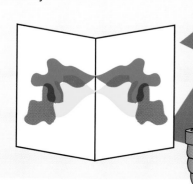

## Boot Weather
By Judith Vigna
Published by Albert Whitman & Company, 1988

*"Boot weather!" announces Kim's father, and thus her adventures begin. She steps into her snow boots and then imagines herself climbing mountains, sledding down slopes, and floating in space. In boot weather, Kim can go anywhere and still be home in time for lunch!*

Boot little imaginations into high gear after reading this spirited story. Place pairs of adult-sized winter boots in a center along with a variety of props, such as a hockey stick, a small sled, or a construction worker's helmet. Invite students to put on the boots and then imagine a place the boots can take them. Encourage youngsters to use the props to act out their fantasies. For a writing extension, place some paper and crayons in the center and have students illustrate their adventures. Have boots, will travel!

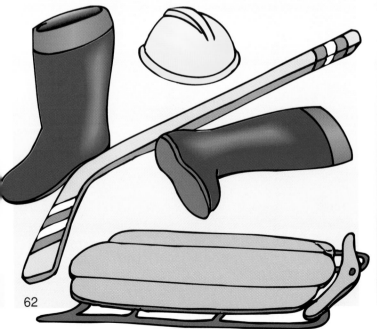

## Thomas' Snowsuit
By Robert N. Munsch
Illustrated by Michael Martchenko
Published by Firefly Books, 1989

*When Thomas' mother brings him a new brown snowsuit, Thomas refuses to wear it, yelling, "NNNNNO!" After a struggle with his mother, Thomas is zipped into the dreaded snowsuit and sent off to school. But once at school, Thomas tangles with his teacher and the principal, who also try to get the boy into the suit. Each fight ends with increasingly hilarious results, until Thomas finally remedies the situation himself.*

After reading the story, create this class book that will really suit your youngsters! For each child, make a construction paper copy of the snowsuit pattern on page 65. Have the child cut out the pattern and write his name in the provided space. Direct him to color the face to resemble his own. (Or cut out the facial area and glue the child's photo behind the paper so that his face shows through the circle.) Invite the youngster to add small buttons, sequins, or other decorative items to trim the suit. To create a front cover for the book, mask the text on the snowsuit pattern; then make a construction paper copy. After cutting out the pattern, draw or glue your own photo in the facial area; then decorate the page as desired. Create a back cover by tracing the snowsuit pattern onto construction paper and cutting on the resulting outline. Program the inside of the back cover as shown. Stack the children's pages between the covers, staple the book at the top, and then add a title. Finally, place the book in your reading area and let it snow, let it snow, let it snow!

Our Class's Snowsuits

Michael is wearing a snowsuit.

We're bundled up And ready to go. Let it snow! Let it snow! Let it snow!

# More Toasty Tales

## A New Coat for Anna
By Harriet Ziefert
Illustrated by Anita Lobel
Published by Alfred A. Knopf, Inc.; 1990

*Although the stores are empty and there's no money, Anna's resourceful mother finds a way to get a new coat for her daughter. Anna, and readers, are treated to the art of trading goods for services as a beautiful coat materializes in the process.*

## The First Snowfall
By Anne F. and Harlow Rockwell
Published by Aladdin Paperbacks, 1992

*Snow falls throughout the cold and quiet night. When morning arrives, an excited young girl bundles up in her cold-weather wear for a snowy-day adventure. Simple text and illustrations invite readers to gear up and join the fun!*

## The Rag Coat
By Lauren A. Mills
Published by Little, Brown and Company; 1991

*Minna proudly wears her new coat to school, for it was lovingly created by the Quilting Mothers. But to her surprise, her classmates laugh at her rag coat. Before long, though, the children come to respect Minna and to admire her beautiful coat as she shares the special stories represented by each piece of cloth.*

## Caps, Hats, Socks, and Mittens: A Book About the Four Seasons
By Louise Borden
Illustrated by Lillian Hoban
Published by Scholastic Inc., 1992

*"Winter is a lot of stuff to put on and a lot of stuff to get off!" This delightful sensory overview of the four seasons provides the perfect resource for comparing and discussing clothing appropriate for each season.*

A _____ crawled in my sock.

Then I crawled in my sock and took a warm winter nap.

_____ is wearing a snowsuit.

# It's Circus Time!

Come one! Come all! It's circus time! Capture the excitement and thrill of the big top with this collection of circus-related books and activities.

*ideas by Mackie Rhodes*

## Engelbert Joins the Circus

By Tom Paxton
Illustrated by Roberta Wilson
Published by Morrow Junior Books, 1997

*When Engelbert the elephant visits his American cousin, he accidentally stumbles into the circus spotlight. Unfazed by his fumble, this fun-loving elephant steals the show with an enormously entertaining performance. Encore!*

After reading the story, revisit the pages on which Engelbert is packing his belongings for his journey. Ask youngsters to imagine that they have been invited to join the circus. What will they pack in their bags? Provide each child with a sheet of paper and direct her to illustrate the items that she would pack. (Or have her cut out and glue pictures onto the paper.) Next instruct the child to glue her paper onto the right side of a large sheet of brown construction paper. Have her fold the brown paper in half to cover the illustration and then decorate the folded paper to resemble a suitcase. Invite each child to share the contents of her suitcase with the class and explain why she might bring each item. All packed? Let's go!

## The Fabulous Flying Fandinis

By Ingrid Slyder
Published by Cobblehill Books, 1996

*When Bobby visits his strange new neighbors, the Fabulous Flying Fandinis, he makes one excuse after another to decline the circus family's invitations to join in the fun. Then, one day, friendly Fandini hands reach out to help Bobby jump on and join an exciting new adventure. Hooray!*

After a shared reading of the book, involve students in a discussion about trying something new (such as a food or an activity), and the feelings that accompany such undertakings. Encourage each child to think of a time he tried a new experience and how he felt when it was over. Was he happy? Proud? Surprised? Next make a class book of new experiences. Give each child a sheet of paper and have him draw a picture of himself engaged in the new experience. Stack the completed pages and bind them between two covers. Title the book; then read it aloud during group time. Place the book and a copy of *The Fabulous Flying Fandinis* in your class library. Jump on! Join in!

## Zorina Ballerina

By Enzo Giannini
Published by Simon & Schuster Books
for Young Readers, 1993

*Every day little Zorina sits ringside watching the older el-ephants rehearse their polka. She secretly practices the dance with coaching from the clowns. So when the star dancer gets sick on opening night, who fills her place in the spotlight? None other than Zorina the Ballerina! A star is born!*

Turn your energetic youngsters into troupes of dazzling dancers! To prepare, tape several different lines—such as straight, curvy, zigzag, and dashed—onto the floor. Read the story; then divide your class into small groups. Give one group at a time a supply of bandanas or scarves. Help each student in the group tie a few bandanas around her waist to create a dance costume. When your youngsters are outfitted, have each child stand on a line. Then play assorted musical selections, such as classical, polka, and jazz. Invite each child in the group to creatively dance to the music, using her line as a guide for her dance patterns. Periodically encourage students to switch lines as they twist, twirl, and tiptoe to the music. Rotate the groups so that each one has a chance to perform and observe the circus dance. Bravo!

Order books online. www.themailbox.com

## Barnyard Big Top

By Jill Kastner
Published by Simon & Schuster Books
for Young Readers, 1997

*The arrival of Uncle Julius and his Two-Ring Extravaganza generates a flurry of excitement and commotion for Ben, his farm animal friends, and the entire town. This farm may never be the same again!*

Challenge the imagination and creativity of your students as they assemble the greatest show on earth—a barnyard big top! After reading the story, ask students to brainstorm a list of farm animals that might be found in a circus. Ask them to imagine the acts they might see in a circus of only farm animals. Next instruct pairs of students to each select an animal from the list. Encourage the pairs to make up circus acts for their animals. Then have them assemble simple props and costumes for their acts. For example, students pretending to be turkeys on a tightrope might make paper beaks and use child-safe umbrellas. Allow students some time to practice their acts; then don your own ringmaster costume. With circuslike fanfare, introduce your barnyard big top and let the show begin!

# Pink Pigs Aplenty

By Sandy Nightingale
(This book is out of print. Please check your local library.)

*This alliterative counting book features a pack of pink piggies performing their circus stunts and skills. And what might the grand finale of this swell swine show be? A perfect piggy pyramid!*

This beanbag game has youngsters counting with the greatest of ease. To prepare, make ten copies of the pig pattern on page 71; then color and cut them out. Label each cutout with a different numeral from 1 to 10; then laminate them for durability. Tape the cutouts onto the floor in a pyramid shape.

To play, name an action such as the following: Hop on one foot. Spin around. Clap your hands. Then invite each child, in turn, to toss a beanbag onto the pig pyramid. Have him read aloud the numeral on which his beanbag landed. Then have him perform the action that many times. This little piggy jumps one time. This little piggy jumps three. How many jumps for this little piggy? Just toss the bag and see!

# Circus

by Lois Ehlert
Published by HarperCollins Publishers, Inc.; 1992

*Step right up! This stupendous show is filled with stately characters, stellar performances, and show-stopping shapes. Imaginative colors and figures combine to make this Lois Ehlert creation a colossal delight.*

Shape up youngsters' circus savvy with these creative collages. After reading the story, divide youngsters into small groups. Provide each group with an assortment of shape tracers, brightly colored construction paper, and decorative gift wrap. Invite students to trace and cut out a variety of shapes. If desired, refer students to the book for inspiration. Then instruct each group to form a circus collage by cooperatively gluing their shapes onto a sheet of black bulletin board paper. Invite each group to tell about its collage; then display the completed works with the title of this book.

# Star of the Circus

By Michael and Mary Beth Sampson
Illustrated by Jose Aruego and Ariane Dewey
Published by Henry Holt and Company, 1997

*One animal after another claims center ring to arrogantly announce his status as "Star of the Circus." But the performers learn a valuable lesson about cooperation and respect when they discover that it takes all of them to create a star circus.*

Highlight your students' fantasies of big-top fame with this star-studded idea. After reading and discussing this story, give each child a yellow construction paper copy of the star pattern on page 70. Help him cut out his star and the circle as indicated. Label the star with the child's self-appointed circus name, such as "Lion-Taming Leeron." Have the child use crayons, glitter pens, and craft items to decorate his star to correspond with his circus title. Then glue his photo to the back of the star so that the face shows through the circle. Later, invite each child to share his star and a sample of his star performance with the class. Then display the stars on a big-top background with the title "Now Starring..."

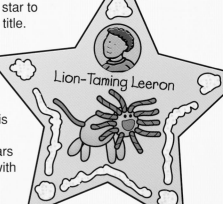

Lion-Taming Leeron

# And the Show Goes On and On!

Share some of the books from this collection of circus literature for a three-ring reading extravaganza!

## Ginger Jumps

By Lisa Campbell Ernst
Published by Aladdin Paperbacks, 1996

*Ginger loves the circus life, but she longs for a little girl companion. Then, one day, she's given a spotlight stunt—and the opportunity to be noticed by the girl of her dreams! Will fear and the snooty Prunella stand in Ginger's way? Readers will be on the edge of their seats as they cheer this circus pup's determination and courage.*

## Mirette on the High Wire

By Emily Arnold McCully
Published by The Putnam Publishing Group, 1997

*Tutored by the world-renowned Monsieur Bellini, Mirette becomes a skillful tightrope walker. But when she discovers that Bellini is overcome with fear on the wire, Mirette begins to feel fear and doubt herself. The beautiful blend of art and text in this Caldecott Medal book will touch the heart of every reader.*

Order books online. www.themailbox.com

## Emeline at the Circus

By Marjorie Priceman
Published by Alfred A. Knopf, Inc.; 1999

*During a circus field trip, Miss Splinter teaches Emeline's class all about the exotic animals, entertaining performers, and daring feats. But where's Emeline? Get into the act right along with Emeline with this hilarious big top adventure.*

## Circus Classics

### If I Ran the Circus

By Dr. Seuss
Published by Random House, Inc.; 1956

### Bearymore

By Don Freeman
Published by Puffin Books, 1979

### Harold's Circus

By Crockett Johnson
Published by HarperCollins Publishers, Inc.; 1959

69

# Star Pattern

Use with *Star of the Circus* on page 68.

Cut
this
out.

# The Alliteration

Hop aboard! Take a rollicking ride with your class through this assortment of alliterative stories. Along the way, youngsters will enjoy inspirational illustrations, teasing text, and a collection of creative curriculum-related ideas. Toot! Toot!!

*by Ada Goren and Mackie Rhodes*

Wanda wears wavy wigs.

## Six Sandy Sheep
By Judith Ross Enderle and Stephanie Gordon Tessler
Illustrated by John O'Brien
Published by Boyds Mills Press, Inc.; 1997

*Several sheep saunter to the beach on a sunny day and share some seaside shenanigans in the sand and surf.*

Students will be eager to show off their own ideas of sheep shenanigans, so be sure to showcase these projects in a special display in your classroom. After reading the story, ask youngsters to brainstorm a list of action words beginning with *S*. List their responses on chart paper. Then invite each child to select a word from the chart. Have her draw a sheep engaging in that action on a sheet of construction paper. After she completes her drawing, encourage her to embellish her picture with craft items, such as cotton balls, wiggle eyes, pipe cleaners, and fabric scraps. Label her picture to describe the sheep's activity and then display all the pictures with the title "Sheep Shenanigans."

## Watch William Walk
By Ann Jonas
Published by Greenwillow Books, 1997

*Take a walk along the beach with William, Wanda, Wally, and Wilma to find out which character is water bound. The overhead perspective of this frolicking foursome creates some interesting illustrations.*

After sharing this story jam-packed with *W* words, revisit each page and ask students to tally all the words that begin with *W*. They'll soon notice that *every* word in this story begins with *W!* Try this follow-up activity to see if your little ones have as much success in making sensible sentences with *W* words. First, have youngsters brainstorm as many *W* words as they can. As you record the words, put them into three lists: nouns, verbs, and adjectives. Then give each child a cutout in the shape of a *W*. Guide each child to choose four words— two from the things or people list, one from the action list, and one from the describing list—to make a sentence, either sensible or somewhat silly! Have her copy her four words onto the four lines of her *W* cutout. Then display these wacky works from your wordsmiths on a bulletin board. Wow!

sing
slurp
swing
skip
sleep
shake
stomp
shiver
smile
snore
ski
skate
swim
surf
sneeze

sheep skating

# Station

## Dinorella: A Prehistoric Fairy Tale
By Pamela Duncan Edwards
Illustrated by Henry Cole
Published by Hyperion Books for Children, 1999

*On her way to the dance, dainty Dinorella spies a disgraceful deinonychus dragging the duke away. Will her daring deeds of bravery save the duke?*

After sharing this prehistoric version of the classic Cinderella story, invite your little ones to decorate some "d-stinctive" eyewear so they can imitate the divinely dressed Dinorella! For each child, photocopy a glasses pattern from page 76 onto tagboard. Have each child cut out her pattern. Then have her use a hole puncher to punch a hole as indicated to form the letter *d* at each upper corner of her glasses. Also have her punch a hole inside the eyehole area on each side as a starting point before cutting out the eyeholes with scissors. Then provide glue, sparkling sequins, plastic gems, and glitter. Encourage each student to decorate her glasses as desired. When the glue is dry, give each child a sparkly silver pipe cleaner. Have her cut it in half; then direct her to wrap the end of one half around each side of the glasses to create the earpieces. Invite your diminutive dinosaurs to don their glasses and wear them while digging in the sand, drawing pictures, dining on a snack, or playing dress-up! How "d-lightful"!

## A Pair of Protoceratops
By Bernard Most
Published by Harcourt Brace & Company, 1998

*Journey through the day with a pair of protoceratops, from preparing for preschool to putting on pajamas for a peaceful night's sleep.*

Prompt lots of imaginative play with these protoceratops headpieces. In advance, cut out several tagboard copies of the protoceratops pattern on page 77 to use as tracers. Share the story; then give each child a 12" x 18" sheet of construction paper to fold in half. Ask her to trace the protoceratops on one side of her folded paper. Then have her cut out the shape through both thicknesses. Invite her to add a wiggle eye, yarn mouth, and pom-pom nostril to each cutout, as shown, so that each is a mirror image of the other. After the glue dries, have the child glue the two pieces together along the top of the head and down the beak. To make a headpiece, staple the protoceratops head onto a fitted sentence-strip headband as shown. Then pair your little dinosaurs and invite each pair to participate in activities beginning with *P,* such as puzzles, painting, or packing pails with sand.

For more ideas using books by Bernard Most, see pages 240–241.

## Some Smug Slug

By Pamela Duncan Edwards
Illustrated by Henry Cole
Published by HarperTrophy, 1998

*This self-important slug is so smug that even the most serious of warnings can't stop him from slithering up a steep slope. So, stationed at the summit, the slug is greeted by a shocking surprise. Slurp!*

After reading this story, page through it once again with youngsters to spot the hidden *S* shape in each picture. Afterward, invite students to create their own hidden letter pictures. To begin, ask each child to draw a large, bold *S* on a sheet of paper. Then have her convert her letter into an animal or an object, or to draw a scene around the letter to "hide" it in her picture. Challenge a few classmates to find the hidden *S* in the child's picture. Later, display all the pictures along with a challenge for admirers to find the hidden letter in each illustration.

## Miss Spider's ABC

By David Kirk
Published by Scholastic Trade Books, 1998

big blue bicycle

*Tiny creatures from ants to a zebra butterfly anticipate Miss Spider's birthday celebration. Imaginative illustrations highlight this insect-inspired alliterative alphabet book.*

Inspire youngsters to imagine some surprise gifts they might give Miss Spider for her special celebration. After sharing the story, encourage students to think of alliterative gift ideas, such as a big blue bicycle, a purple pinwheel, a yellow yo-yo, a heart-shaped hat, or a speedy skateboard. Ask each child to secretly illustrate his gift idea for Miss Spider on a sheet of white construction paper. Then write his dictation on his drawing. Next, have each child make some gift wrap for his gift by coloring a unique marker design on another sheet of paper. Help each child staple his gift wrap to his birthday gift illustration along one edge. If desired, invite him to add ribbon and a bow to embellish his gift wrap. Then have each child give clues about his "wrapped" gift to help the class guess what it might be. After several guesses, have the child fold back the gift wrap to reveal the special surprise beneath it.

## Four Famished Foxes and Fosdyke

By Pamela Duncan Edwards
Illustrated by Henry Cole
Published by HarperTrophy, 1997

*Fosdyke favors French food over fox food. And that's fortunate for his four foolish siblings who return home famished after a night of failed fowl hunting.*

These creative cuisine collages are perfect for reinforcing beginning letter sounds. After sharing the story, write the letter of your choice on chart paper; then have youngsters brainstorm a list of foods beginning with that letter. List their responses on the chart. Repeat the activity for several different letters; then assemble a student group for each letter. Give each group a poster board labeled with the assigned letter. Then ask students to cut out pictures from magazines and grocery store flyers that begin with the appropriate sound. Have them glue their pictures onto the poster to create a food collage. Invite each group to share its collage during group time. Then display the posters with the title "Food Favorites."

## Look Out, Bird!

By Marilyn Janovitz
Published by North-South Books Inc., 1997

*Snail's little slip starts a circular series of events that leads right back to him. Then, suddenly startled, snail slips again....*

What kind of chaos will snail's slip cause in your class? Find out with this idea. In advance, make a class supply of a page programmed with the sentence starter "Snail slipped and…" After reading the story, ask each child to creatively illustrate a programmed page with a picture of a snail and an object from which it slipped. Then have him imagine that the snail's slip caused something to happen, but what? Encourage the child to think of an action beginning with the same letter as his first name. Label a separate sheet of paper with his alliterative response, such as "bumped Bruce." Then ask him to illustrate his page to show the consequence of snail's slip. Afterward, sequence and bind all the student pages into a class book titled "Look Out!" Invite each child to read his pair of pages to the class; then place the book in your reading center for individual and shared reading enjoyment.

Snail slipped and...

Ouch!

bumped Bruce.

Order books online.
www.themailbox.com

# Glasses Patterns
Use with *Dinorella: A Prehistoric Fairy Tale* on page 73.

**Protoceratops Pattern**
Use with *A Pair of Protoceratops* on page 73.

# Nature's

Summer is the ideal season to get out and about to explore, discover, and experience the countless wonders of nature. And this collection of literature and related activities is the perfect complement to your nature studies.

*by Mackie Rhodes*

## Bugs! Bugs! Bugs!
By Bob Barner
Published by Chronicle Books, 1999

*A colorful collection of collages and simple rhyming text brings readers up close and personal with a variety of bugs. The handy Bug-o-Meter in the back of the book provides additional information about each bug.*

Use this book as a springboard to find out what your youngsters know about bugs common to your area. In advance, create a Bug-o-Meter (similar to the one in the back of the book) on a sheet of chart paper. Use your own questions in the left column and leave blank spaces for the bugs' names at the top. Then gather a class supply of plastic tweezers and a shoebox.

After sharing the story, take students outdoors to observe local bugs. Invite each child to transfer any dead bugs he finds into the box with tweezers. Back in the classroom, have youngsters use magnifying lenses to examine the bugs in their collection. Afterward, have them decide which bugs to list on the Bug-o-Meter. Label each column with a different bug's name. To complete the Bug-o-Meter, discuss student responses to each question and then write the most popular response in each box. Extend this activity by having your class re-search each bug to check the accuracy of their responses.

| Bug-o-Meter | Beetle | Cricket | Butterfly |
|---|---|---|---|
| Does it have wings? | no | no | yes |
| How many legs? | 6 | 6 | 6 |
| What does it eat? | dirt | grass | flowers |
| Where does it live? | under-ground | in grass | near flowers |

## My Father's Hands
By Joanne Ryder
Illustrated by Mark Graham
Published by Morrow Junior Books, 1994

*A young child admires her father's big, strong hands—the hands that shape a garden from the earth—which turn soft and gentle when small treasures are discovered and presented. Soft illustrations and tender text convey the warm, trusting affection a child has for her father.*

What child doesn't enjoy having a surprise presented to her in cupped hands—or surprising someone else with a treasure hidden in her own cupped hands? Here's a guessing game that incorporates both kinds of surprises! To begin, collect a variety of toy bugs that easily fit into a child's hands. Then share this sweet story with students. After the story, divide your class into small groups. Instruct one child in each group to secretly select a bug from the collection and hide it in her hands. To play, the child gives clues to help group members identify the selected bug. Then she opens her hands to reveal the surprise inside. Play the game until each group member has had a turn to hide a bug. No peeking!

# Stories

## Jack's Garden
By Henry Cole
Published by Greenwillow Books, 1995

*Cumulative text and illustrations follow the growth stages of Jack's garden from tiny seeds to splendid blooms. Garden-related items and creatures spill out of and border each illustration, making this book a storehouse of scientific information. As a bonus, the author provides a simple guide on how to start your own garden.*

Plant seeds of creativity in your students with this multisensory activity. In advance, gather some potting soil, an assortment of seeds, tagboard (one piece per child), and a variety of craft items, such as cotton balls, yarn, pipe cleaners, stamp pads, construction paper, scissors, glue, markers, and tissue paper. After reading the story, invite each child to use the provided materials to create his own garden. First, have him glue a layer of soil along the bottom portion of the tagboard. Then encourage him to show the various growth stages of his garden, as well as a few garden-dwelling creatures. For example, he might glue seeds and yarn worms onto the soil. Then he might use pipe cleaners, construction paper, and tissue paper to create flowers as shown. Label each child's picture with "[Child's name]'s Garden" and then invite him to share his picture with the group.

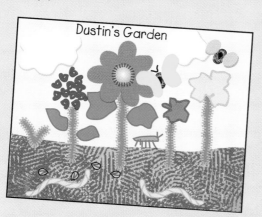

Dustin's Garden

## Bugs for Lunch
By Margery Facklam
Illustrated by Sylvia Long
Published by Charlesbridge Publishing, Inc.; 1999

*Bugs for lunch? That's right! Bugs are a part of many creatures' diets. This interesting book allows children to meet a variety of bug eaters, from birds and insects to plants and even people. Enjoy the story and then use the handy reference in the back of the book to learn more about each creature.*

Bugs may not sound very appetizing to your youngsters, but they'll work up an appetite for counting with this buggy game. To prepare, put a supply of toy bugs in a lunchbox and then gather some paper plates. Read the story; then invite small groups of students to join you for a lunch of bugs. To begin, give each child a plate. Then recite the rhyme below, filling in the first line with the name of a child and the second line with a number.

[Child's name, child's name], it's time for lunch.
Take [number] bugs to munch, munch, munch!

Have the child count out the appropriate number of bugs from the lunchbox and then place them on her plate. Repeat the rhyme for each child in the group. Conclude the activity with a snack of Gummy Worms® candy. Yummy!

# Chickens Aren't the Only Ones

By Ruth Heller
Published by Grosset & Dunlap, 1981

*Chickens lay eggs, but they aren't the only ones! This brightly illustrated book introduces a variety of egg-laying creatures, from birds, reptiles, and insects to more unusual animals, such as the spiny anteater and the duckbill platypus.*

Share this informative book with students and then invite them to create a spectacular display showing what they've learned about egg-laying animals. To begin, cut out a large egg shape from bulletin board paper. Then have several students sponge-paint the egg to make it look speckled. When the paint is dry, cut the egg in two so that it appears to be cracked. Write "Chickens Aren't the Only Ones" on the top half of the egg and "_____ Lay Eggs, Too!" on the bottom half. Staple the bottom half of the egg to the bottom of a bulletin board and then staple the top half of the egg to the board as shown.

After reading and discussing the story, give each child a half sheet of paper. Have her illustrate an egg-laying animal and then write (or dictate) its name. During group time, invite each child to share her page with the class. Then staple the illustrations to the display for everyone to enjoy.

# Where Butterflies Grow

By Joanne Ryder
Illustrated by Lynne Cherry
Published by Puffin Unicorn Books, 1989

*Imaginations soar in this green, leaf-covered growing place as readers follow the life cycle of a caterpillar from its beginnings as a small egg to its majestic emergence as a beautiful black swallowtail butterfly.*

Help youngsters learn the stages of a caterpillar's metamorphosis with these interactive pictures. To prepare, make tagboard tracers of the butterfly patterns on page 82. Provide each child with a sheet of blue construction paper; a sheet of construction paper in his color choice; a strip of sandpaper; and small pieces of green, yellow, brown, and white construction paper. Each child will also need access to the butterfly tracers, scissors, crayons, glue, and a hole puncher. After sharing the story, help each child follow the steps below to create a picture.

1. Trace the caterpillar onto yellow paper and the cocoon onto brown paper. Cut out each shape.
2. Trace the butterfly onto the colored sheet of paper (folded) as shown. Cut out the butterfly.
3. Color the caterpillar and butterfly as desired.
4. Cut the sandpaper strip to resemble a tree branch. Glue it to the middle of the blue paper.
5. Add a few green leaf cutouts to the branch, making sure that the tip of one leaf is glued over the branch.
6. Punch a hole in the white paper. Glue the white paper dot (the caterpillar's egg) onto the tip of the leaf.
7. Position the caterpillar along the branch so that it covers the egg. Glue only the bottom end of the caterpillar to the branch.
8. Fit the cocoon over the caterpillar and then glue only the top end of the cocoon to the branch. (Make sure you do not trap the caterpillar in the glue.)
9. Align the butterfly over the cocoon; then glue only the tips of the left wing to the paper.

To use, the child folds the butterfly back to uncover the cocoon. Then he folds the cocoon up to expose the caterpillar and the caterpillar down to reveal the egg. Encourage each child to use his picture as he describes to his family the life stages of a caterpillar.

## Pond Year

By Kathryn Lasky
Illustrated by Mike Bostock
Published by Candlewick Press, 1995

*Two young girls share the richness of pond life throughout the year. From catching warm-weather critters to skating on the frozen water in the winter, the girls' love for the pond and for each other bonds them together as "best friends, pond buddies, scum chums forever."*

After sharing the story, turn to the two-page spread showing the girls "dipping" in the pond in June. Explain that when the girls step into the pond they stir up the mud on the pond floor. The loosened particles then cling to the girls' legs, darkening them so that they appear to be covered in socks or stockings. Invite youngsters to create these personal ponds in order to observe firsthand how the water changes when a pond is disturbed.

In advance, gather a class supply of quart-sized Ziploc® freezer bags; corn starch; green craft foam; plastic grass; red, blue, and green food coloring; scissors; wide tape; and a class supply of metal binder clips. To make a pond, cut out a lily pad from craft foam. Pour one-fourth cup of corn starch and one cup of water into a plastic bag. Add one drop of blue food coloring, two drops each of red and green food coloring, a few strands of grass, and the lily pad to the mixture. Seal the bag and then reinforce the seal with wide clear tape. Gently knead the water and cornstarch to mix them together. Attach a binder clip to the top of the bag and then hang it on a bulletin board with a pushpin.

Encourage students to periodically check their ponds for settling. After the cornstarch mud settles completely, invite each youngster to poke his pond bottom and observe the results.

## The Very Quiet Cricket

By Eric Carle
Published by Philomel Books, 1990

*A little cricket tries to answer the greetings of numerous insects, but nothing happens when he rubs his wings together. Then he meets another cricket, and his wings magically create a beautiful greeting. Chirp!*

Youngsters will chirp with delight when they find the matching crickets in this game. To prepare, make two enlarged tagboard copies of the insect cards (page 82) for each small group. Color and cut out each card. After reading the story, invite student groups to play Memory with the insect cards. When a player matches the cricket cards, invite him to chirp and rub his "wings" (arms) together. After all the matches are found, challenge each child to name the insects on his cards.

# Butterfly Patterns
Use with *Where Butterflies Grow* on page 80.

cocoon

caterpillar

butterfly

Place on fold.

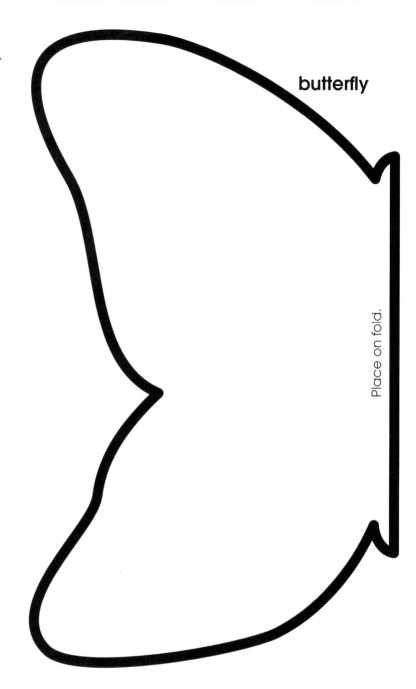

# Insect Cards
Use with *The Very Quiet Cricket* on page 81.

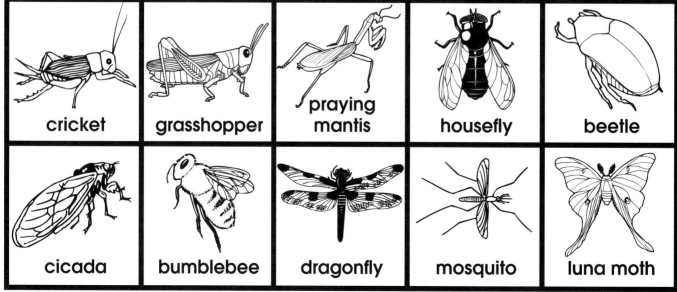

| | | | | |
|---|---|---|---|---|
| cricket | grasshopper | praying mantis | housefly | beetle |
| cicada | bumblebee | dragonfly | mosquito | luna moth |

©The Education Center, Inc. • *THE MAILBOX®* • *Kindergarten* • June/July 2000

# Thematic Units
# and Special Features

# HANGING OUT IN SCHOOL

Aahhh! Nothing says comfort like the feel of a favorite T-shirt! Bring this same comfort into your classroom during the first days of school with these T-shirt theme ideas that are one-size-fits-*all*!

*ideas by Lucia Kemp Henry*

### Welcome!

Show your new students that you are eager to meet them with these special T-shirt greetings. Make a class supply of page 88 on colored construction paper. Personalize each T-shirt, sign your name, and then cut it out. If desired, cut a small slit at the top of the T-shirt's pocket and insert a treat—such as a new pencil, a lollipop, or a stick of gum—as shown. Then tape the treat to the back of the cutout to hold it in place. This timely note from you is sure to make each child feel like he'll fit right in!

### This Must Be the Place

Your kindergartners will know right where to go when they see this lineup of colorful T-shirts outside your door. To make the display, cut out two narrow lengths of bulletin board paper and tape them to your wall to resemble clothesline poles. Next, attach the ends of a length of thick yarn to the poles to serve as the clothesline. Cut out eight large T-shirt shapes from different colors of construction paper. Use a wide-tipped marker to label each of the seven shirts with a different letter from the word "Welcome." Then label the eighth shirt with your name and room number. Mount each shirt to the wall so that it slightly overlaps the clothesline. Finish the display by clipping colorful clothespins to the shoulders of each shirt, as shown. Glad you're here!

### Attendance Online

Put your attendance online—the *clothesline,* that is! To make this handy chart, glue white construction paper clouds to the top of a large sheet of blue poster board. Use markers to write "Who's Hanging Out?" across the clouds. Next, attach the ends of several pieces of yarn to the sides of the poster board to resemble lengths of clothesline. From construction paper, cut out a class supply of white T-shirts and a class supply of colored T-shirts. For each child, label one white and one colored T-shirt with her name. (If desired, attach matching stickers to the shirts to help with name recognition.) Store the colored shirts in a small plastic "laundry" basket. Glue the white T-shirts to the poster board just under the clotheslines. To finish the chart, hot-glue a wooden spring-type clothespin above the clotheslines near the top of each white T-shirt, as shown. Then mount the chart to a bulletin board or wall within youngsters' reach.

As you welcome each child on the first few days of school, help her find her colored T-shirt and then encourage her to pin it to her space on the chart. As your youngsters become accustomed to using this chart every day, taking attendance will be a breeze!

## Special Tees

Celebrate a birthday, a lost tooth, a student of the week, or some other favorite happening by making a whimsical T-shirt for the honoree to wear during the school day. Use fabric paints and any other embellishments of your choice to decorate a shirt for the designated occasion. (You may want to have two or three birthday shirts on hand, just in case!) Then invite the special student to wear this special tee on his special day. Afterwards, simply wash and dry the shirt for the next celebration. "Zip-a-*tee*-doo-dah, Zip-a-*tee*-ay! My, oh my, what a wonderful day!"

## They Come in All Colors

What better way to display colors in your classroom than with T-shirts? Cut out a large T-shirt shape from a piece of 12" x 18" colored craft foam in each color you want to represent. Use fabric paint, glitter glue, or a permanent marker to label each T-shirt with its corresponding color word. If desired, tape a small hanger to the back of each shirt. Then display the shirts on a bulletin board or wall along with a title.

## "Plen-tee" of Helpers

Continue the T-shirt theme throughout your room with this classroom job display. Photocopy page 88. Mask out the text on the T-shirt; then use the modified copy to duplicate a construction paper T-shirt for each job in your classroom. Label each shirt with a different job title and a corresponding illustration. Then cut out the shirts and laminate them for durability. Use an X-acto® knife to cut a small slit at the top of each pocket.

To make name cards, write each child's name (or use photos) on a separate 1 1/2" x 2 1/2" piece of card stock. Laminate the cards if desired. Then glue a craft stick to the back of each name card.

To use the helper display, insert a child's name card into the pocket of each T-shirt. Then simply switch the names periodically to give everyone a turn at being a "migh-tee" fine helper!

## T-Shirt Show-and-Tell

Break the ice with this short-sleeved sharing session. As youngsters bring in their favorite T-shirts (from "Welcome!" on page 84), collect them in a laundry basket. During your first circle time, hold up a shirt and ask its owner to stand or come to the front of the group. Encourage him to say his name, describe his T-shirt, and then explain why it is his favorite. Be sure to include yourself in the sharing, too! At the end of the introductions, have each child wear his shirt and sing the movement song below.

## A T-Shirt That's Just for You

*(sung to the tune of "Daisy, Daisy")*

Find a T-shirt, any ol' color will do.
Find a T-shirt. Pick one that's old or new.
Then put on your shirt. You can do it!
There's really nothing to it.
You're off to school.
You look so cool.
In a T-shirt that's just for you!

*Point finger in different directions as if choosing.*
*Pretend to hold up a shirt.*
*Pretend to put on a shirt.*
*Cheer with arms.*
*Walk in place.*
*Smile and strut.*
*Hold hands out to the side and turn in a circle as if modeling.*

## Meet Our "Facul-tee"

Extend the sharing in "T-Shirt Show-and-Tell" to include members of your school staff as a fun way of introducing them to your youngsters. Arrange for each staff member that your students need to meet—such as the school secretary, librarian, custodian, principal, and music teacher—to bring her favorite T-shirt to school. Then, after the classroom T-shirt sharing, lead youngsters on a school tour to meet, greet, and hear about other staff members' favorite tees. Now you've given your little ones something to associate with each new face!

## Trendy Tees

Use this idea to practice fine-motor skills and encourage creativity with your little fashion designers. Make several simple T-shirt templates from tagboard (or use the T-shirt pattern on page 88). Have each child choose a color of construction paper; then help her trace and cut out a shirt shape. Use a marker to label each child's shirt with her name. Then provide a variety of decorative materials—such as glitter glue, sequins, buttons, stickers, and fabric scraps—for each child to use to decorate her T-shirt. When the projects are complete, remove the T-shirts that spell "Welcome" on the clothesline created in "This Must Be the Place" (page 84). Then hang the new T-shirt collection on the clothesline. (You might need to add another clothesline to accommodate everyone's shirt.) Finish the display by adding the title "Look Who's Hanging Out in Our Room!" These one-of-a-kind T-shirts are sure to be conversation starters for anyone hangin' around in the hallway.

# LOOK WHO'S HANGING OUT IN OUR ROOM!

Katie · Cassie · Noah · Allen · Jamar · Devon

## T-Shirt Tales

You'll get to know your new students even better as they work on these individual booklets. And your new students will be getting to know some of their thinking, fine-motor, and artistic skills! To prepare, duplicate pages 89–91 for each of your students. Encourage each child to complete his pages. (See the directions below.) Then help each child cut out his pages, stack them in order, and staple them together along the left side. Invite each child to share his book with the group, then take it home to share with his family. "Tee-rific" bookmaking!

**Cover:** Write your name in the space provided.
**Page 1:** Color the shirt your favorite color.
**Page 2:** Cut out a magazine picture of your favorite food; then glue it to the page.
**Page 3:** Write your age on the shirt.
**Page 4:** Color the head to look like yourself. Then write (or dictate) to complete the sentence on the shirt.

## T-Shirt Pattern

Use with "Welcome!" on page 84, " 'Plen-tee' of Helpers" on page 85, and "Trendy Tees" on page 87.

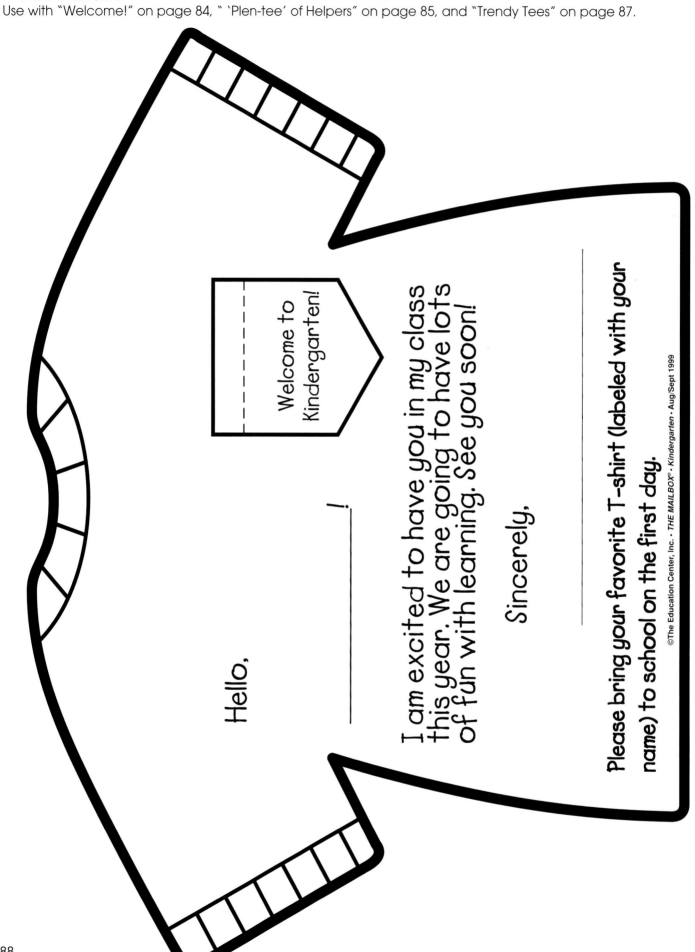

Welcome to Kindergarten!

Hello,

_____!

I am excited to have you in my class this year. We are going to have lots of fun with learning. See you soon!

Sincerely,

_____

Please bring your favorite T-shirt (labeled with your name) to school on the first day.

©The Education Center, Inc. • THE MAILBOX® • Kindergarten • Aug/Sept 1999

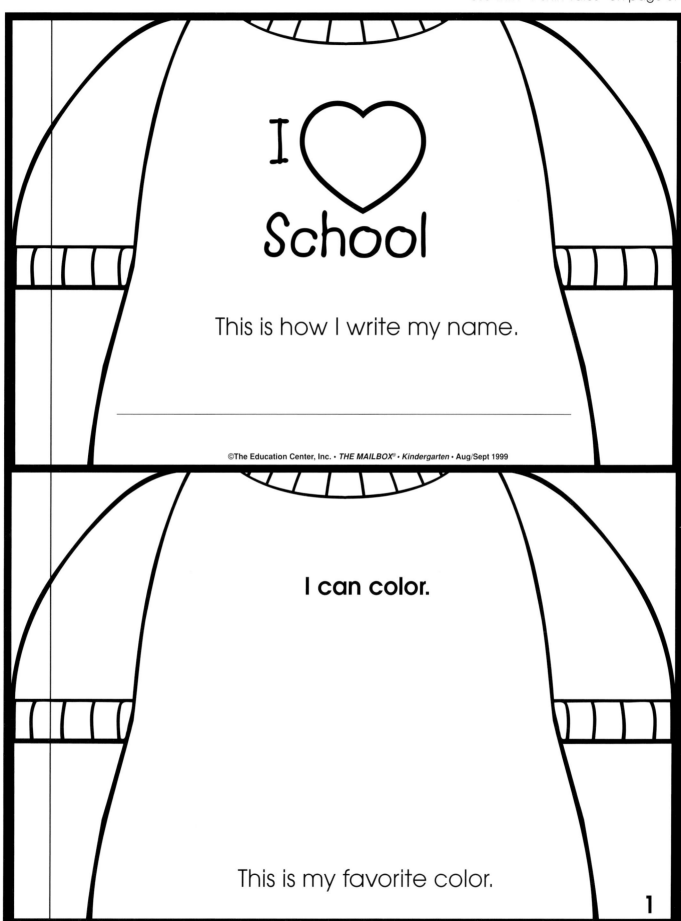

I ♥ School

This is how I write my name.

_____

©The Education Center, Inc. • *THE MAILBOX®* • *Kindergarten* • Aug/Sept 1999

I can color.

This is my favorite color.

1

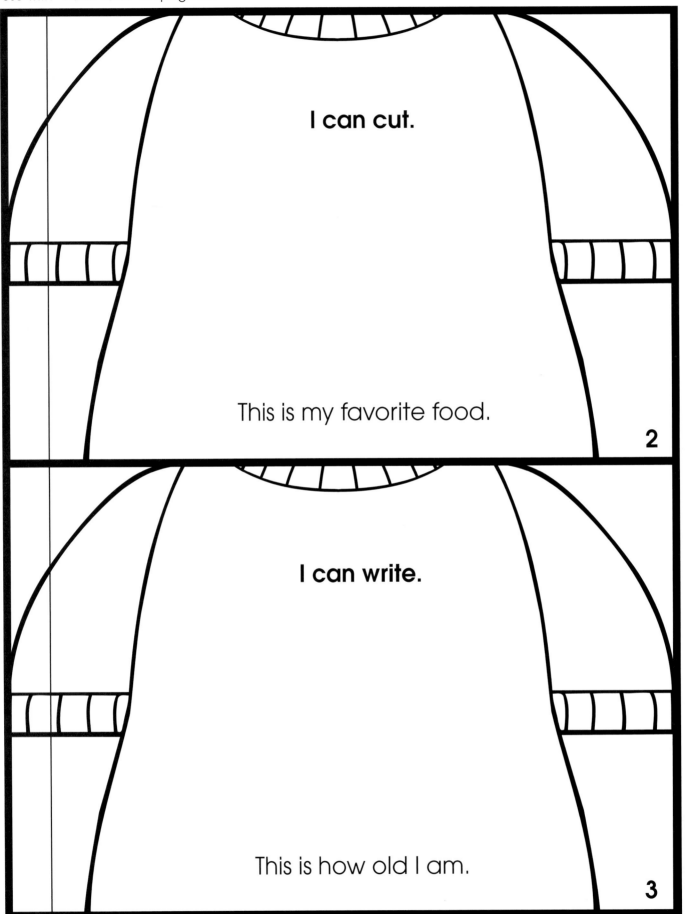

I can cut.

This is my favorite food.

2

I can write.

This is how old I am.

3

I like to

4

# There's No Place

## Ideas to Help Young Children Feel at Home in the Classroom

The first days of a new school year are often exciting for both teachers and students. But with that excitement, have you noticed that some youngsters arrive with a slight case of "the first-day jitters"? Choose from among this collection of ideas designed to ease those jitters by helping your little ones get to know you, each other, and their new school environment.

*ideas contributed by early childhood teachers*

## Before the Big Day

### Oh, You'll Know!

Every parent who has dealt with the question, "How will I know who my teacher is?" will be forever grateful to you for this idea! Choose a symbol from a classroom theme or a book that you plan to read on the first day. Then design something with that symbol that you can wear. For example, if you plan to read *The Cat in the Hat,* make a red-and-white striped hat from a paper plate and construction paper. (See additional suggestions below.) A couple of weeks before school starts, jot a quick note to each child telling her that you will be the teacher wearing (for example) the tall, red-and-white striped hat. They'll know just what to look for!

- For a teddy bear theme, wear a headband with teddy bear ears.
- For a T-shirt theme, wear a very colorful, oversized T-shirt. (See pages 84–91 for more T-shirt ideas.)

Deb Scala—Gr. K
Mt. Tabor Elementary School
Mt. Tabor, NJ

### A Special Space

Foster a sense of classroom ownership and belonging by inviting each child to create his own special space in your classroom. A couple of weeks before school starts, mail each child a notecard inviting him (and his parent) to drop by your classroom on a designated date. (Use your Open House date if your school holds one before classes start.) In the note, ask the child to bring requested school supplies with him on that day. When the child arrives, show him his cubby and where any larger supplies of his will be kept. Then give him a strip of tagboard labeled with his name. Encourage him to use an assortment of simple art supplies, such as stickers and stamps, to decorate his nametag. Then help him post his nametag on his cubby or at a table space. Youngsters will rest easy knowing they have a special space in their new kindergarten classroom. And you'll rest easy knowing all those sets of school supplies are organized before that hectic first day of school!

adapted from an idea by
Kiva English—Gr. K
Cato-Meridian Central School
Elbridge, NY

This is my dog, Pepper.

Camping with my daughter.

### All About You!

You've all had those precious little ones that respond with shock when they learn that teachers actually *leave* the school building in the evenings and do ordinary things, such as shop in grocery stores, walk their dogs, or eat at restaurants. Create an all-about-you book to help your new batch of kindergartners get to know you and feel more comfortable in your classroom. In advance, gather a collection of photos that show you in settings or situations that children are likely to find interesting, such as with your family, friends, pets, or on a vacation. Arrange and mount the photos on sheets of construction paper. Then add simple captions for each picture. Laminate the pages; then bind them together behind a laminated cover. Display this book during meet-the-teacher times and the first few days of school. This book will be in high demand!

Angela Van Beveren
Alvin, TX

Ben

# Like Kindergarten!

## On the Big Day...and After

### Mingling Manager

On that first day of school, do you have every intention to meet and greet each new child and parent with warmth and security only to be barraged by too many things happening at once? Here's a suggestion to ease that dilemma. Before students arrive, set up several play dough stations on your tables. (For lots of play dough ideas, see pages 108–113.) If desired, offer written suggestions at each station to get the dough rolling—so to speak! When children and parents arrive, ask them to choose a place to work with the play dough. Because each parent and child is involved in this activity, you'll be able to meet and mingle at your leisure. You're also likely to find that this environment is a great one in which students and parents get to know each other as well. So let's get that dough rolling!

Leslye Davidson—Gr. K
Alameda, CA

### Are We There Yet?

"Is it lunchtime yet?" "When can we go outside?" "Is it time to go home?" Sure, all of these are very important questions to a kindergarten child—but they also take up a lot of your time, don't they? This idea will help children understand the pace of each day as well as reinforce meaning and print. In advance, laminate a long strip of butcher paper. Glue a school cutout to the left side and a house cutout to the right side. Then use wipe-off markers to program significant times of your day along that strip. Next add words, simple drawings, and/or pictures to depict your schedule for the first day of school. As you go through the first day, use reusable adhesive to post a cutout (such as a bus or other theme-related item) along the timeline. At the end of the day, program the timeline for the next day. As children become accustomed to this process, ask a child to move the cutout as the day progresses. "I can read just where we are!"

Angela Lavy Joel—Gr. K
Marlowe Elementary
Falling Waters, WV

### The Magic Apples of My Eye

Let each child know how important he is to you with this "magic" idea that plants a seed of wonder. In advance, cut out a large tagboard apple for each child in your class. Using a craft blade, cut out a square from the center of each apple. (Judge the size of the apple and the cutout square by the size of your Polaroid® pictures—described later.) If desired, add a stem and leaf to each apple. Then mount a large tree cutout on a classroom wall. On the first day of school, take each child's picture with a Polaroid camera. Invite each child to hold his picture by the edges and watch as the "magic" happens! When each photo has developed, glue it to the back of an apple and write the child's name on the front of the apple. Mount each apple on the tree and title the display "The Apples of [your name]'s Eye!" After explaining the meaning of the title to your students, watch them shine with pride!

Lou Monger—Gr. K
Glen Allen Elementary
Glen Allen, VA

10:00 Library    12:00 Lunch    1:00 Centers

## Our Mission Statement

Class spirit and pride abound when youngsters help to author a mission statement for your classroom! To begin, lead youngsters in a discussion about why they come to school and what they hope to learn. Write their responses on the board. Next condense that list into a sentence or two that everyone agrees upon. Write this newly created mission statement on chart paper. Then invite each child to sign the statement. Mount the signed statement on a sturdy colorful background and post it in a prominent place in your classroom. Periodically, read the statement aloud, encouraging children to join in the reading as they are able. Later, choose a different child each day to read/recite the statement during your morning group time.

Genie Merrer—Gr. K
Oldsmar, FL

Our Mission Statement
We will work together and learn to read and write and do math. We will also be safe.
David   Cori   Matt   Tony
Loe   Metta   Aliki   EliSKA
Hien   JeriSarah
             MUhammed

## Name Games

Doesn't everybody feel a little more secure when they're in a place where everyone knows their name? Use these name-related ideas to facilitate just that!

### Higgety, Biggety Bumblebee

Can you say your name for me? This catchy rhyme draws the attention of your linguistic and auditory youngsters while the movement keeps those kinesthetic kids involved. To begin, seat students in a circle. Say the rhyme below; then toss a soft ball or beanbag to a child. Ask that child to say his name. As abilities permit, encourage the whole class to repeat that name, whisper that name, clap the syllables, and say the beginning sound. Then say the rhyme again, asking the child who is currently holding the ball to toss it to another child when the rhyme has been said. Continue in this same manner until each child's name (and yours!) has been said.

Higgety, biggety bumblebee—
Can you say your name for me?

Melissa Jackson—Gr. K
Miano School
Los Banos, CA

### Mary Wore Her Red Dress

Feature each child's name and chosen specialty of the day with this familiar song. First share the book *Mary Wore Her Red Dress and Henry Wore His Green Sneakers,* adapted and illustrated by Merle Peek (Houghton Mifflin Company). Then have each child stand, in turn, and say her name and what she would like the class to sing about. Then sing away! Extend the use of this song by using it in call-and-response style to encourage children to remember their classmate's names. To do so, sing the song asking a question, such as "Who is wearing stripes today?" or "Who is wearing brown boots?" Encourage the class to respond by singing, for example, "Jess is wearing stripes today, stripes today, stripes today..."

Judy Richmond—Gr. K
Good Shepherd Lutheran
Pekin, IL

Megan   rlos   Bobby   Lia

### Duck, Duck, Who?

That old favorite game of Duck, Duck, Goose is a great one to use when it comes to learning names! First play the game in the traditional way. Then add little twists. For example, when It sits down, ask him to say the name of his chaser. At another time, announce that It must say the goose's name as he chooses her. Or even write each child's name on a goose cutout. Place all the cutouts in a box. Then have It secretly choose a goose from the box. Have him whisper the name to you (for confirmation) and then choose that person as the goose during his turn. You'd better run!

Kelly J. Sickle—Gr. K
Oak Grove Primary
Oak Grove, MD

## The Literature Link

*Franklin Goes to School*
Written by Paulette Bourgeois
Illustrated by Brenda Clark
Published by Scholastic Inc., 1995

*I Don't Want to Go Back to School*
By Marisabina Russo
Published by Greenwillow Books, 1994

*I'll Go to School If...*
Written by Bo Flood
Illustrated by Ronnie Walter Shipman
Published by Fairview Press, 1997

*Jamie Anderson Wouldn't...*
Written by Carol Meredith
Illustrated by Lorrie Szekat
Published by Annick Press Ltd., 1998

*Little Bear Goes to Kindergarten*
By Jutta Langreuter & Vera Sobat
Published by The Millbrook Press, Inc.; 1997

*My First Day of School*
By P. K. Hallinan
Published by Ideals Children's Books, 1987

*Never Spit on Your Shoes*
By Denys Cazet
Published by Orchard Books, 1990

*Spider School*
Written by Francesca Simon
Illustrated by Peta Coplans
Published by Dial Books for Young Readers, 1996

## All Join Hands!

Here's an activity that will reinforce listening skills and honor diversity as well as similarities among your students. Begin by seating your children in a circle. Call out a direction such as one of those suggested below. When the specified children stand, ask them to move to the middle of the circle and join hands. Then have them sit down where they are. Repeat this process many times, having children move from group to group. Make your last direction one that will include everyone, such as "Stand if you are a student in [Ms. Wiklendt's] class." Have all the children join hands and form a circle like the one they were in at the beginning of the activity. Guide children to summarize that they are all alike and different in many ways, but they are all part of the same class!

Stand and hold hands if:
• you are wearing [sneakers]
• you have [blue] eyes
• you like [chocolate] ice cream
• you have a [brother]
• you have a [dog]

Jamie Wiklendt—Gr. K
Chattahoochee Elementary
Duluth, GA

## Here Are My Hands

Dip your hands into this first-day memento that will mean a lot to both children and parents. To begin, copy the poem below on white paper; then duplicate it for each child. Next have each child select a color of paint and make handprints on the top part of a sheet of construction paper. When the paint is dry, glue the poem to the bottom part. Read the poem together, inviting each child to read along. Also encourage each child to count the ten fingers in her handprints and on her own hands. That sounds like a very good day!

Here are my hands with ten fingers in all—
My first mark in school to hang on the wall.
As years go by, I'll remember and say,
"My hands and I had a very good day!"

Melissa Jackson—Gr. K
Miano School
Los Banos, CA

## Hugs & Kisses

No matter how old you are, making it through the first day of school deserves a hug and a kiss! In advance, purchase a supply of Hershey's® Hugs® and Kisses® candies. For each child, wrap a Hug and a Kiss together in a square of tissue paper; then tie the tissue paper closed with a length of curling ribbon. At the end of the first day, tell your youngsters that they each deserve a hug and a kiss—and then hand them out!

Sandra Rice—Gr. K
Trinity Lutheran School
West Seneca, NY

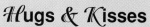

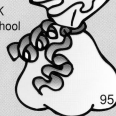

# Rainbow Dragon

Rainbow Dragon is coming to your classroom with
this first-class collection of colorful learning fun!

*ideas contributed by Lori Kent*

**Kimberly
Richard**

## Rainbow Tail

What's that dragon waggin'? His colorful tail, of course! Youngsters will explore six (or more!) colors when they make this creative dragon booklet.

**To prepare:**

Photocopy the dragon body and tail patterns (pages 100–101) on construction paper. Then, for each child, cut a 4" x 5" page from red, orange, yellow, green, blue, and purple construction paper. (Add additional pages of color if desired.)

**To make the booklet:**

Color and cut out the dragon body and tail. Then work with one colored page at a time. (This works well as a center activity spread over several days.) Write/copy/dictate the appropriate color word on the bottom of the page. Then cut out magazine pictures of that color and glue them to the page. When each page contains a collage of color, tape the pages together as shown, leaving just a slight space between pages. Then glue the attached pages to the dragon body where indicated. To close the booklet, accordion-fold the inside pages.

Invite small groups of children to read their books aloud to you. Then display each booklet (extended) on a board titled "Rainbow Dragons."

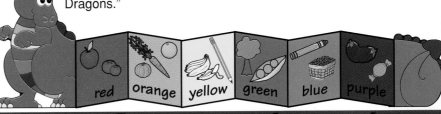

## Rainbow Dragon's Wagon

With Rainbow Dragon as the host, show-and-tell has never been so colorful! In advance, enlarge and duplicate the dragon pattern (page 102) onto white construction paper. Then color, cut out, and laminate the dragon body. To make a wagon, cover the edges of a shallow box with the desired color of construction paper. Add cardboard wheels, a laminated construction paper handle, and a color word card to the wagon. Then post Rainbow Dragon near the wagon.

Each week, encourage children to bring correspondingly colored show-and-tell items to display in Rainbow Dragon's wagon. During group time, invite each child to tell about his item. Then change the color of the wagon and repeat the process. After you've featured all the colors, cover the wagon with a variety of colors and announce that week as rainbow week. (If desired, give a guideline, such as "Each show-and-tell item must have at least three different colors in order to be displayed in Rainbow Dragon's wagon.")

## Rainbow's Sing-Along Song

This little ditty will capture your kinesthetic kids right from the start—and all listening ears will be fine-tuned to catch their cues! In advance, photocopy the dragon pattern (page 102). Color the dragon's front with rainbow colors and add other details as desired. Cut out and laminate the pattern; then glue a large craft stick to the back to make a stick puppet. Next, copy the song to the right on chart paper. (If desired, use the corresponding color for each color word.) Then cut a class supply of crepe paper streamers in the colors mentioned in the song. When you're ready to sing this song, distribute the streamers among your students. Instruct each child to wave his streamer in a wide rainbow arch when he hears that color in the song. Once children are familiar with the song, invite them to exchange streamers and sing the song again using their new colors. It's really quite a sight!

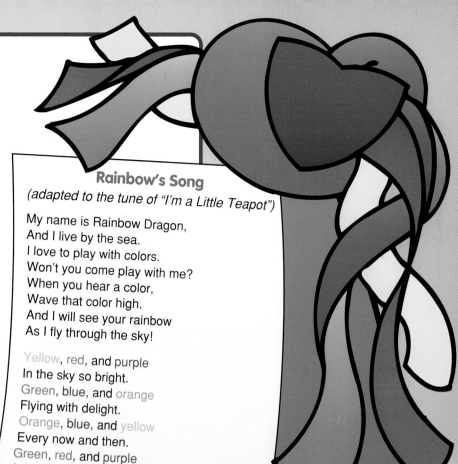

### Rainbow's Song
*(adapted to the tune of "I'm a Little Teapot")*

My name is Rainbow Dragon,
And I live by the sea.
I love to play with colors.
Won't you come play with me?
When you hear a color,
Wave that color high.
And I will see your rainbow
As I fly through the sky!

Yellow, red, and purple
In the sky so bright.
Green, blue, and orange
Flying with delight.
Orange, blue, and yellow
Every now and then.
Green, red, and purple
Coming back again.

## Fit for a Dragon!

Your children will construct all sorts of color concepts when they design a home that's fit for Rainbow Dragon! To prepare, stock your block center with a supply of colorful scarves, sheer gauzy fabric, and crepe paper streamers. When children visit this center, encourage them to use the supplies to design a home for Rainbow Dragon. If desired, invite children to use art supplies to make dragons to house in the delightful dragon homes!

## Rainbow Drops

Scoop up a bunch of color practice with this activity that also reinforces fine-motor skills. To prepare, fill a large bowl with assorted colors and sizes of pom-poms. Arrange the large bowl in a center along with an ice-cream scoop, a pair of tongs and/or chopsticks, and paper bowls. To do this activity, have a child use the ice-cream scoop to scoop a bunch of pom-poms into a paper bowl. Then encourage the child to use the tongs or chopsticks to separate the scoop of pom-poms into different color groups. When his work has been checked, have the child return the rainbow drops to the large bowl and mix them up to prepare for the next center visitor.

adapted from an idea by Elaine Sheerin
New Bedford, MA

## Beyond the Rainbow!

Fly above and beyond the colors of the rainbow with this classification activity. To prepare, place a box of 64 or more assorted crayons in a center along with a supply of white 6" x 6" construction paper squares. When a child (or small group of children) visits this center, encourage her (or them) to sort the crayons into groups of colors that are similar—or in the same family. Have each child select which color group she'd like to work with and then color one white square using all the colors in that color group. Next help each child mount her work on a larger square of a dark color of construction paper. Mount each child's work on a board titled "Beyond the Rainbow!"

Note: *The Crayola® Counting Book* by Rozanne Lanczak Williams (Creative Teaching Press, Inc.) provides a complementary literature extension for this activity.

adapted from an idea by Maureen Tiedemann—Gr. K
Holy Child School, Hicksville, NY

## Dragon Puffs

Any dragon would be proud to puff out these fluffy treats! To make one, use different colors and combinations of food coloring to color several different bowls of water. Then cut two marshmallows in half. Color three of the marshmallow halves by using toothpicks to dip the marshmallows in the colored water. (The fourth half is yours for snacking!) Next arrange the three colored marshmallow halves on a graham cracker square. Microwave the graham cracker–marshmallow combination for five to eight seconds. When they're cool, these dragon puffs make a colorful tasty treat!

## The Magic School Bus®:
### Liz Makes a Rainbow
### Written by Tracey West
### Illustrated by Jim Durk
### Published by Scholastic Inc., 1999

From the animated TV series based on The Magic School Bus books comes this colorful tale featuring an active little dragon named Liz. Two hardworking children are stumped when they attempt to paint a rainbow with only four different colors of paint. But leave it to Liz to show the way to save the day! Extend this story with the activity described in "Rainbow Stew" on page 99.

## Magic Dragon Drink

Rainbow Dragon loves this magical drink—and your students will too! In advance, mix up about a quart each of red, blue, and yellow Kool-Aid®. To each flavor, add a few drops of corresponding food coloring to make each color more intense. Then freeze a supply of ice cubes in each of these colors. Next, mix up a pitcher each of regularly colored red, blue, and yellow Kool-Aid. To do this activity, invite each child to ladle or pour his choice of Kool-Aid into a clear plastic cup, being sure to leave room for ice! Then encourage him to add a couple of colored ice cubes to his cup. Next, invite each child to skewer a few maraschino cherries onto a plastic straw and use the straw to stir his magical brew. As each child stirs, encourage predictions! What colorful concoctions!

## Books About Dragons

*Anna and the Little Green Dragon*
*Where Are You, Little Green Dragon?*
By Klaus Baumgart
Published by Hyperion Books for Children

*Dragon Naps*
Written by Lynne Bertrand
Illustrated by Janet Street
Published by Viking

*The Dragons Are Singing Tonight*
Poetry by Jack Prelutsky
Illustrated by Peter Sis
Published by Greenwillow Books

*The Paper Bag Princess*
Written by Robert Munsch
Illustrated by Michael Martchenko
Published by Annick Press Ltd.

*There's a Dragon in My Sleeping Bag*
Written by James Howe
Illustrated by David S. Rose
Published by Atheneum

## Rainbow Stew

It might look a little slimy and yucky to you, but if you were a dragon, you'd *love* rainbow stew! Follow the directions below to whip up a batch of rainbow stew and color it. Then arrange the bowls of stew in a center along with three serving spoons, sturdy Ziploc® bags, and duct tape. When a child visits this center, invite her to scoop a spoonful of two different colors of rainbow stew into a Ziploc bag. Then help her squeeze out the excess air and seal and tape the bag closed. Encourage her to squish and squash the stew until a new color appears! Encourage each child to record her experience in print as shown. Then post the written information along with each resulting color.

1 cup cornstarch
1/3 cup sugar
4 cups water

Mix the dry ingredients together in a saucepan. Slowly add the water and stir over medium heat until the mixture becomes thick and clear. Let the mixture cool; then divide it into three different bowls. Use food coloring to color each batch of stew a different color: red, yellow, or blue.

# Dragon Body Pattern
Use with "Rainbow Tail" on page 96.

Glue here.

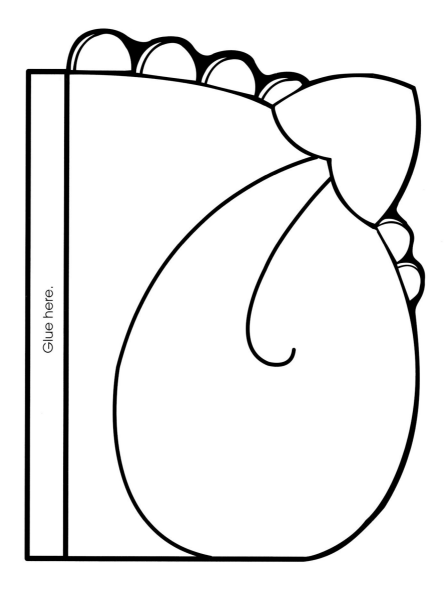

Glue here.

# Dragon Pattern

Use with "Rainbow Dragon's Wagon" on page 96
and "Rainbow's Sing-Along Song" on page 97.

# Now & Then

Have you ever found yourself—at the *end* of a school year—looking back to those days when your new group of students first arrived? Did you fondly recall when names were sometimes no more than squiggles on a page and the task of lining up required a herculean effort? The ideas in this unit are designed to help you and your students reflect on those days and see how far they've come!

*ideas by Susan A. DeRiso*

## My Kindergarten Career—on Record!

What better way to keep a record of each kindergartner's progress than to publish a book about it! Photocopy pages 105–107. Program your copy of the title page with the date (month and year) that your children will be working on these books. Then copy all the pages for each child. Have each child complete the pages as his abilities permit (see the suggestions below). Then help him staple his pages together in just one corner. Invite each child, in turn, to share his book with you; then file it in his portfolio. Repeat this process a few times during the year. At the end of the year, make one book for each child by stapling all his books together in chronological order. Then staple the pages along the left edges. Encourage each child (and parent) to read his book and delight in his progress. What a kindergarten career!

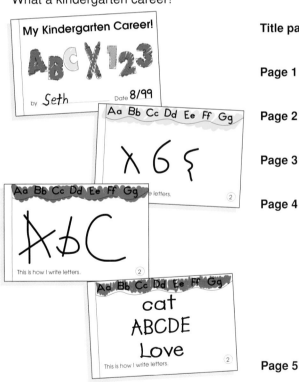

**Title page**    Have each child color his title page and write his name in the space provided.

**Page 1**    Invite each child to draw a picture of himself and write his age in the space provided.

**Page 2**    Ask each child to write all the letters that he can on the page.

**Page 3**    Ask each child to write all the numbers that he can on the page.

**Page 4**    Group children in pairs. Have one child in each pair lie on the floor while his partner uses a strip of butcher paper (or adding-machine tape) to measure him. Instruct the child who is measuring to draw a line on the butcher paper to indicate his partner's height and then cut along that line. When each child has a strip of paper to represent his height, have him glue one end of that strip in the space provided. Then instruct him to accordion-fold the loose end of the strip.

**Page 5**    Ask each child to draw all the shapes he can on the page. Encourage creative arrangement and coloring of the shapes!

## What Do You Know?

Everyone will be amazed at how this "stack of knowledge" grows through the year! Begin by labeling a recipe box "What Do You Know?" At the end of each week, write questions that are relevant to that week's studies on index cards. Then put the cards in the box. When you need a five-minute filler, take the stack of cards from the box and ask children questions from the cards. Each subsequent time that you remove the stack of cards, emphasize how the stack is growing! At the end of the year, use the cards to highlight how much everyone has learned. Wow—look how much you know!

# Let Us Entertain You!

Start preparing for this end-of-the-year performance now and, without even realizing it, your little ones will be ready to give the performance of a kindergarten lifetime! During calendar times, teach your children the appropriate verse from "The Months at School" (see below). Periodically, have youngsters sing all the verses that they've learned so far. At the end of each month, make a note of the skills worked on and save a few pieces of related work. (Large pieces of work that can be seen from a distance are best.)

For the performance, arrange students in choir fashion. Have the whole group sing one verse of the song at a time. (Change the verb of being from *is* to *was* if desired.) After each verse, have designated children come to the front holding their work. Have each child briefly tell about her project and what she learned. You might also like to have smaller groups of children sing other skill-related songs, recite poetry, or perform large-motor skills. Then have those featured children return to the choir group and sing the next verse all together. Continue in this manner until the last verse of the song. After the last verse, have all your children join hands and take a bow!

# The Months at School

*(adapted to the tune of "She'll Be Coming Around the Mountain")*

September is the first month here at school.
September is the first month here at school.
We are making brand-new friends
And the learning never ends.
Oh, September is our first month here at school.

October is the next month here at school.
October is the next month here at school.
Leaves are falling from the trees.
What a colorful sight to see!
Oh, October is the next month here at school.

November is the next month here at school.
November is the next month here at school.
There are turkeys with bright feathers
Getting ready for cold weather.
Oh, November is the next month here at school.

December is the next month here at school.
December is the next month here at school.
It's the time we like to say
Have a happy holiday!
Oh, December is the next month here at school.

January is the next month here at school.
January is the next month here at school.
It's the time we sing and cheer.
Have a wonderful New Year!
Oh, January is the next month here at school.

February is the next month here at school.
February is the next month here at school.
Hearts are hanging everywhere.
Love is floating in the air.
Oh, February is the next month here at school.

March is the next month here at school.
March is the next month here at school.
Fluffy clouds are blowing by
In the windy, windy sky.
Oh, March is the next month here at school.

April is the next month here at school.
April is the next month here at school.
Raincoats keep us dry
When the rain falls from the sky.
Oh, April is the next month here at school.

May is the next month here at school.
May is the next month here at school.
Blooming flowers can be seen
And the earth is turning green.
Oh, May is the next month here at school.

June is the last month here at school.
June is the last month here at school.
We had all these months to grow
And just look how much we know!
Oh, June is the last month here at school.

*by Susan A. DeRiso*

104

# My Kindergarten Career!

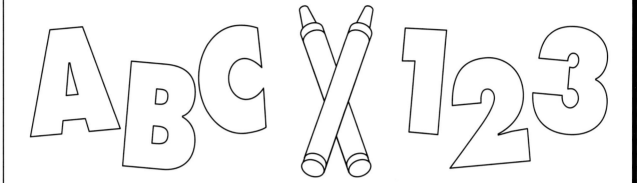

by _____ Date _____

Me     Me     Me     Me

This is me! I am _____ years old.     ①

## Book Pages 2 and 3

Use with "My Kindergarten Career—on Record!" on page 103.

Aa Bb Cc Dd Ee Ff Gg

This is how I write letters.

(2)

1 2 3 4 5 6 7 8 9 10

This is how I write numbers.

(3)

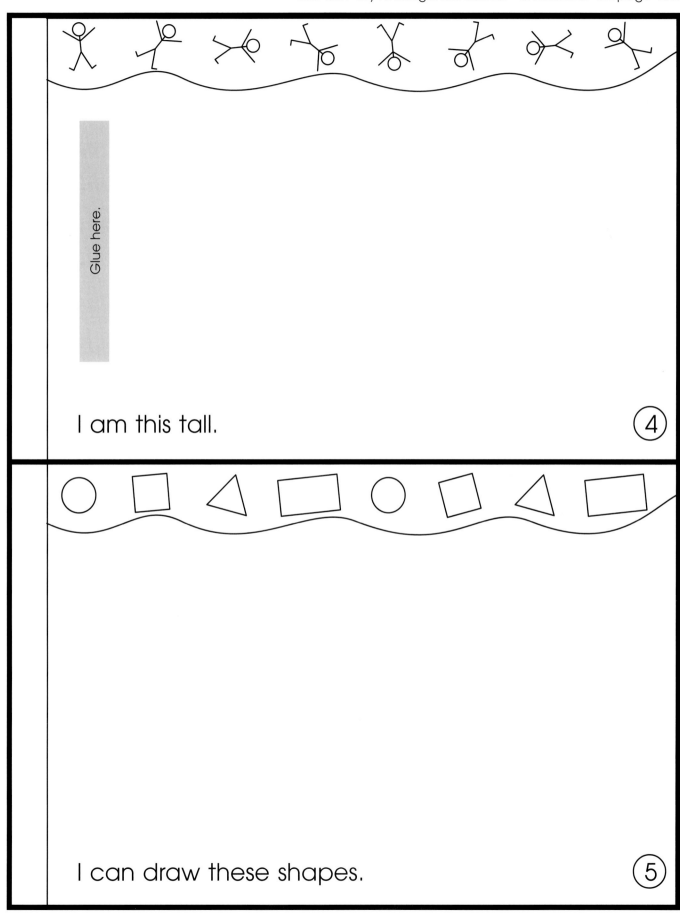

Glue here.

I am this tall.

④

I can draw these shapes.

⑤

# Just "Dough" It!

## Using Play Dough for Lots of Learning Fun

Check out these dough recipes and center activities to keep little fingers kneading, pushing, pressing, and rolling the whole year through!

*ideas contributed by Anna Lisa Damminger, Carole H. Dibble, Diana L. Kempe, Angie Kutzer, Kathy H. Lee, Patti Moeser, and Dr. Suzanne Moore*

Working with play dough strengthens finger and hand muscles that are important for fine-motor development.

Working with play dough develops eye-hand coordination and control that is important for writing.

### No-Cook Dough

**Ingredients:**
4 cups flour
1 cup salt
1 3/4 cups warm water tinted with food coloring

**Preparation:**
Combine the flour and salt in a bowl; then add the warm water. Knead the dough for ten minutes. Keep the dough refrigerated in an airtight container. (This dough will air-dry in one to five days, depending on the humidity in your area and the thickness of the project.)

### Peanut Butter Play Dough

**Ingredients:**
1 cup peanut butter
1 cup honey
1 cup powdered milk
1 cup oatmeal

**Preparation:**
Combine all of the ingredients in a large bowl. Encourage your youngsters to make something special with this dough...and then eat it!

Working with play dough invites creativity.

**Cornstarch Dough**

Ingredients:
1 cup cornstarch
2 cups baking soda
1 1/2 cups cold water
1/2 cup additional cornstarch

Preparation:
Mix the first three ingredients and cook over medium-low heat, stirring constantly, until the mixture looks like mashed potatoes. Let the dough cool. Then knead it, adding small amounts of additional cornstarch as necessary to reach the desired consistency. Store the dough in an airtight container.

Working with play dough reinforces the concepts of shape and form.

Working with play dough encourages exploration with tools (traditional and unconventional).

Working with play dough can relieve tension and produce a calming effect.

**Kool-Aid® Dough**

Ingredients:
2 1/2–3 cups flour
1/2 cup salt
1 package unsweetened Kool-Aid
1 tablespoon alum
2 cups boiling water
3 tablespoons corn oil
1 cup additional flour

Preparation:
Mix the first six ingredients into a dough. After the dough cools, knead it—adding small amounts of the additional flour as necessary—until it reaches the desired consistency. Store the dough in an airtight container.

# Things to Do the Whole

## August

- Encourage children to use play dough to form the letters in their names.
- Add school supplies, such as scissors and rulers, to the play dough center for children to use to manipulate the dough. Cutting play dough with scissors is especially good practice for those children who still struggle with scissors!
- Bring back memories of those summer days at the beach! Provide pebbles, seashells, party favor flags, and small sand molds for youngsters to use with play dough to create their own sculptures. For a beachy display, sprinkle the finished projects with sand and arrange them on a flat surface covered with a thin layer of sand and a few seashells.

## September

- Set out red, green, and/or yellow play dough and invite youngsters to make a basketful of apples. Then, as a group, sort and graph the pretend fruit.
- Mix numeral-shaped metallic confetti into your play dough and encourage students to use the dough to form numerals.
- Celebrate Labor Day in your play dough center by adding supplies, such as toothpicks, craft sticks, and plastic construction tools. Then have youngsters "build" a house. Provide an opportunity for each child to show his construction to the class as he tells about its features and who might live there.

## October

- Happy Columbus Day! Challenge students to experiment with a ball of commercially made Play-Doh® or clay to create a floating vessel. (Homemade dough does not float.) Provide a water-filled container to test the innovations.
- Tint a batch of play dough orange; then provide collage materials—such as large sequins, buttons, and colored pasta pieces—for children to use in creating jazzy jack-o'-lanterns. These projects are sure to light up faces in students' homes during Halloween!
- Have each child make a set of five pumpkins from play dough and then use them to act out the "Five Little Pumpkins" poem.

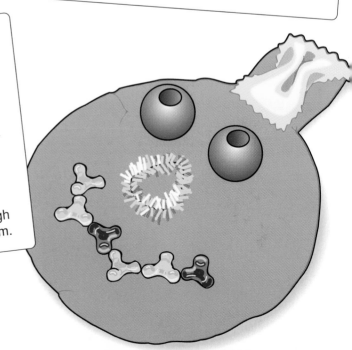

# Year Through!

## November

- Invite your youngsters to make decorative wreaths for autumn. To begin, have children collect nature items during a walk. Return to the classroom and direct each child to make a circle with a thick rope of play dough. Have her flatten it out slightly; then show her how to press her items into the play dough to cover the ring. These wreaths make great candle rings for table centerpieces during the holidays.
- In your dramatic play center, provide play dough in a variety of colors. Encourage students to make lots of fruits, vegetables, and other dough foods to prepare a pretend Thanksgiving feast.
- As you discuss Native Americans, have youngsters create these beaded necklaces. To make one, roll out several balls of play dough. Use a straw to poke a hole through each ball. Let the dough harden; then thread the beads on a length of yarn. Students will be as proud as peacocks (or turkeys!) to wear their necklaces during fall festivities.

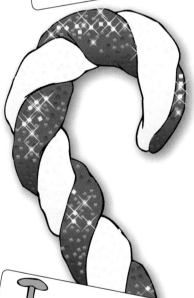

## December

- Have youngsters twist red and white dough ropes together to form candy canes. For added fun, mix in red glitter with the red dough and clear glitter with the white dough. These cute creations make great decorations for your classroom tree!
- Encourage your students to make reindeer from brown play dough. (You may also want to have some red dough on hand for those students who want to create the most famous reindeer of all!) As a finishing touch, have each child add small twigs for his reindeer's antlers. These reindeer sculptures are sure to be included in the holiday decor of many kindergarten households.
- It's baking season! Be sure to add rolling pins, cookie cutters, cookie sheets, tart tins, measuring spoons, and collage materials to the play dough center so that your little confectioners can cook till their hearts are content.

## January

- Add silver glitter to your play dough, and watch for glistening snowmen to appear!
- Have a student flatten a piece of white dough (snow) and then make tracks in the snow with items such as forks and small cooking utensils. Can she make a pattern?
- Promote peace and cooperation during Martin Luther King's birthday month by having pairs or a small group of students work together in the play dough center to create a birthday cake for Dr. King. For each cake, make a small sign that says "Happy Birthday, Dr. King!" and then list the little bakers' names. Display the cakes with their signs around your school as reminders of this special day.

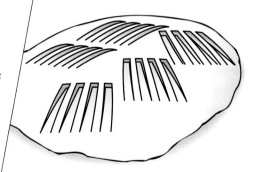

# February

- Have your youngsters use play dough to pretend to be groundhogs! With a washable marker, draw a simple face on each child's index finger, as shown. Have him mold some play dough into a mound. Then have him use his finger to push through the mound and pop out to take a peek. Does the groundhog see his shadow?
- In observance of National Cherry Month, prepare the Kool-Aid® dough recipe (page 109) using cherry-flavored Kool-Aid. Then practice size differentiation and seriation by challenging youngsters to use the dough to make a set of five different-sized cherries.
- Recognize our presidents by having students make impressions of coins in play dough, then examining them to point out similarities and differences.

# March

- Since this is the month of lions and lambs, it's a great time to work on opposites in your play dough center. Encourage students to make a *tall* structure and a *short* structure, a *fat* rope and a *thin* rope, a *bumpy* surface and a *smooth* surface, etc.
- Everything is turning up green! Mix green glitter into a batch of green play dough for youngsters' shamrock-molding fun.
- Add a variety of seeds, artificial flowers, small plastic pots, and several handheld gardening tools to the play dough center and watch spring sprout up all over!

# April

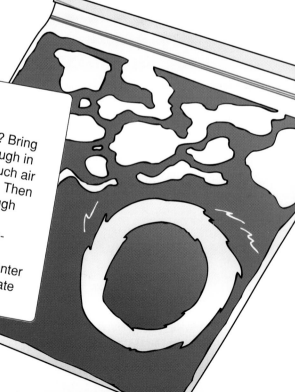

- What do you do once your play dough is a rather nondescript color? Bring on the April showers to make mud! Place a small handful of play dough in a resealable plastic bag and add a little rain (water). Press out as much air as you can before sealing the bag. Tape the bag's seal for durability. Then encourage students to use their fingertips to squish and squash through the mud as they form letters and shapes.
- Add lemon extract to your favorite play dough recipe to give it a spring-fresh scent.
- Place several different styles of chocolate bunnies in the play dough center along with a few colors of dough. Invite children to hop on over and create play dough versions of these delicacies to take home.

# May

- Play dough for Mother's Day? You bet! Have each youngster use colored Crayola® Model Magic® modeling compound to make a flower. Let the flower air-dry for approximately 24 hours. Then attach a piece of magnetic tape to the back of it to create a marvelous magnet for Mom!
- Since strawberry patches are bursting with juicy fruits by this time of year, a batch of strawberry-scented play dough might be in order. Read *The Little Mouse, the Red Ripe Strawberry, and the Big Hungry Bear* by Don and Audrey Wood (Child's Play) to your youngsters. Encourage them to make a few strawberries in the play dough center. Then provide plastic knives or craft sticks for students to practice cutting their strawberries into *halves, thirds,* and *fourths.*
- You won't find that hungry bear in the play dough center, but you may find some very hungry caterpillars! Provide pipe cleaners, collage materials, and colored play dough to invite some cocooning in the center. Then make a display of what emerges!

# June

- 'Tis the season for sunflowers. Mix gold glitter into a batch of yellow-tinted dough. Have each youngster form a sunflower shape with the dough. Then, before the dough hardens, direct her to poke real sunflower seeds into the center of the flower and insert a craft stick (stem) into the bottom of the flower. Display the flowers along your classroom's window sills; then watch for sunshiny smiles!
- Place a collection of five or more seashells or other beach objects that have different textures and patterns in the play dough center. Have a pair of students visit the center and take turns playing this guessing game. One child closes her eyes while the other child makes an impression with one of the objects in a mound of dough. The child then opens her eyes and tries to guess which object her partner used.
- Encourage youngsters to practice counting and making sets with these ladybugs. Make several ladybug cards similar to the ones shown. (Laminate the cards for repeated use.) Program each card with a numeral, number word, or addition fact. Tint a batch of the cornstarch play dough (page 109) with washable, black liquid tempera paint. Have each student use the black play dough to put the correct number of dots on each ladybug.

# July

- Display a flag in your play dough center. Invite youngsters to try to replicate it using red, white, and blue play dough; star-shaped cookie cutters; rolling pins; and plastic knives.
- Direct each youngster to wrap a layer of green play dough around a ball of red or pink play dough to create a watermelon. Then give each child a plastic knife to slice up some juicy fun. Who cut the most slices?
- We all scream for ice cream! Make a few pretend sugar cones from tagboard. Set out two or three pastel colors of play dough. Have each youngster roll some of the play dough into balls to resemble scoops of ice cream. Then challenge her to stack as many scoops as she can on a cone. How many scoops can a kindergartner scoop?

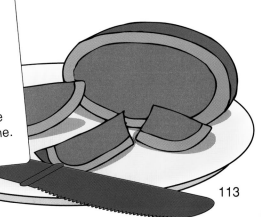

# "Shiver Me Timbers! Me Spies a Treasure!"

'Tis the season for pretending, parading, and picking up plenty of prizes. Need an alternative to Halloween festivities? Sail to this imaginary island full of cross-curricular activities. Your little fortune seekers will treasure the fun and you'll treasure the learning taking place. No tricks here!

*—ideas contributed by Cheryl Jones and Mackie Rhodes*

## Portrait of a Pirate

Being a pirate was not a glamorous or coveted profession by any stretch of the imagination! Give youngsters a glimpse into a pirate's life by sharing your choice of the information from the books listed below. Your students will probably decide that while dressing up as pirates is great fun, they're awfully glad to be landlubbers!

*Order books online. www.themailbox.com*

*A Pirate's Life for Me! A Day Aboard a Pirate Ship*
Written by Julie Thompson and Brownie Macintosh
Published by Charlesbridge Publishing

*Pirates: Robbers of the High Seas*
Written by Gail Gibbons
Published by Little, Brown and Company

*Pirates*
Written by Greg Nickles
Published by Crabtree Publishing Company

## Let's Pretend!

Once your youngsters have heard how horrible pirates really were, invite them to do some creative role reversals. Use the list below to stock your dramatic play center with lots of pirate-related garb and invite youngsters to dress as pirates. Then encourage them to act out what *friendly* and *helpful* pirates would do on the high seas. What if they found a trading ship in trouble? What would they do? Can your pirates actually turn into princes and princesses?

**The Latest Look in Pirate Wear:**
— bandanas for headgear
— long scarves for waist sashes
— pillowcase shirts with ragged edges around the bottoms, sleeves, and necklines
— eye patches made from black craft foam and yarn
— white tube socks to make pants into breeches
— costume jewelry
— face paints to add dirt smudges, mustaches, and whiskers
— cardboard tube telescopes and/or binoculars
114 — toy tools, such as flashlights, shovels, and rakes

# Words to Treasure

This treasure chest of words is a valuable way to teach and reinforce a variety of language arts skills. To begin, create a treasure chest for class use (see "Treasure Chests From the Heart"). For each word you want to represent, label a separate notecard and include a picture cue. Word selections might be taken from word families, environmental print, color and/or number words, or unit-related words, such as *treasure, hunt, gold, map,* and *compass.* Place the programmed notecards in the chest.

To use, ask a child to open the chest and remove a card. Help her identify the word; then ask her to respond to your question or direction related to that word. For instance, you might ask her to say a rhyming word, to count the syllables in the word, or to name the initial or final sound in the word. You might prompt her to find a particular letter, count the letters, or to spell the word out loud. What a loot of literacy learning!

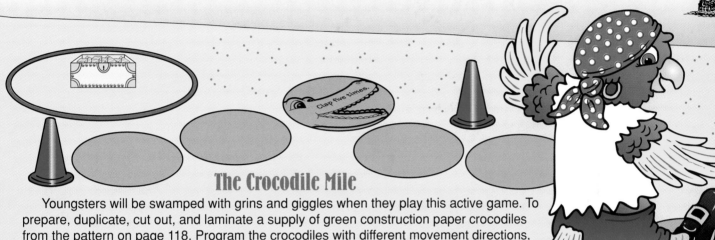

# The Crocodile Mile

Youngsters will be swamped with grins and giggles when they play this active game. To prepare, duplicate, cut out, and laminate a supply of green construction paper crocodiles from the pattern on page 118. Program the crocodiles with different movement directions, such as "Jump three times," "Flap your arms like a duck," or "Hop back three spaces." Set up a balance beam bridge. Then create a winding path by placing crocodiles at each end of the bridge, as shown. At the end of the path, place a Hula-Hoop® to represent Treasure Island. Fill the class treasure chest (from "Words to Treasure") with an assortment of candies wrapped in gold foil. Then put it inside the hoop. If desired, add a few safety-cone trees along the path.

To play the game with a small group of students, each player, in turn, rolls a die and then advances down the path the corresponding number of spaces. The player follows the directions from the crocodile on which he lands. When a player reaches Treasure Island, he gets his share of the treasure from the chest. Watch out for those crocs!

# Treasure Chests From the Heart

Brainstorm a list of things that might be considered valuable—from the economic (gold, jewelry, and coins) to the sentimental (letters, photos, and special gifts). Then invite youngsters to create these treasure chests. To make one, paint a shoe box and its lid. (If desired, you can use a baby wipes container instead—no painting!) When the paint is dry, decorate both pieces with a variety of craft items, such as buttons, sequins, metallic confetti, rickrack, and die-cut shapes.

Use these special treasure chests as home-school connections to promote self-esteem and verbal expression. Send each child's treasure chest home along with a parent note requesting that the child return the chest with a special item (or illustration of an item) inside. During sharing time, invite each child to show and tell the class about his cherished treasure.

# Bullions in the Balance

Here's a sweet way to practice measurement and counting skills. Collect an assortment of foil-wrapped chocolate candies (or use the leftovers from "The Crocodile Mile" on page 115) to represent *bullions*—bars of gold—and gold nuggets. Place each type of candy in a separate container. Then label each of ten notecards with a different numeral from 1 to 10. Put the candy, a balance scale, and the cards in your math center.

Explain to your class that some lost treasures might contain gold. Show them a candy bullion and nugget and then have youngsters speculate on which weighs more. To find out, invite students to visit the math center to weigh them on the scale. While there, challenge each little prospector to pick a card and then count out the corresponding number of gold nuggets onto the scale. Have her balance the scale with the bullion. To extend the activity further, have the child weigh a few classroom objects using the candy as nonstandard units of measurement. This activity is definitely worth its weight in gold!

Clevell Harris

**Map Symbols**

~~~~~ water
△ tree
▨▨▨ grass
▬ bridge
⌂ house
○ rock

Polly

# X Marks the Spot!

What are your little pirates going to do with that huge, heavy chest full of valuable jewels? Hide it, of course! This activity is a great introduction to mapmaking. To prepare, stock your sand table with miniature landscaping items, small toys, and craft materials. Paint an empty matchbox gold and then fill it with rhinestones to represent the treasured jewels. Collect a paper lunch bag for each child. Draw and label several simple topographical symbols on chart paper, and place the chart and some crayons near the sand table.

Encourage each youngster to create a scene in the sand, hide the treasure, and then make a map to represent the treasure's location. To make a map, tear off the bottom of a paper lunch bag. Then tear the bag down one side, open the bag, and press it flat. Use the symbols on the chart (or create your own symbols) to replicate the scene in the sand table. Then draw a line showing the way to the hidden treasure. Be sure to mark the hiding place with an **X.** Crumple the map and then smooth it to give it a vintage look.

Later, invite students to show their maps to the class and to describe the route to the hidden treasure. Display the maps with the title "Yo-Ho-Ho! A-Treasure Hunting We'll Go!"

## Which Way Next?

Reinforce the concepts of *port* and *starboard* (that's *left* and *right* to me and you) with this listening and problem-solving activity. To prepare, cut out a tagboard circle for every two students. Label each circle as shown to create a Kinder-compass. Begin the activity by showing your class a real compass and explaining its purpose—to determine directions. After examining the device, give each pair of students a Kinder-compass and demonstrate how to hold it correctly. For practice, call out a few directions such as "Take two steps to the left and then hop forward once." Encourage each pair to refer to their compass to follow the directions.

For a more challenging activity, position each pair of students at a different starting point in your classroom. Assign a destination, such as the door, a bookshelf, or the sink. Then have partners work cooperatively, using their compass, to find their way to the designated location. If desired, equip the pairs with paper, pencils, and clipboards so that they can record the directions they take. Let's see, five steps to the right...

## Tasty Treasures

Once your little buccaneers have practiced hiding their plunder, take them on this real search for buried treasure. In advance, prepare a mixture of vanilla pudding and crushed vanilla wafers to resemble wet beach sand. For each child, place a Nestlé® Treasures™ chest-shaped candy in the bottom of a small cup. Then add several spoonfuls of the pudding mixture to "bury" the treasure. Sprinkle some crushed wafers on top of the pudding to resemble loose sand. If desired, finish the effect by inserting a gold foil-wrapped chocolate coin into the pudding. Put the cups in your cafeteria's refrigerator. Then tape a large **X** cutout to the refrigerator door.

To prepare the hunt, use the following list of clues, or make up your own according to your school's layout. Write each clue on a separate card and hide it in the location described in the previous clue. To get the hunt started, have the first clue mysteriously fall out of a book about pirates (see "Portrait of a Pirate" on page 114) that you are reading aloud. Then gather up your fortune seekers and get started. Once the snacks are found, equip each child with a spoon shovel and then watch for the surprise when she digs her way to the bottom of her cup. Shiver me timbers!

**Possible Clues:**

1. I've buried me treasure in your school.
   Use this clue as a tool.
   Go to where bookworms hang out,
   But be careful not to shout!
   If you find the next clue there,
   Then me treasure I will share.

2. You found it, like I knew you would.
   On to the second clue—this one's good!
   Think of where you like to go
   When it's raining or there's snow.
   A place to play and get wiggles out.
   The teacher here lets you move about.

3. On the playground is where you'll find
   The next clue *if you use your mind.*
   Think of a word that rhymes with *glide*—
   These can be narrow or really wide.
   Think of the opposite of *top.*
   Now look for that clue and do not stop!

4. On to the fourth clue, this is fun!
   Now listen closely to this one.
   It's time to visit a place that's busy…
   Lots of people—makes me dizzy!
   Kids and parents and teachers and guests,
   All have things that need addressed.
   At times this place may seem quite scary,
   But just look for the secretary!

5. You've made it to the last clue,
   Now you know just what to do.
   Figure out the place that helps bodies grow,
   And you'll know just where to go.
   Once you're there think chilly, think cold;
   Then look for the X—be brave and bold!

6. Here is the treasure, thanks to you.
   You solved each and every clue!
   A scoop of the island you will get—
   Some sand, maybe gold—but we're not through yet.
   Everyone should take a cup,
   Then, with a spoon, dig and eat up!

117

# Crocodile Pattern
Use with "The Crocodile Mile" on page 115.

# Shoe BEE Doo WOP!

Look out Daddy-o! Here's a well-polished shoe unit that will have your youngsters doing the jitterbug! Tie these beboppin' ideas and activities in with your curriculum, and get those little feet up and learning!

## Step Right Up!

Step into your shoe unit with this lively circle-time game. Have students stand in a large circle. Sing the song below. As you mention the various types of shoes, direct youngsters wearing those shoes to step inside the circle.

*(sung to the tune of "Johnny Works With One Hammer")*

If you're wearing [brown] shoes,
[Brown] shoes, [brown] shoes,
If you're wearing [brown] shoes,
Step right [in]!

Continue singing additional verses substituting the word *brown* with other colors or shoe descriptors, such as *buckled, tennis,* and *slip-on.* After all children are standing inside the circle, sing the song again substituting *out* for *in.* Direct your little ones to step back to the edge of the circle as their shoe types are mentioned.

Jill Rich and Rhonda Clark
West Elementary School
Valley Center, KS

## Left and Right

Learning will happen left and right with this idea! Place a pair of children's shoes at a center. From construction paper, make ten cutout insoles for each shoe. Label each cutout "left" or "right" accordingly; then laminate the cutouts. Set the insoles near the shoes and invite your little ones to place the insoles inside the corresponding shoe. For an added challenge, label each cutout in each set with a different number from 1 to 10. Direct students to place the cutouts in numerical order inside the corresponding shoe. What a perfect fit!

Jill Rich and Rhonda Clark

## SOCK HOP TONIGHT!

## These Shoes Were Made for Walkin'

Take a walk on the wild side with this unique story starter. Bring several different types of worn, threadbare shoes to class. During circle time, show your youngsters each of the shoes. Have them brainstorm some places each shoe may have been and some things it may have done. Then invite each child to illustrate the shoe of his choice in an imaginary setting. Encourage the child to think of a statement the shoe might make if it could talk; then write his dictation on his paper. Show off these shoe stories by mounting them on a wall or bulletin board. Or bind the illustrations together with a cover to create a class book.

Karen M. Smith
Pace, FL

## Ring Around the Shoes

Here's a really far-out center activity that will reinforce a variety of math skills! Make a large supply of the shoe pattern on page 123. Color and cut out the shoes; then laminate them. Tape the shoe cutouts to the floor and place a few embroidery hoops or plastic rings nearby. To play, a child tosses a hoop over the shoes, then counts how many are inside the ring after it has landed. For a variation, have the child count how many shoes of each color are inside the ring. Or invite the child to toss two rings, then figure the sum of the shoes in both rings. Any way you toss, it all adds up to fun!

Jill Rich and Rhonda Clark
West Elementary School
Valley Center, KS

## On Your Mark, Get Set,...

...go! Your little cool cats will really dig this number sequencing activity. Make ten copies of the shoe pattern on page 123. After coloring the shoes, program each one with a different number from 1–10. Laminate the shoes and then tape a tongue depressor to the back of each one. Fill a large cardboard gift box with packing foam; then use a permanent marker to draw a path on the lid of the box. Write "start" at one end of the path and "finish" at the other end. Next use a craft knife to cut ten slits from one end of the path to the other. Set the shoe cutouts beside the track and challenge your youngsters to sequence them by inserting the tongue depressor in the appropriate slit on the box.

Jill Rich and Rhonda Clark

## All Sorts of Shoes!

Sharpen math skills with this hands-on learning activity. Stock a center with a variety of shoes, such as hiking boots, ballet slippers, sneakers, and sandals. Then invite youngsters to sort the shoes by style, color, or size. As an extension, provide a tub of Unifix® cubes near the shoes and encourage your little ones to measure the length of each shoe. For an added challenge, have students estimate how many cubes will fit inside a shoe; then have them fill the shoe with cubes and count the number needed.

Tracy Gates
Hoxie Elementary School
Hoxie, AR

## Shoe and Sock Hop

This lively game is sure to knock the bobby socks off your little ones! Divide your class into teams. Have each child remove one shoe and place it in a pile in front of her team. Next line up each team facing its pile of shoes. At the start signal, the first child in line hops on one foot to the pile and finds the shoe of the next student in line. She hops back to the line, places the shoe on that child's foot, and then moves to the end of the line. The child with both shoes then hops on one foot to the pile and finds the shoe of the next person in line. The game continues in this manner until all students in line have both shoes. Crazy, man!

Karen M. Smith
Pace, FL

## A Very Special Shoe Tree

Let your little ones show off their shoes with this nifty display. Provide each student with a large sheet of white construction paper. Direct her to trace both of her shoes onto the paper, then cut on the resulting outlines. Next have her use markers to decorate the cutouts so they resemble her own shoes. If the child has lace-up shoes, help her punch shoelace eyelets in her cutouts. Add gummed reinforcers over the holes; then have her lace a length of yarn through each set of holes. From bulletin board paper, cut out a large tree shape. Mount the tree onto a wall or bulletin board; then add the construction paper shoes and a title. What fancy footwork!

Our Class Shoe Tree!

## A Definite "Shoe-In"

This song and follow-up activity will be an instant hit with your little ones. Play Raffi's tune "Something in My Shoe" and have students follow along with Raffi. Next duplicate the patterns on page 123 (make enlargements of the patterns, if desired). Color the patterns, laminate them, and cut them out. Glue a strip of felt on the back of each cutout; then set the cutouts and a recording of the song near your flannelboard. Invite your youngsters to play the song and use the flannelboard pieces as they follow along. As an extension, have youngsters illustrate other silly objects that might get caught inside their shoes. Look! There's an elephant in my sneaker!

"Something in My Shoe"
Sung by Raffi
*Rise and Shine;* Troubadour Records, Ltd.
Available from Educational Record Center, Inc.
To order, call 1-800-438-1637.

## Delicious Shoes?

Your youngsters will get a kick out of this creative snack idea! To make one shoe snack, spread white frosting on the top of a Nutter Butter® cookie. Then place a large marshmallow in the frosting at one end of the cookie. Break a string of licorice into small pieces and arrange them in the frosting to resemble laces on the shoe. Admire *briefly;* then eat! Scrumptious!

## Shiny Shoe Stories

*A Pair of Red Sneakers*
Written by Lisa Lawston
Published by Orchard Books

*Red Dancing Shoes*
Written by Denise Lewis Patrick
Published by Mulberry Books

*Shoes, Shoes, Shoes*
Written by Ann Morris
Published by Mulberry Books

*Shoes, Shoes, Shoes*
Written by Anne Schreiber
Published by The Millbrook Press, Inc.

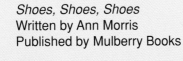

# Flannelboard Patterns

Use with "A Definite 'Shoe-In'" on page 122.
Use the shoe pattern with "Ring Around the Shoes" and "On Your Mark, Get Set,..." on page 120.

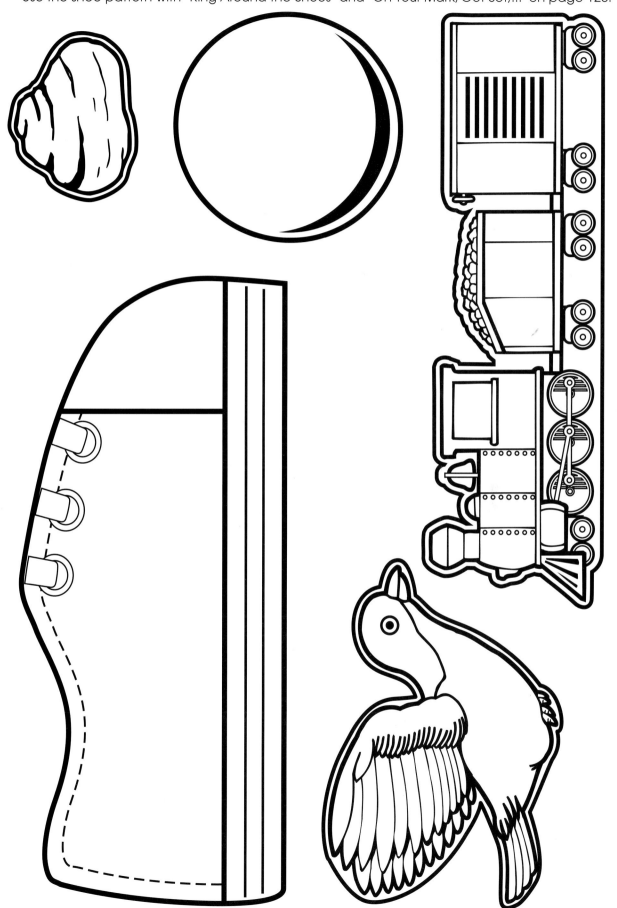

# CELEBRATE

Throw a curve into your curriculum during the World Series. These baseball-related activities will help you score big with your Little Leaguers. Play ball!

*—ideas contributed by Cindi Zsittnik*

## Who Are You Pullin' For?

Once the two teams are decided for the World Series, invite your fans to show their true colors in this graphing activity. On the first school day of the games, have youngsters come to school dressed in their favorite team's colors. During circle time, make a graph to see which team has more fans. Then wrap up the activity by singing "Take Me Out to the Ballgame."

## Play It Safe

Need a safe alternative to real baseballs? Try these nifty sock balls. To make one, stuff a sock into the toe of a white tube sock. Twist the toe of the sock to create a ball; then pull the cuff of the sock over the ball. Twist the sock again and pull the cuff over the ball again. If you still have some cuff left over, repeat the twist-and-pull process as needed.

## Home Run Reading

Order books online www.themailbox.com

**The Baseball Counting Book**
Written by Barbara Barbieri McGrath
Published by Charlesbridge Publishing, Inc.

**The Baseball Star**
Written by Fred G. Arrigg Jr.
Published by Troll Associates, Inc.

**The Jungle Baseball Game**
Written by Tom Paxton
Published by Morrow Junior Books

**Nana Hannah's Piano**
Written by Barbara Bottner
Published by G. P. Putnam's Sons

**Home Run: The Story of Babe Ruth**
Written by Robert Burleigh
Published by Harcourt Brace & Company

**Take Me Out to the Ballgame**
Original lyrics by Jack Norworth
Published by Aladdin Paperbacks

## Game Day

Help youngsters suit up for the big game in your dramatic-play area. Stock the center with lots of props (see the list below) and watch for a wide variety of players, spectators, and vendors to appear. If you set the stage, they will perform!

### Possible Game Day Props

For players:
—ball caps
—batting helmets
—batting gloves
—jerseys
—baseball pants
—baseball gloves
—foam or Wiffle® balls
—plastic or foam bats
—sweatbands
—catcher's equipment

For spectators:
—sunglasses
—seat cushions
—pennants
—binoculars
—souvenir team shirts and hats
—programs

For vendors:
—aprons
—paper hats
—popcorn boxes
—drink cups
—serving trays
—play money

# THE SERIES

## Strike Zone

Relief pitchers will be warming up in the bullpen with this gross-motor activity! Set up a classroom bullpen by suspending a Hula-Hoop® in front of a wall. (Hang the hoop so that the top edge of it is approximately four feet from the floor.) Then use colored tape to make a line on the floor about eight feet in front of the hoop. Position a bucket of sock balls (see "Play It Safe" on page 124) near the line. Encourage youngsters to take turns practicing their pitching finesse by throwing the balls through the hoop strike zone. Can anyone pitch three strikes in a row?

For added fun, turn this into a whole-group activity and integrate some math skills. Invite a child to step up to the line and pitch while the group tallies *strikes* (pitches that go through the hoop) and *balls* (pitches that go outside the hoop). After ten pitches, compare to see which type of pitch was thrown more often.

## A Series Snack

Hit a line drive straight to little tummies with this snack idea. Invite youngsters to help you prepare the recipe below and then, if desired, serve the snack in these handy mitts. Loosely trace each child's hand (with fingers together) onto brown construction paper to resemble a glove, as shown. Cut out the gloves; then glue a nut cup into the palm of each one. Distribute snack-filled gloves to your MVPs before reading a title from "Home Run Reading." Who needs peanuts and Cracker Jack®?

### Grand Slam Trail Mix
—mini marshmallows (baseballs)
—pretzel sticks (bats)
—bite-size shredded wheat cereal pieces (bases)

*Combine the ingredients in a large bowl. Then serve individual servings in nut cups.*

## A Double Play

Here is a fielder's choice—use this matching activity to help children practice letter recognition *or* rhyming skills. Make several baseballs on construction paper. Cut out the balls and then cut each one in half. Program each half with a matching uppercase/lowercase letter or with a rhyming picture. If desired, label the back of each half with an identical sticker for self-checking. Store the ball pieces in a real glove and invite each student to take a turn fielding a basic skill.

# Thanksgiving

Thanksgiving is a time for friends, family, food, and fun. But it's also a time to remember our long-celebrated Thanksgiving friends—the Pilgrims and Native Americans. Use the ideas in this unit to teach your youngsters about the history of one of our most beloved American holidays.

*ideas contributed by Allison Ward*

## Telling the Tale

The story leading up to the very first Thanksgiving is certainly a tale worth telling! Share the history of Thanksgiving with your children by reading Ann McGovern's *The Pilgrims' First Thanksgiving* (Scholastic Inc.). The simple text and realistic illustrations introduce youngsters to the trials and triumphs leading up to that historic day. If this title isn't available, see the list of additional realistic-fiction books below. Then tell the tale!

*Across the Wide Dark Sea*
Written by Jean Van Leeuwen
Illustrated by Thomas B. Allen
Published by Dial Books for Young Readers

*On the Mayflower*
Written by Kate Waters
Photographs by Russ Kendall
Published by Scholastic Inc.

*The Story of the Pilgrims*
Written by Katharine Ross
Illustrated by Carolyn Croll
Published by Random House, Inc.

*Three Young Pilgrims*
Written & Illustrated by Cheryl Harness
Published by Aladdin Paperbacks

These books are currently out of print but definitely worth checking for in your local library:

*Mayflower II: Plimoth Plantation*
Photographed by Ted Curtain
Published by Fort Church Publishers, Inc.

*The Pilgrims at Plymouth*
Written by Lucille Recht Penner
Illustrated by S. D. Schindler
Published by Random House, Inc.

# The Mayflower

## Making a Mayflower

Hoist the sails on creativity as children design a rich dramatic-play experience. After sharing the story of the first Thanksgiving (see "Telling the Tale"), invite small groups of children to share in creating a classroom *Mayflower*. Begin with a large box. Encourage groups of children to paint the outside of the box to resemble the *Mayflower*. (Keep your collection of Thanksgiving books handy for children's reference.) Then encourage student groups to use art supplies to create the ship's details (see the illustration). This ship will launch youngsters on hours of Thanksgiving dramatic play!

Jennifer Miller—Grs. K–1 Special Education, Alann Elementary School, Reston, VA

## Mayflower Menu

Mealtime on the *Mayflower* was no picnic—so to speak! Since there was no refrigeration on the ship, the Pilgrims had to bring food that would not spoil during the long journey. Give your youngsters just a sampling of *Mayflower* fare. When you share another realistic Thanksgiving book, serve your children beef jerky, hard cheese, and crackers. Invite each child to snack on these *Mayflower* foods while you read. Afterward, ask children for their comments. Not bad for a day or two? How about 66 days!

# Remembered

## Packing Pilgrims

What would you take to a brand-new land if you were traveling on a very crowded ship? Pose this question to your children, reminding them that the Pilgrims were going to a land where there would be no refrigerators, houses, or stores. In fact, they were going to a wilderness! Encourage each child to imagine that she is a Pilgrim and illustrate one thing that she would pack to bring on the ship. (If desired, suggest realistic ideas from the list below.) Then have each child cut out her illustration and glue it to the inside of your classroom *Mayflower*. By the way, did you know that one *Mayflower* passenger brought along 126 pairs of shoes? Of course, he shared!

### On Board the Ship

| | |
|---|---|
| sacks of cabbages, turnips, dried peas, flour | tools |
| barrels of salted meat, smoked fish | books |
| rounds of cheese | farm animals |
| seeds | two dogs |
| gardening tools | one cat |
| cookware | |

Jennifer Miller—Grs. K–1 Special Education

## Ship Shape

With a little creative artistry, these *Mayflower* look-alikes take on fine form. To make one ship, photocopy the ship pattern (page 130) on brown construction paper. Cut out the pattern; then place it on a large sheet of blue paper. Arrange one end each of three craft sticks behind the ship (to resemble masts). Next, cut out an assortment of sail shapes from paper, wallpaper, or fabric scraps. Then glue all the pieces in place. Use these ships for the activity described in "What's in a Name?"

## What's in a Name?

Most researchers think that the *Mayflower* was named after the pretty white flower that grows on the hawthorn tree and blooms in May in England. These researchers also think that there was probably a picture of that flower painted on the *Mayflower*. After discussing this with your children, encourage each child to think of a meaningful name for her own ship (made in "Ship Shape"). Then have her draw a picture, cut it out, and glue it onto her ship. Also invite each child to use markers to add colorful details to her ship if desired. Then have each child hold her finished project and "sail" it in front of her as you all sing "Sail, Sail, Sail Our Ship" (on page 128). Then encourage youngsters to take their finished projects home and share the whole Thanksgiving story and song with their families.

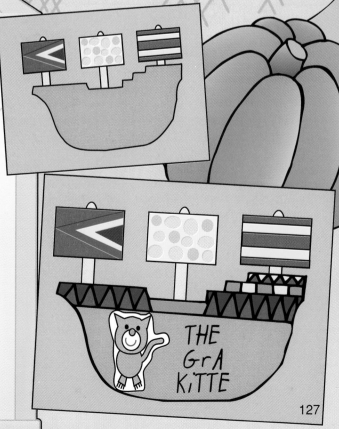

THE GrA KiTTE

## Sail, Sail, Sail Our Ship

Here's a little sailing song that your pretend Pilgrims might like to sing as they journey at sea.

*(sung to the tune of "Row, Row, Row Your Boat")*

Sail, sail, sail our ship
Across the deep blue sea.
We're sailing to America
Where we can all be free.

## Thanks, Squanto!

Corn chips, corn dogs, cornflakes, corn bread—where would we be without corn? And more to the Thanksgiving point, where would we be without Squanto? Squanto was a Native American who spoke English. After he met the Pilgrims, he decided to stay with them and help them survive in the new land. Among many other important things, Squanto taught the Pilgrims how to grow corn. Without this corn, the Pilgrims would have starved. So take a moment to recognize Squanto with this creatively corny art project. Stock your art area with colored and regular popcorn kernels, popped popcorn, tagboard pieces, and craft glue. Encourage each child in the center to squeeze a glue design onto a piece of tagboard. Then have him arrange the popped popcorn and the kernels along the glue lines. When the glue is dry, back each creation with another color of tagboard. Then mount all the projects on a board titled "Thanks, Squanto!" Encourage your little ones to share Squanto's story with classroom visitors.

## Three Days of Thanks

After the Pilgrims' first very difficult winter in the new land, they were so thankful to be alive and to have a bountiful fall harvest that they celebrated for *three days in a row!* After explaining this to your youngsters, launch three days of thanks in your classroom. To prepare, cut out a large butcher-paper basket and mount it on a board titled "Thinking Thankful Thoughts." Then enlarge and duplicate a supply of the food patterns (page 131) on colorful construction paper. Prompt children to begin thinking about what they are thankful for in their lives. On the first of your chosen three days, have each child choose a food cutout and write or illustrate a thankful thought on it. Then help him mount it in the basket. Repeat this activity on the second and third days, creating an overflowing display of thankful thoughts.

## Are Ye Ready? Are Ye Set?

Eating wasn't the only thing going on during that first Thanksgiving celebration—there were lots of fun and games, too! Running races and tug-of-war are two activities that have held people's interest from way back then until now. This year when you take your youngsters out for a few running races and a couple rounds of tug-of-war, add a touch of the old days to the festivities. To start off each game or race, call out "Are ye ready? Are ye set? Go!"

## Pumpkin Delight

Although pumpkin pie is standard fare for Thanksgiving these days, historians think that the *pie* part might not have been around until a couple years after the very first Thanksgiving. So if you're planning to have a classroom feast, try adding this form of pumpkin to your menu. First cut the top off a baking pumpkin. Then have your youngsters help remove the seeds and pulp. Next fill the pumpkin with apple chunks, raisins, walnuts, and cranberries. Sprinkle the filling with cinnamon and sugar, and dot with butter. Replace the pumpkin top and bake the pumpkin on a cookie sheet in a 350° oven for approximately 1¹/₂ hours. To serve, scoop out the warm fruit as well as the pumpkin. Mmm…delightful!

Pam Crane

*I wd lik to milk a got.*

*I can sit down to eat.*

## Thanksgiving-Related Stories

*1, 2, 3 Thanksgiving!*
Written by W. Nikola-Lisa
Illustrated by Robin Kramer
Published by Albert Whitman & Company

*Albert's Thanksgiving*
Written & Illustrated by Leslie Tryon
Published by Atheneum

*Thanksgiving Treat*
Written & Illustrated by Catherine Stock
Published by Aladdin Paperbacks

*Today Is Thanksgiving!*
Written & Illustrated by P. K. Hallinan
Published by Ideals Children's Books

*Thanksgiving at the Tappletons'*
Written by Eileen Spinelli
Illustrated by Maryann Cocca-Leffler
Published by HarperCollins Publishers, Inc.

*Turkey Pox*
Written by Laurie Halse Anderson
Illustrated by Dorothy Donohue
Published by Albert Whitman & Company

Order books online. www.themailbox.com

## Looking Back

Get your modern-day pilgrims pondering the past with this thought-provoking activity. To set the stage, read aloud a book that realistically depicts life in the new land. Some especially good choices include *Sarah Morton's Day, Samuel Eaton's Day,* and *Tapenum's Day* by Kate Waters (Scholastic Inc.). Photographed in full color at Plimoth Plantation—a living history museum—these books accurately offer an up-close look at different children's days in 17th-century America.

After sharing the book(s), prompt your students to brainstorm a list of activities in which children participated in those early days. Write their comments on chart paper. Then give each child a large sheet of construction paper and ask her to fold it in half. On one half, encourage each child to write about and illustrate one thing from the past that she wishes she could do in the present. On the other half, have her illustrate one thing that she is happy she does not have to do now. Bind all the pages between construction paper covers titled "Now & Then." Invite each child to share her page with the group. Ah, this is the life…or was *that?*

# Ship Pattern

Use with "Ship Shape" on page 127.

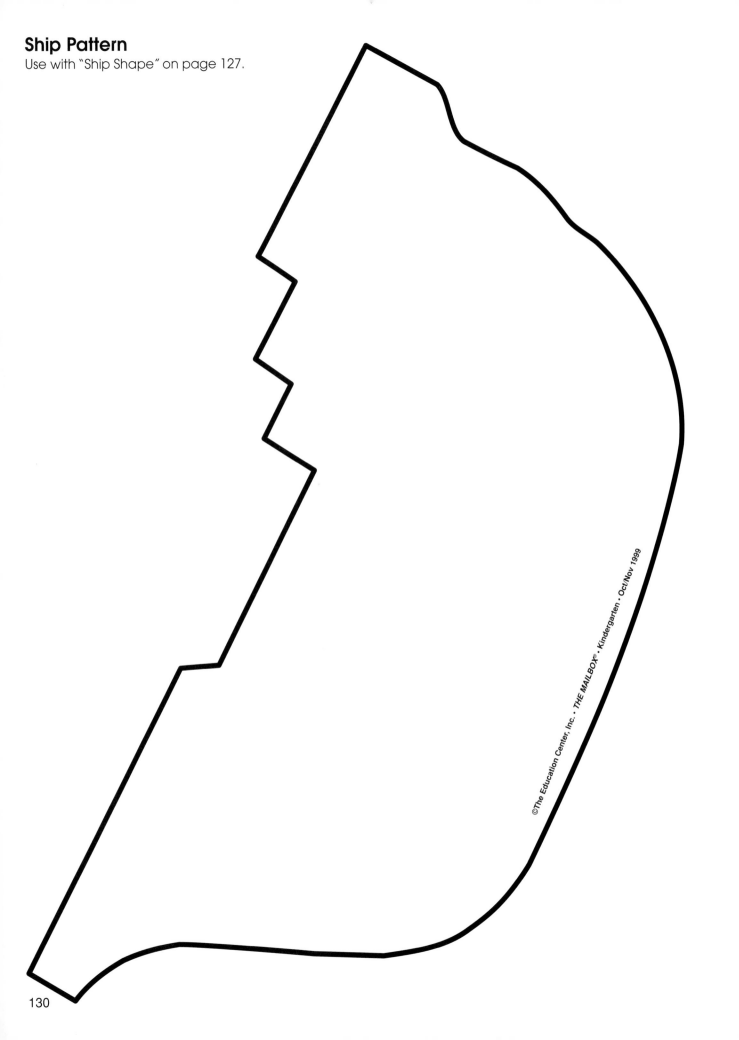

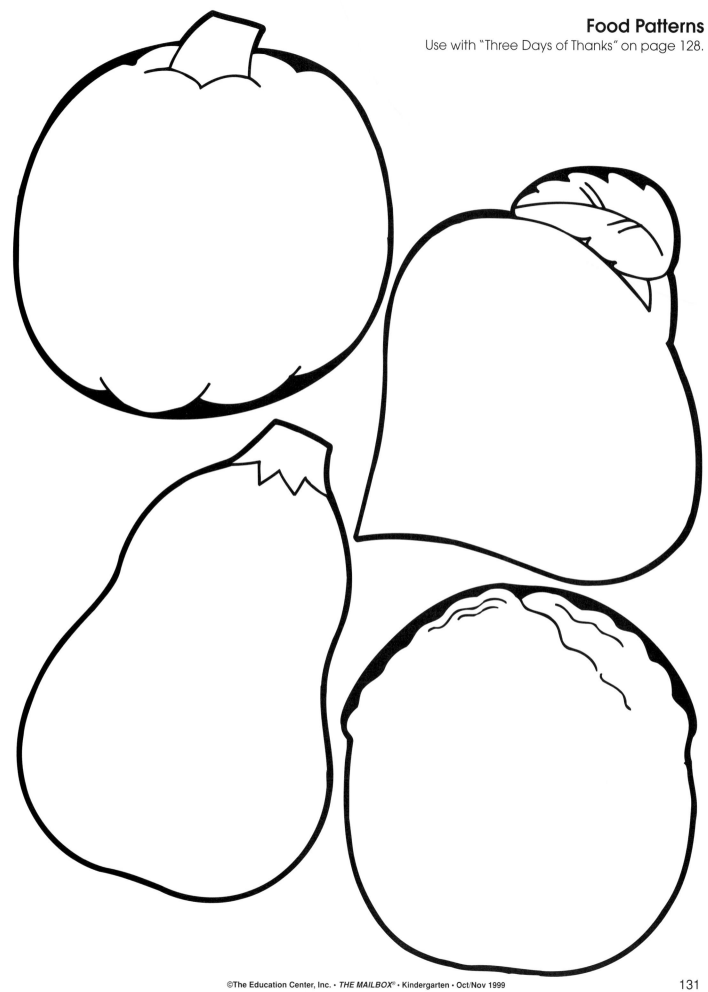

# A Bumper Crop of Readers!

As kindergarten teachers, you constantly plant the seeds of reading as you busily cultivate your way through each day. So in recognition of National Children's Book Week, we asked you to send us your favorite ideas for harvesting a bumper crop of readers in your classroom. Here's the field—take your pick!

## Oh, Dear!

Does your class participate in DEAR* time? If so, here's a fun variation on the theme. (If not, why not start now!) Every once in a while, announce that your DEAR time for a specific day will be round-robin style. Then divide your class into groups of three or four. Give each group member a book from your class library and start DEAR time. Then, in a few minutes, ring a bell signaling children to pass their books one person to the right. Continue in this manner until each group member has had a chance to "read" all the books in his group. If desired, conclude your DEAR time by having each group member report on one of the books that he read.

Bonita Strope—Gr. K
Montour Falls, NY

*DEAR is an acronym that stands for *drop everything and read!*

## Forest Reading

Enchant children to read by transforming your independent reading area into a forest. Make a variety of large tree trunks cut from brown bulletin board paper or grocery bags. Have students bring in an assortment of real leaves and glue them onto the trees. Also add child-made, construction paper leaves to the trees. Complete the area by placing several comfortable pillows or beanbag chairs on the floor. Finally, invite students to visit the forest and get lost in a book!

Anne Marie Johnson, Tipp City, OH

## Tales to Tote

What's the best thing about this portable, color-coded library? Organization, organization, organization! In advance, sort the books in your class library by themes. Place each set of books in a plastic two-sided tote or a large plastic tub. Next label each tote with its corresponding theme. Finally, color-code each set of books by attaching matching dot stickers on the cover of each book and on the tote. If desired, place a specific tote at a table to create a special-interest reading area for students. With this system, finding books, cleaning up, and staying organized is as simple as a tote!

Kathy Levy, Jacksonwald Elementary
Reading, PA

## Book 'Em!

If you order books regularly from children's book clubs, this idea is for you! Use the free books you receive from the club as prizes in a weekly book drawing. Write each child's name on a strip of paper and put all the strips in a seasonal container. At the end of each week, have a student draw one child's name out of the container. Invite the chosen child to pick a book to keep as his own. All students will be motivated to read and the child whose name was selected will love hearing you say, "Book him (or her)!"

Taryn Way—Gr. K
Los Molinos Elementary
Los Molinos, CA

Robert

The Reading Railroad

Choo! Choo! Meghan (childs name) has hopped aboard the Reading Railroad! We read Pumpkin, Pumpkin together.

Dawn Roberts (Parent signature)

## I've Been Reading on the Railroad!

This home-school connection will have your little ones reading all the live-long day! At the beginning of each week, allow a few students to each check out a book from your class library. Place each child's selected book in a small canvas bag along with a construction paper railroad car similar to the one shown. If desired, add a sheet of fun follow-up activities that a parent can do with her child. Send these book bags home with a note inviting each parent to read the book to her child and complete a follow-up activity (if included). Direct the parent and child to sign the railroad car, and then return the bag and its contents by the end of the week. When the child returns the bag, add his railroad car to a construction paper engine that has been mounted on a wall in your classroom. (See "Two Thumbs Up!" below for a related extension activity.)

Catherine Turpin—Gr. K, Mohave Valley Elementary
Bullhead City, AZ

## Two Thumbs Up!

Sharpen story comprehension by having your little book critics give two thumbs up to their favorite books. At the beginning of each week, invite a few students to each check out a book from your class library. Send the book home along with a note asking parents to read the book to their children. (See "I've Been Reading on the Railroad!" above for a related home-school connection idea.) After the child has heard the story and returned the book, invite him to review the book for the class. Then have him rate the book with a thumbs down, thumbs up, or *two* thumbs up! As an extension, ask the child to draw a picture from the story or illustrate a new cover. Then display the pictures around your room. At the end of the year or each semester, count the total number of books reviewed. Wow! Two *hundred* thumbs up!

adapted from an idea by Sarah Simpson—Gr. K
Pinar Elementary, Orlando, FL

# Penguins on Parade

Waddle, dive, slide, and glide through the curriculum with these chilly ideas that are black, white, and fun all over!

What are penguins?
rodents |
birds ||||| ||||
fish |||

## Pondering About Penguins

Introduce your penguin unit and dive into a little critical thinking with this group activity. During your circle time, write a penguin question on chart paper and then list several possible answers. After a little pondering, invite each child to place a tally mark beside the answer he believes is correct. Then share the correct response with your group, adding any relative information. If desired, use the facts listed in "Penguin Particulars" to continue this activity each day of your unit.

Lynn Creede—Gr. K, Benton Heights Elementary, Monroe, NC

## Penguin Particulars

Share these interesting facts that are peculiar to penguins. If desired, use illustrations from picture books and reference books as visuals (see the booklist on page 138). At the conclusion of the discussion, have each student identify the penguin fact that she finds most interesting. On a sheet of paper, write her dictation about what she has learned and then have her illustrate the page. Display students' work on a bulletin board titled "We Know Plenty About Penguins!"

- Penguins are birds, but they cannot fly.
- There are 17 different kinds of penguins.
- Penguins are found only *south* of the equator.
- Most penguins do not live in ice and snow.
- Penguins live together in *colonies* or *rookeries*. (There can be as many as one million penguins in a colony.)
- Mother and father penguins share the job of hatching, protecting, and feeding penguin chicks.
- Penguin families recognize each other by their voices.
- Penguin parents feed only their own chicks.
- Penguins eat fish, squid, and krill.
- Penguins have spiky tongues that help them hold on to slippery fish and make sure the fish go down headfirst.
- Penguin chicks huddle closely together in large groups called *crèches* to keep safe and warm while their parents are away hunting for food.
- Penguins' black-and-white patterns help camouflage them from predators.
- Their enemies include the leopard seal, killer whale, and skua.
- Penguins can change directions in an instant. They can escape an enemy by zigzagging as they swim.
- A penguin can hold its breath underwater for about three minutes. (Emperor penguins have been known to stay under the water for as long as 18 minutes!)
- Adélie penguins can push themselves, or *toboggan,* on their bellies faster than they can walk (and faster than a man can run!).

## Up on the Iceberg
*(sung to the tune of "Up on the Housetop")*

Into the ocean, penguins go.
They spy seals way down below.

Zip through the water with no delay,
Zigzagging penguins swim away.

Oh, oh, oh! Go penguins, go!
Oh, oh, oh! Go penguins, go!

Leap to the iceberg, quick, quick, quick!
Back to the crèche to feed your chick.

adapted from an idea by Susan Daley
Narragansett Elementary School
Warwick, RI

**Kimberly Richard**

## Slip and Slide

Predicting and experimenting get a little slippery with this science activity. To prepare, freeze a 9" x 13" pan of water to create a pretend ice floe. Then collect a variety of small objects—some that will slide on the ice and some that will not. (Be sure to include a penguin figurine that will slide.) Divide a sheet of chart paper into three columns and then label the columns as shown.

Show each object to the group and then write the objects' names on the chart. Poll students on whether or not they think the first object will slide on the ice. Write their predictions on the chart. Then have a student volunteer test the object. Write the outcome on the chart. Continue in this manner for the rest of the objects. Then refreeze the water and set it out again during center time. Invite students to explore and find other objects that will slide on the ice. It's slippery science!

Marci Matchett, Lakeland, FL

**Will It Slide?**

| Item | Prediction | Outcome |
| --- | --- | --- |
| Cotton ball | yes-12 no-8 | no |
| Lima bean | yes-10 no-10 | yes |

## Counting Penguins

Extend the penguin theme into your learning centers with this easy-to-make matching game. Enlarge the penguin and egg patterns on page 139. Make ten copies of each of the enlarged patterns on construction paper. Color, cut out, and then laminate them. Program each of the penguins with a different numeral. Use sticky dots to make a dot set on each egg to correspond with one of the numerals. Direct students at this center to match each penguin with its egg.

For a more challenging activity, tie a length of cord between two chairs to resemble a clothesline. Provide clothespins for children to use to attach the penguins to the line sequentially and for clipping on the matching eggs. Follow up this math practice with a reading of *Splash! A Penguin Counting Book* by Jonathan Chester and Kirsty Melville (Tricycle Press).

Susan A. DeRiso—Gr. K
John W. Horton School
Cranston, RI

## Eye-to-Eye

Adult penguins vary in size. The smallest, the little blue penguin, averages 11 inches, while the largest, the emperor penguin, averages 35 inches. Most of the other species of penguins—including the Adélie penguins—are in the 16- to 20-inch range. Make these sizes concrete for your youngsters with this informative display.

Enlarge the penguin face pattern on page 139. Make three copies and then cut them out. Mount one face on a classroom wall at 35 inches above the floor; then mount the second face at 18 inches and the third at 11 inches. Label each face with the corresponding species name (see above paragraph). Then invite students to compare their heights to the penguins' heights. Can they see eye-to-eye with an emperor penguin?

Joanna Rivera, McAllen, TX

Emperor Penguin

Adélie Penguin

Little Blue Penguin

## Glacier Graphing

Use this independent activity to encourage your youngsters to waddle into some graphing practice. To prepare, make ten penguins by painting lima beans black on one side and white on the other. Store the penguins in a cup. Cut a piece of white construction paper or craft foam to resemble a patch of ice. Then draw a two-column graph—with each column having ten spaces—on a sheet of paper. Label one column "Black" and the other "White." Duplicate a graph for each child. Place the penguins, ice, graphs, and some crayons in a center.

To complete this activity, a student empties the cup, letting the penguins "slide" onto the ice. He then graphs the penguins according to the colors showing. When finished, have each child share his graph with you and encourage him to use math terms, such as *more than, fewer,* and *equal to.* Reward efforts with a black-and-white Oreo® treat.

Lynn Creede—Gr. K
Benton Heights Elementary
Monroe, NC

## Give Me a *P!*

Reinforce upper- and lowercase letter recognition with the help of these hungry penguins. To prepare for this small-group activity, enlarge the penguin on page 139 onto an 11" x 17" sheet of paper. Label the penguin's tummy with "PENGUIN" and then duplicate it onto 12" x 18" construction paper for each child. Duplicate, color, and cut out a set of fish (page 142) for each child. Pile the fish facedown in the center of the playing area and then give each child a penguin. Designate a child to go first. Have her pick a fish from the pile. If she needs that fish to match a letter on her penguin, she keeps it and places it below the matching letter. If the child doesn't need that particular letter, she asks the group, "Who needs a(n) [g]?" The first child to respond gets the letter. Play continues with each child taking a turn until everyone has spelled *penguin* in lowercase letters. Wow, what a fishy feast!

Lynn Creede—Gr. K

## Lunchtime!

Need an enjoyable way to review basic skills? Try this chilly game where students become penguins trying to keep their fish. Duplicate and cut out the gameboard halves on pages 140 and 141. Glue the halves together as indicated and then laminate the gameboard. If desired, glue Poly-Fil® onto the gameboard to give it a snowy effect. Make game markers by using a fine-tipped permanent black marker to draw penguin faces and wings on lima beans. Then hot-glue each penguin to a different colored button, as shown. Duplicate the fish on page 142. Mask the letters on the fish; then duplicate and cut out a set of them for each player. Program a set of flash cards with letters, numerals, colors, or any other desired skill. To set up the game, place the gameboard and a die on a table, have each player choose a marker, and then give her a set of fish.

To play the game, show the first player a flash card. If she correctly identifies it, have her roll the die and move the corresponding number of spaces. If she lands on a penguin, she loses one of her fish. If she identifies the flash card incorrectly, her turn is over. Play continues until each player reaches the end of the path. Once at the end of the path, invite each player to swap any remaining fish for fish-shaped snack crackers. Yummy!

adapted from an idea by Karen Cook—Resource K–1
McDonough Primary School
McDonough, GA

## A Tacky Race

Tacky means terrific in this story-extension activity. After enjoying *Tacky the Penguin* by Helen Lester (Houghton Mifflin Company) with your students, gear up for this unique relay race. Divide your class into two or three teams and line them up on one side of the room. On the other side of the room, assemble tacky outfits including a shirt, pants, socks, and a hat. Designate an outfit for each team.

On your signal, the first player on each team runs to his pile of clothes, dresses, runs back to the team, and undresses. Then the next player dresses, runs to the other side of the room, undresses, and runs back to the team. Play continues until everyone has had a turn to be tacky. Ready, set, go!

Lynn Creede—Gr. K

## Waddle, Waddle, Waddle

Here's a tune that will make everyone want to get the waddles out. After teaching the song (below), give each child a large rubber band to put around his ankles. Encourage him to move around the room and explore the movement capabilities. Then sing the song together again and watch your little penguins waddle!

*(sung to the tune of "I'm a Little Teapot")*

I'm a little penguin, short and fat.
I waddle like this and I waddle like that.
I am always dressed in black and white.
Don't you think I'm quite a sight?

Susan A. DeRiso—Gr. K
John W. Horton School
Cranston, RI

## Waddle On Home

Create this activity bag to extend the penguin theme into students' homes. Duplicate the parent note on page 142. Then pack a bag (or a small cooler) with the items listed below. During a group time, read aloud *Cuddly Dudley* by Jez Alborough (Candlewick Press). Show the activity bag to your children and explain its contents. Then give each child an opportunity to take the bag home and slide and glide into activities with his family. When each child returns the bag, share his journal page with the class. Then collect the pages and bind them into a class book for your reading center.

### What to include:
— parent note (page 142)
— copy of *Cuddly Dudley*
— stuffed penguin toy
— journal page (program an enlarged copy of the penguin on page 139, as shown)
— crayons
— scissors
— glue
— several Oreo® cookies

Susan A. DeRiso—Gr. K
John W. Horton School
Cranston, RI

For a yummy penguin treat, see the recipe on page 267.

## Chilly Reading

Use the literature list below to inform and entertain your little ones as you toboggan with penguins through the curriculum.

### Nonfiction
*The Penguin (Life Cycles)*
Written by Sabrina Crewe
Published by Raintree Steck-Vaughn
　　Publishers

*Penguins!*
Written by Gail Gibbons
Published by Holiday House, Inc.

*See How They Grow: Penguin*
Written by Mary Ling
Published by Dorling Kindersley, Inc.

*Penguins* (A First Discovery Book)
Translated by Jennifer Riggs
Published by Scholastic Inc.

### Fiction
*Solo*
Written by Paul Geraghty
Published by Crown Publishers, Inc.

*Antarctic Antics: A Book of Penguin Poems*
Written by Judy Sierra
Published by Harcourt Brace & Company

*Penguin Pete*
Written by Marcus Pfister
Published by North-South Books Inc.

*The Funny Red Christmas Stocking:
A Lift-the-Flap Story*
Written by Harriet Ziefert
Published by Little Simon

*Little Penguin's Tale*
Written by Audrey Wood
Published by Harcourt Brace Jovanovich

Order books online.
www.themailbox.com

# Penguin Pattern

Use with "Counting Penguins" on page 135, "Give Me a *P!*" on page 136, and "Waddle On Home" on page 138.

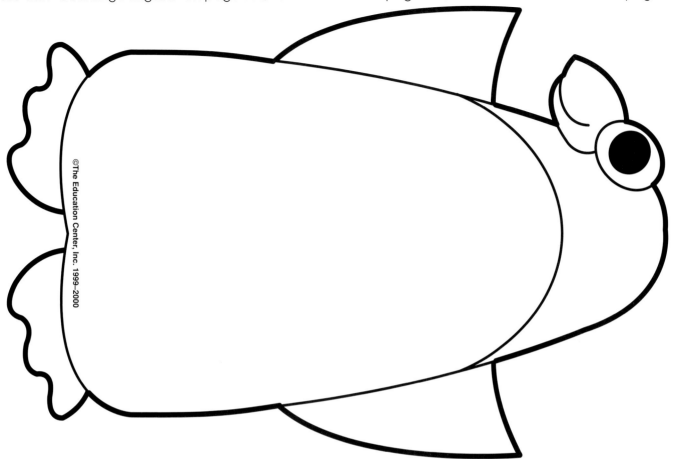

©The Education Center, Inc. 1999–2000

## Face Pattern

Use with "Eye-to-Eye" on page 135.

## Egg Pattern

Use with "Counting Penguins" on page 135.

# Gameboard

Use with "Lunchtime!" on page 137.

**START**

©The Education Center, Inc. • *THE MAILBOX*® • *Kindergarten* • Dec/Jan 1999–2000

Overlap here and glue.

FINISH

## Fish Cards
Use with "Give Me a *P!*" on page 136 and "Lunchtime!" on page 137.

## Parent Note
Use with "Waddle On Home" on page 138.

Dear Parents,
Penguins are parading in our classroom! We're having lots of fun learning about penguins and using the penguin theme to practice basic skills. Please join the parade by hosting Dudley overnight and then helping your child complete the activities below. Return all of the materials—including the completed journal page—to school tomorrow. Have fun!

- Read the book *Cuddly Dudley* to your child.

- Look around the house and help find something black and something white. Have your child draw these items on the journal page where indicated.

- Search the p-p-paper (newspaper) for some *P*s. Have your child cut out several of them and glue them to the penguin's feet.

- Write on the journal page your child's dictation about what Dudley did during his stay. Encourage your child to illustrate the story.

- Enjoy the black-and-white treat with your child. Yummy!

Black

White

Mom's black pot

My dog's bone.

Dudley and I played on my swingset. Then we ate pizza and walked my dog. He slept in a soft basket beside my bed. Dudley had a cuddly time!

Kyle

# Happy New Year 2000

All over the world, in all sorts of ways, people joyfully welcome each new year. And this particular new year marks an exciting milestone! Use the ideas in this unit to learn about and celebrate this very special occasion.

*ideas contributed by Susan DeRiso*

Alright!

## Cheer for the Year

As the new year approaches—or is already upon you!—build new year spirit and delight by singing this song with your students. Each time you repeat the song, encourage students to substitute a different word of cheer for the under-lined word.

*(sung to the tune of "If You're Happy and You Know It")*

If you're ready for the new year,
Give a cheer—[hooray]!
If you're ready for the new year,
Give a cheer—[hooray]!
If you're ready, give a cheer
For the next 1,000 years.
If you're ready for the new year,
Give a cheer—[hooray]!

## We're All Out of Months!

Begin a discussion about the new year by asking children how we know a new year is coming. Then show a 1999 calendar and flip through the months as children recite them together. After they say "December," exclaim in mock alarm that we're all out of months! Ask what happens next. Prompted by your students, bring out a 2000 calendar. Guide children to state that after every December comes a new year that begins with January. Explain that the number of the year also changes on January 1. Then write "January [today's date], 2000," on the board. Have each child copy this date at the top of a large sheet of construction paper. Use this page for "I Resolve!"

January 3, 2000
I will et ol my diner.

Abbie

## I Resolve!

What's a new year without New Year's resolutions? Introduce and discuss this topic with your students. Ask each child to think of resolutions she might like to make this year. Then have each child write about and illustrate her ideas on the page she prepared in "We're All Out of Months!" Bind each completed page behind a cover titled "Our New Year's Resolutions." Invite each child to share her page with the group. In a month or so, read this book again as a class. How's everybody doing?

## Give 'em a Hand!

Lend a hand in spreading New Year's wishes with these cute crafts! To make this craft, paint a child's hand with his choice of a bright color of paint. Then have him make a handprint by pressing his hand onto a sheet of tagboard. When the paint is dry, instruct the child to cut around the print. Have his glue a photo of himself to the palm. Then, using a thin, permanent black marker, have the child write a New Year's greeting similar to the one shown. Finally, instruct the child to attach a strip of magnetic tape to the back of the print. Encourage each child to choose a special recipient for his gift of new year cheer.

## Celebrate With a Snack!

Just how much is *2,000?* Youngsters will find out with this educational snack! In advance, ask each child to bring a bag of 100 pieces of a small snack, such as Cheerios®, raisins, chocolate chips, or peanuts. (If you have fewer than 20 students, you'll need to provide some snacks too. If you have more, enjoy the extras!) As you circulate with a large bowl, have each child pour his snack into the bowl while the class counts aloud by 100s. Continue with this process until you reach 2,000. After children examine the 2,000 total, enjoy the snack with a New Year's book, such as *Cider Apples* by Sandy Nightingale or *P. Bear's New Year's Party* by Paul Owen Lewis.

Carole Dibble
Marietta, GA

### Kindergarten Capsule

Keep kindergarten memories alive with these kindergarten time capsules. To begin, instruct each child to paint a paper towel tube. Next have each child complete, color, and cut out a copy of the label on page 145. (Have her label the time blank with a date that is 12 years in the future.) When the paint is dry, have her glue the label to her capsule and add stick-on stars or other decorations as desired. Next, have each child complete the survey found on page 146. Demonstrate how to roll up the survey along with a selected piece of schoolwork and a personal note from you. (If your school has a color copier, include a copy of your class photo too!) Insert the rolled-up materials in the tube; then seal the tube by taping a construction paper circle over each end. Instruct each child to take her time capsule home and put it in a safe place. Imagine the smiles as these memories are opened up when your students are seniors in high school!

For a New Year's bulletin board idea, see page 9.

_____'s

## Kindergarten Time Capsule

*Do not open until _____!
(date)

©The Education Center, Inc. • *THE MAILBOX®* • *Kindergarten* • Dec/Jan 1999–2000

_____'s

## Kindergarten Time Capsule

*Do not open until _____!
(date)

©The Education Center, Inc. • *THE MAILBOX®* • *Kindergarten* • Dec/Jan 1999–2000

_____'s

## Kindergarten Time Capsule

*Do not open until _____!
(date)

©The Education Center, Inc. • *THE MAILBOX®* • *Kindergarten* • Dec/Jan 1999–2000

# My Kindergarten
## Time Capsule Survey

My name is _____.

I am _____ years old.

My school's name is _____.

My teacher is _____.

My friends are _____.

My favorite thing to do is _____.

My favorite book is _____.

What I like best about school is _____

_____.

I like to eat _____.

I don't like to eat _____.

When I grow up I'd like to be _____.

### Here is a picture of me!

Glue photo here.

# Special You, Special Me!

Snowflakes and children are both one of a kind. This blizzard of activities focuses on self-esteem and will help your youngsters see that to be *different* is to be *special*.

*ideas contributed by Susan A. DeRiso, Carole Dibble, and Kathy Lee*

## A Special Sharing

Celebrate the uniqueness of each student during circle time with this special touch. In advance, create this snowflake wand using a sheet of 1-inch Styrofoam®, a 12-inch wooden dowel, two wiggle eyes, and red felt. To make the wand, use a serrated knife to cut out a snowflake from the Styrofoam®. If desired, use the pattern on page 150 as a template. Insert the dowel into the bottom of the snowflake to create a handle. Then glue on the wiggle eyes and a felt mouth, as shown.

Have students pass the wand around the circle while singing the tune below. Encourage the child holding the wand at the end of the verse to share something special about himself. Continue singing the verse until each child has had a turn to share.

### I'm Something Special

*(sung to the tune of "London Bridge")*

Share with us some special news,
Special news, special news.
Share with us some special news,
About you!

Pam Crane

## Fingerprinting Flurry

Frolicking fingers make a flurry of snow in this activity. Explain to your little ones that fingerprints and snowflakes are similar because there are no two flakes nor fingerprints that are exactly alike. Give each child a sheet of dark-colored construction paper and provide access to white washable paint. Demonstrate how to draw several lines on the paper that intersect at the same point. Encourage the child to use the lines as guides and make fingerprints (or use toes!) along and beside the lines to create her own unique snowflake. Cut out the flakes and display them together with the title "A Flurry of Fun!"

147

# A Snowstorm of Successes

Many things make us unique. Often we are differentiated by things we can and cannot do. By focusing on the *cans* with this snowy mobile, your youngsters will be shoveling up mounds of self-esteem. Gather the necessary materials listed below. Then assist each child in completing the directions. Hang the finished mobiles from your ceiling to create a constant reminder of "I can!" Wow, there's a real feeling of success in the air!

**Materials needed for each student:**
— 24" x 3" tagboard strip
— 4 copies of the snowflake pattern on page 150
— 4 pieces of white yarn cut in different lengths
— 3 pieces of blue yarn cut the same length
— stapler
— hole puncher
— crayons

**Directions:**
1. Write your name and "can…" on the tagboard strip.
2. Staple the ends of the strip together to form a cylinder.
3. Punch four holes around the bottom of the cylinder and three holes around the top.
4. On each snowflake, write/dictate and illustrate a different activity that you can complete successfully.
5. Cut out the snowflakes, and then punch a hole at the top of each one.
6. Attach each snowflake to the bottom of the cylinder with a white piece of yarn.
7. Tie one end of each piece of blue yarn to a different hole in the top of the cylinder; then tie the loose ends together.

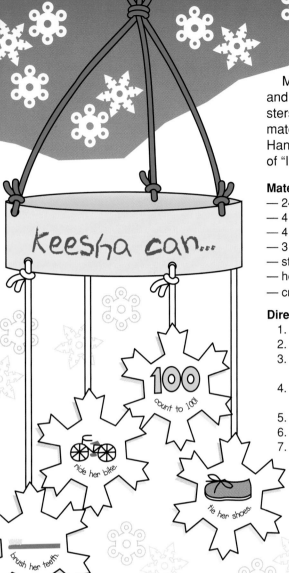

# A Blizzard of Praise

Shake up spirits with these rewarding jars of praise. In advance, collect a class supply of clean baby food jars (with the labels removed). Also, duplicate and cut out the snowflake pattern below for each child.

To make a praise jar, cut a child's photo to fit the inside of the jar's lid. Then laminate the photo and hot-glue it to the inside of the lid. Next fill the jar with water, add some silver glitter, and secure the lid. Finally glue the snowflake to the top of the lid.

Keep the jars on students' desks or tables and use them as magical, motivating rewards. To give praise and attention to a deserving child, simply turn his jar upside down. Now *that's* something to cheer about!

# Double the Pleasure, Double the Fun

This version of the traditional memory game gets up close and personal to help students refine their visual-discrimination skills. To prepare the game, duplicate the snowflake cards on page 151 on tagboard and then cut them apart. Make two copies of each child's photograph. Cut out the duplicated photos and mount them on separate tagboard cards that are the same color as the snowflake cards. Mix the snowflake and photo cards together and arrange them facedown on a tabletop. (If there are too many cards, divide them to make two games.) Then invite each child in a small group to try to find a matching pair. Look carefully!

**Pattern**

Hooray for ME!

## Snowflake Snacks

Your little ones will love creating these uniquely different treats. Gather the ingredients and supplies listed below. Have each child place part of a doily on top of her cupcake. Then help her sift powdered sugar over the doily. Carefully remove it to reveal a snowflake design. No two treats will be the same!

**Ingredients/supplies needed:**
1 chocolate cupcake per child
powdered sugar
sifter
doilies

## If You Were a Snowflake...

Hmmm, what would you do? Youngsters will have no trouble pretending to be snowflakes in this creative-thinking activity. Duplicate page 152 for each child. Pose the question, "What do snowflakes do?" during a group time and brainstorm the possibilities. Have each child imagine that he is a snowflake and record his dictation on his page. Encourage the child to illustrate his story. Then bind the completed pages together to make a class book. Share the stories during the next circle time, being sure to acknowledge the author-illustrator of each page.

If I were a snowflake...

I'd whirl right to the tip of my mom's nose!

by

David

## Sing a Song of Self-Esteem

Now that your youngsters know that being different makes them special, they have something to sing about! So teach this little ditty and sing up a snowstorm.

*(sung to the tune of "She'll Be Coming 'Round the Mountain")*

We all are very different, yes, we know.
Yes, we know! *(shout)*
We all are very different, yes, we know.
Yes, we know! *(shout)*
From our heads down to our toes—
Like the little flakes of snow—
We all are very different, yes, we know.
Yes, we know! *(shout)*

# Snowflake Pattern

Use with "A Special Sharing" on page 147 and "A Snowstorm of Successes" on page 148.

# If I were a snowflake...

by

_____

**Note to the teacher:** Use with "If You Were a Snowflake…" on page 149.

# Count on Quilts

Cover your math curriculum with a quilt! This unit pieces together patterning, geometry, counting, and more to create a pleasing patchwork of fun and learning.

*ideas contributed by Suzanne Moore*

## Getting Ready

Gather together a collection of quilts in all different shapes, sizes, and patterns for your children to observe and analyze. Friends, family members, and other teachers may be willing to add to the collection—with the promise that you'll be extra careful! Also check your local library for resource books featuring photographs of quilt designs. Display the most treasured quilts out of students' reach and have the less frail ones available for dramatic play, your reading area, resting, and use in several of the activities that follow.

## Take a Look

Set the stage for making observations as youngsters count and name the colors, shapes, and patterns of a quilt. Spread a quilt on the floor and invite students to sit around its edges. Then sing the following song to help them focus on the quilt's attributes. Pause after each verse to discuss the answers. Extend this activity by singing the song again using a different quilt.

*(sung to the tune of "Skip to My Lou")*

How many colors do you see?
How many colors do you see?
How many colors do you see?
Count and name them all for me.

How many [circles] do you see?
How many [circles] do you see?
How many [circles] do you see?
Can you count them all for me?
*(Repeat this verse using other shapes such as diamonds, squares, and stars.)*

What kind of patterns do you see?
What kind of patterns do you see?
What kind of patterns do you see?
Can you point one out for me?

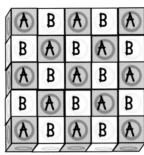
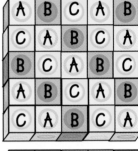

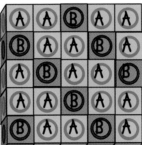

## Patterning Pizzazz

Most quilts are made out of blocks of fabric. Some quilt blocks are stitched together to form a pattern over the entire quilt. Other quilt blocks are patterns in and of themselves. Give your students an opportunity to make patterned quilt blocks with linking cubes. Have each child choose two or three colors from a set of cubes. Then encourage her to form a simple pattern—such as ABAB, AABB, or ABCABC—and continue it for five rows to make a square, as shown. Invite the student to compare her block to other blocks to see who used the same pattern.

## A Patchwork of Patterns

Help youngsters replicate the patterned blocks made in "Patterning Pizzazz" in this collaborative quilt. Cut a supply of one-inch squares from construction paper in each of the colors represented in the linking cube set. Then cut out a five-inch construction paper square for each child. Have him refer to his pattern block and record the pattern he created by gluing smaller squares in the appropriate colors and order onto his larger square. Display the squares together on a length of bulletin board paper to resemble a patchwork quilt. For an interactive display, label a tagboard strip with the appropriate pattern sequence for each block. Store the strips near the display and encourage students to take turns matching each strip to its corresponding block.

## Shapely Quilts

Reinforce shape recognition and counting with this simple small-group activity. To prepare, make a display of several different quilt block designs on a sheet of posterboard. Then provide a supply of small counters, such as dried beans. Direct students' attention to one of the quilt blocks on the display, and then call out the name of a shape. Have youngsters find the designated shapes in the block and put a counter on each one. Then have a volunteer count the number of shapes aloud. Repeat the activity with different shapes, quilt blocks, and volunteers. For independent practice, have each child complete a copy of page 157.

## It's "Geo-rific!"

Use Geoboards to help students better understand the relationship between shapes and quilts. Provide each child with a Geoboard and several rubber bands. Call out the name of a shape (without rounded edges) and direct each student to create the shape on her board using only one rubber band. Explain that many quilt blocks are made of repeated shapes. Then demonstrate how to make the blocks shown here (a transparent Geoboard on an overhead projector is ideal for this) and challenge youngsters to make them on their own boards.

Nine Patch
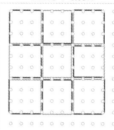

Broken Dishes
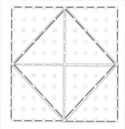

Rail Fence
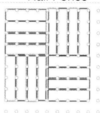

Honeycomb
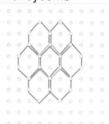

*(sung to the tune of "Ten Little Indians")*
How *many* ways can you cover this shape?
How *many* ways can you cover this shape?
How *many* ways can you cover this shape
Using other pattern blocks?

## The Great Cover-Up

Many quilters use the math concept of *equivalence* when designing new patterns for quilts. Here's a fun way to introduce this concept to students in a small-group setting. Start by placing a set of pattern blocks in the middle of the group. Have each child place a yellow hexagon in front of him; then sing the song in the speech bubble above.

Encourage each child to use the various pattern blocks to cover the hexagon and then share his discoveries with the group. Explain that because the smaller shapes fit *exactly* on top of the hexagon, together they are *equivalent* to the hexagon. Now you see it, now you don't!

## Switcheroo

Switch it, change it, rearrange it! Fractions, fine-motor skills, and visual-discrimination skills get a workout here as youngsters create quilt blocks. To prepare, each child will need a four-inch construction paper square and a four-inch wallpaper square. (Make sure the wallpaper squares are all different.)

Direct each child to fold the wallpaper square in the middle, being careful to match the edges. Then have her unfold the square and trace the fold line with a crayon. Explain that her square is now divided into *halves.* Next have the child refold the square and then fold the square in half again. Direct her to unfold her square completely and trace the new fold line with a crayon. Explain that her square is now divided into *fourths.* Finally have the child cut on the fold lines to make four small squares. Then challenge her to cut each square in *half* by folding opposite corners, as shown. Each child should have eight triangles.

And now for the big switcheroo! Have each child glue four of her triangles to her construction paper square, as shown. Then encourage her to pick a partner (you may need to participate if there's an odd number of students) and exchange the remaining four triangles. Have each child finish her quilt block by gluing on the newly acquired four triangles. For added fun, display the completed squares all together and invite youngsters to identify the partners. Quilting is always more fun with a friend!

Finished Square
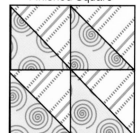

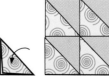

## The Need for Symmetry

Introducing *symmetry* to your little ones ties right in to using quilts to teach math. Find some examples of symmetrical designs in your quilt collection and in quilting reference books. Show one of the quilts to your youngsters. With masking tape divide the quilt in half. Then explain that whatever shape, fabric, or pattern the quilter put on one half, she also put in the same place on the other half. Encourage your students to look at other quilt examples and point out instances of symmetry.

Make symmetry even more concrete for your students by having partners create symmetrical designs with pattern blocks. Give each pair of students a nine-inch construction paper square divided in half. Direct each child to take a turn adding a block to his side and having his partner copy him and then vice versa until the square is completed.

## Let's Go Crazy!

Now that your students have a good grasp on how important pattern, shape, equivalence, and symmetry are to quilting, throw caution to the wind and get a little crazy…with crazy quilts! Popular in the late 1800s, these exceptions to the rules consisted of random colors of random fabrics cut in random shapes and placed randomly on the quilt. Show children a crazy quilt illustration. Then invite small groups to play this crazy quilt game. Give each child a nine-inch construction paper square. Put a large supply of pattern blocks in a bag. To play the game, each child takes a turn reaching into the bag, pulling out a shape, and arranging it on his square. Continue until all of the squares are covered. The winner is determined by the child's square that has the least amount of white space showing. Craaa-zy!

## Read More About Them

The following titles are good sources for a quick and concise look at the history of quilting. For more in-depth information, you may want to search the Internet. There are numerous sites on various topics related to quilts.

*Eight Hands Round: A Patchwork Alphabet*
Written by Ann Whitford Paul
Published by HarperCollins Publishers, Inc.

*The Quilt-Block History of Pioneer Days
    With Projects Kids Can Make*
Written by Mary Cobb
Published by The Millbrook Press, Inc.

*Quilting Now & Then*
Written by Karen Bates Willing
    & Julie Bates Dock
Published by Now & Then Publications

*With Needle and Thread: A Book About Quilts*
Written by Raymond Bial
Published by Houghton Mifflin Company

Order books online. www.themailbox.com

Name_____

# A Shapely Quilt

Color by the key.

△ = blue

□ = red

▭ = yellow

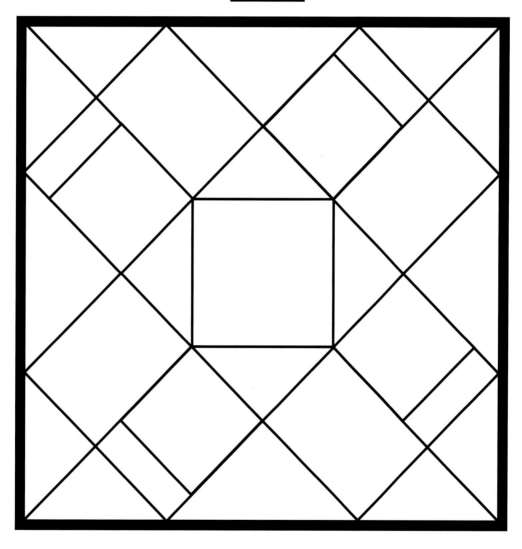

How many?

Count.

Write.

 △ _____     □ _____     ▭ _____

**Note to the teacher:** Use this page as a follow-up to "Shapely Quilts" on page 154.

# Winter Where You Are

Whether your winter is cold and snowy, wet and rainy, or warm and sunny, these cross-curricular ideas and activities will create the perfect learning climate in your classroom.

*ideas contributed by Lucia Kemp Henry*

## It's Winter!
## What's Our Weather Like?

Thunderstorms or snowstorms? How about brainstorms? This circle time activity has youngsters brainstorming words that describe winter in your neck of the woods. To begin, have your students close their eyes and imagine a typical winter day. Invite each child to share a descriptive weather word; then write his response on a sheet of chart paper. Review the completed chart with students before displaying it in your classroom. Refer to the chart again in "Sing a Weather Song" (below).

### Our winter is...

| | |
|---|---|
| rainy | gloomy |
| cloudy | chilly |
| cool | damp |
| wet | muddy |
| dark | stormy |

## Sing a Weather Song

Once students are familiar with your list of weather words (see "It's Winter! What's Our Weather Like?"), have them sing the song at the right, replacing the underlined words with words from the chart. If needed, replace the italicized phrase with another phrase that more accurately describes your winter weather—such as *raindrops pouring* or *sunlight shining*.

(sung to the tune of
*"If You're Happy and You Know It"*)

When it's winter in our town, it is [cold].
When it's winter in our town, it is [cold].
When it's winter in our town, we see
*snowflakes falling* down.
When it's winter in our town, it is [cold].

## Winter Wear for Winter Where?

Would you wear mittens during winter in San Diego? How about shorts on a typical Detroit winter day? Help your little ones sort out winter weather differences with this group flannelboard activity. In advance, obtain pictures of different types of climates, such as rainy, sunny, snowy, and mild. (Calendars are a good source.) Laminate the pictures and then glue a strip of felt to the back of each one. Next, duplicate the clothing patterns on pages 165 and 166. Color, cut out, and laminate the clothing; then glue a strip of felt to the back of each piece. Place the pictures and clothing on a flannelboard; then invite students to match the clothes with the appropriate climate. Discuss the differences in clothing for each climate; then have students determine which set is most like the clothing needed for winter weather in your area.

## Wonderful Winter Wear!

Now that your youngsters have warmed up to the idea of different winter climates, heat up their reading skills with these individual booklets. To prepare, duplicate for each child pages 162–164 and the clothing patterns most appropriate for winter in your area. (See pages 165 and 166. Do not use the hats.) Cut apart the booklet pages; then provide each child with a set of pages and a page of clothing patterns. Have the child follow the directions below to complete his booklet. When the glue is dry, stack the pages in order, and then staple them together along the left side.

**Cover:** Write your name where indicated; then embellish as desired with various craft items.
**Page 1:** Color the page; then glue sand to the bottom of the page.
**Page 2:** Draw raindrops on the page. Squeeze yellow glue on the raincoat and boots; then use your finger to spread the glue over the coat and boots. Cut an umbrella canopy from fabric (see sample) and glue it to the umbrella handle.
**Page 3:** Color the page; glue cotton ball pieces to the coat and the bottom of the page to resemble snow.
**Page 4:** Color and cut out the clothing patterns. Glue them onto the figure and then color the head to look like yourself.

sledding
building snowmen
throwing snowballs
ice skating

# Winter Weather Movements

Surfing, sledding, or splashing around in puddles? What do you like to do in winter? Get your youngsters in the mood for the season with this fun movement activity. Use the pictures from "Winter Wear for Winter Where?" on page 159 and review the different types of winter climates. Tape each picture to a large sheet of paper; then have students brainstorm different outdoor activities appropriate for each climate. Write their responses on the paper. After the brainstorming session, have students recall which picture is most like the winter climate in your area. Then have them act out the activities listed for that climate. As an extension, invite a child to perform an activity from another climate and have the class guess what he is doing. Wow! Winter weather sure is fun!

# The Local Report

Watching winter weather is wonderful! Use the following suggestions to help give your youngsters a wide variety of weather-watching experiences.

- Take a field trip to the weather center at your local television station. Or invite a local weather reporter to come and speak to your class.
- If you have access to cable television in your classroom, watch and discuss The Weather Channel® with your youngsters. If you do not have cable in your classroom, record a segment from The Weather Channel to view with your students.
- Have different students volunteer to watch the evening weather report and relay the report to the class the following day.

# Weather-Watching Center

The forecast for this dramatic-play area calls for fun, fun, fun! After all of the winter weather talk, your little ones will be eager to visit this weather-watching center and practice their forecasting skills. In preparation, duplicate the weather symbols on page 167. Color and laminate the symbols; then cut out each one. Attach a strip of magnetic tape to the back of each symbol.

Place a sign in your designated weather center along with the weather symbols and a large map attached to a magnetic surface. (If a magnetic surface is not available, use Sticky-Tac on the symbols and laminate the map.) Have each little meteorologist observe the weather outside, predict the weather for the next few days, and then place the corresponding weather symbols on the map. Invite her to then use a pointer to give the winter weather report. There's sure to be a downpour of learning at this center!

# All Sorts of Snowmen

Whether or not your winter days bring enough snow for a snowman, your youngsters can still create this classic winter symbol by using the suggested ideas below.

**Sand Table:** Encourage youngsters to make snowmen out of sand. Have them add features using various craft items, such as buttons for eyes and craft sticks for arms.

**Block Area:** Get those little minds thinking creatively! Invite students to build a snowman out of blocks!

**Manipulative Area:** Unifix® cubes are not just for counting! Have your little ones use these manipulatives to create a frosty fellow.

**Play Dough Center:** Stock this center with a variety of circular cookie cutters. Have youngsters use them to create a variety of snowmen with different numbers of segments. As an extension, challenge students to sequence the snowmen according to the number of segments.

# Warm Winter Reading

Whatever the weather, your youngsters will want to curl up with these wonderful wintry stories.

*Is That You, Winter?*
Written by Stephen Gammell
Published by Harcourt Brace & Company

*The First Snow*
Written by David Christiana
Published by Scholastic Inc.

*Six Snowy Sheep*
Written by Judith Ross Enderle and Stephanie Gordon Tessler
Published by Puffin Books

*When It Starts to Snow*
Written by Phillis Gershator
Published by Henry Holt and Company

*Wild Horse Winter*
Written by Tetsuya Honda
Published by Chronicle Books

# Booklet Cover and Page 1

Use with "Wonderful Winter Wear!" on page 159.

Wonderful Winter Wear!

by _____

If winter in my town was hot,

I would wear my shorts a lot.

1

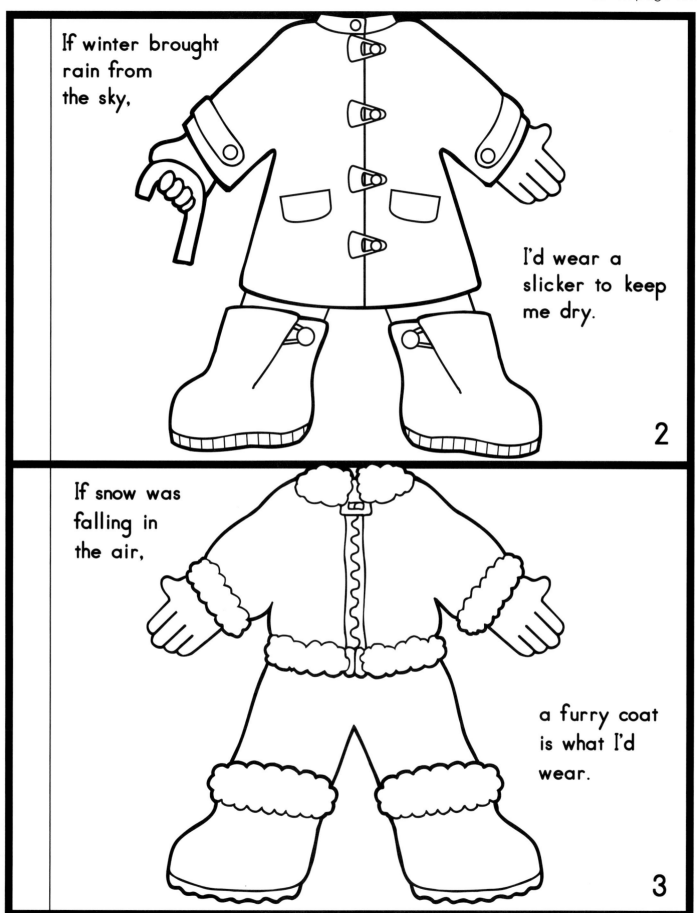

If winter brought rain from the sky,

I'd wear a slicker to keep me dry.

**2**

If snow was falling in the air,

a furry coat is what I'd wear.

**3**

# Booklet Page 4
Use with "Wonderful Winter Wear!" on page 159.

Winter there.
Winter here.

This is my own
winter gear.

# Clothing Patterns

Use with "Winter Wear for Winter Where?" and "Wonderful Winter Wear!" on page 159.

# Clothing Patterns

Use with "Winter Wear for Winter Where?" and "Wonderful Winter Wear!" on page 159.

**Earth Protector Label**
Use with "I'm an Earth Protector!" on page 169.

Earth Protector

# Earth Day 2000!

This April 22 marks the *30th anniversary* of Earth Day—a day set aside to especially preserve and honor our wild and wonderful earth! So use the ideas in this unit to get little hands, feet, and voices in on the Earth Day action. It's Earth Day today—hooray!

## What's It All About?

Earth Day was first observed on April 22, 1970, with the message "Give earth a chance." Special attention was given to restoring and keeping clean the earth's air, water, and living environment. Choose from among the literature recommended at the right to introduce and reinforce various earth-friendly ideas. *The Earth and I* is an especially joyful fiction selection that celebrates the connection between a young boy and the earth. That's what it's all about!

*ideas contributed by Susan DeRiso*

### Earth-Friendly Reading

*Bit by Bit*
By Steve Sanfield
(Philomel Books)

*The Earth and I*
By Frank Asch
(Harcourt Brace & Company)

*Hey! Get Off Our Train*
By John Burningham
(Crown Publishers, Inc.)

*Recycle! A Handbook for Kids*
By Gail Gibbons
(Little, Brown and Company)

*Where Does Pollution Come From?*
By C. Vance Cast
(Barron's Educational Series, Inc.)

*Someday a Tree*
By Eve Bunting
(Clarion Books)

Order books online. www.themailbox.com

## The Three *R*s

Here's a tidy little tune to reinforce some of the Earth Day basics. After discussing each of the concepts, teach this song to your children using the hand motions illustrated below. Repeat the song, singing it a little bit faster each time. Ready? Let's go!

### Reduce, Recycle, and Reuse
*(sung to the tune of "Head, Shoulders, Knees, and Toes")*

Reduce, recycle, and reuse—that's the way!
Reduce, recycle, and reuse—that's the way!
That's the way we'll make a brighter day.
Reduce, recycle, and reuse—that's the way!

## Why Recycle?

By now, most of your children have been exposed to the idea of recycling, but do they know *why* we do this? Try this experiment to see! In advance, be sure that you have several small plastic items, such as juice cups or disposable utensils. After a snack of fresh apples, divide children into groups of four or five. Select one child from each group to save his apple core. Then give each of the following supplies to a different person in the group: a large spoon or small shovel, two large craft sticks, a pencil, and a plastic item. Take your class outside to an area that has soft soil. Instruct each group to dig two holes and place the apple core in one, and the plastic item in the other. Then have a group member label each craft stick and insert them in the ground to mark the locations. Next have each group cover both holes with dirt. About 12–14 days later, have each group dig up its buried trash. What happened in each of the holes? Why do we need to *recycle* certain types of trash?

Cut on dotted line.

## I'm an Earth Protector!

Display the twinkling efforts of your little earth protectors with these creative crafts. In advance, enlarge the earth protector label (page 167) to 110% and then make a class supply on construction paper. Also, use a craft knife to cut a paper plate (as illustrated) for each child. Then instruct each child to paint the center of the *back* of her plate blue. When that paint is dry, have each child paint on green land masses. Then have her paint the rim of the plate black to resemble the night sky. When the paint is dry, instruct the child to write her name on her label, cut it out, and glue it to the rim of her plate. Staple each earth protector project to a bulletin board titled "I'm an Earth Protector!" To create a 3-D look, gently pull forward and slightly crease the top section of the earth. When a child demonstrates an earth-friendly practice, recognize her efforts with a stick-on star to place in the sky section of her project. Twinkle, twinkle, little earth protectors!

## Happy Earth Day to You!

Since April 22, 2000 is the *30th* anniversary of Earth Day, it's the *birthday* of *Earth Day!* Celebrate this day with a specially designed Earth Day cake! Bake a prepared devil's food cake mix in a large Pyrex® bowl at 350° for one hour. Let the cake cool for about 15 minutes; then turn it out onto a platter. When the cake is completely cooled, frost it to resemble the earth. Load it up with 30 candles and you're ready for a rousing round of "Happy Birthday, Dear Earth!" You know the rest!

Note: One cake makes about 20 servings.

## Adopt a Spot

Everybody needs a spot, and that's just what your class will have when you do this activity. In honor of Earth Day, guide your class in selecting an area of your schoolyard to adopt. Then, for the rest of the school year, think of (and carry out) ways to take care of that spot, such as picking up litter, planting plants, or hanging bird feeders. Ah, that's just the spot!

# "Pasta-bilities"

With the learning "pasta-bilities" in this unit, you'll be able to serve entrees of language, math, and problem solving guaranteed to satisfy students' cravings.

*ideas contributed by Lucia Kemp Henry*

### A Potful of Pasta

Begin your kindergarten dining experience with this appetizing guessing game. In advance, purchase one small package each of spaghetti, large elbow macaroni, wheel-shaped pasta, shell-shaped pasta, and bow-tie pasta. Place the uncooked pasta in a pot, mix well, and then replace the lid. During circle time challenge your little ones to guess the contents of the pot using clues you recite from the riddle to the right. Pause dramatically after you recite each line, giving students a chance to state their guesses.

### What Is It?

What do you think is in my pot?

It's something I can cook up nice and hot.

Sometimes it's shaped like a long, skinny string.

Sometimes it's shaped like a tube or a ring.

Sometimes it's shaped like a shell or a bow.

It's often topped with sauce. Now, do you know?

### Noodle Notes

When the mystery from "A Potful of Pasta" is solved, pass the pot of pasta around the circle. While students view the pasta, discuss the different shapes described in the riddle. Then sing the following song until your youngsters' hunger for pasta vocabulary has been satisfied!

### "Lotsa" Pasta
*(sung to the tune of "Yankee Doodle")*

Pasta's yummy and there are
So many kinds of pasta.
[This bow pasta] tastes so good.
Oh, let's eat "lotsa" pasta!

*Repeat the song four times, substituting* this wheel pasta, this shell pasta, this spaghetti, *and* macaroni *for the underlined phrase.*

## Pick a Piece of Pasta

Spice up listening and critical-thinking skills with this descriptive pasta game. Begin by filling two bowls with identical pasta pieces, such as a pasta wheel, a pasta bow tie, a lasagna noodle, and a piece of macaroni. Invite two children to sit back-to-back and hold the pasta bowls. To play, one child selects a pasta piece from her bowl and describes it to her partner. The other child looks in his bowl until he finds the piece described. Then the children switch roles and continue playing until all of the pasta pieces are used.

It's shaped like a curved tube.

One, two, three, four...

## Pour on the Pasta

What do you get when you fill your sensory table with plenty of pasta, add bowls and measuring cups, and sprinkle in some student participation? A recipe for measurement success! Begin by having a small group of students join you at the sensory table. Invite each child to explore the dry pasta by scooping it into bowls using different-sized measuring cups. Encourage him to use the largest cup and count how many cupfuls it takes to fill the bowl. Repeat this process with the other sizes until the child has used all of the measuring cups. Then discuss which cup filled the bowl the fastest. That's the scoop on measurement!

## Cooking Changes Pasta

Discover how cooking changes egg noodles, spaghetti, and macaroni when your pasta lovers dig into this science investigation! In advance, cook one batch of egg noodles, one batch of spaghetti, and one batch of macaroni according to the package directions. After each batch is cooked, rinse it well, add a tablespoon of cooking oil, stir, and store it in a resealable plastic bag. Refrigerate all three bags.

Begin the activity by giving each child one uncooked egg noodle, one uncooked spaghetti noodle, and one piece of uncooked macaroni. Direct them to touch, smell, and look at each piece. Write their descriptions on chart paper. Next give each child a sample of cooked pasta. Have students compare how the pasta changed in shape and texture. Write these conclusions on chart paper next to the previous list. Wow! Cooking really does change pasta!

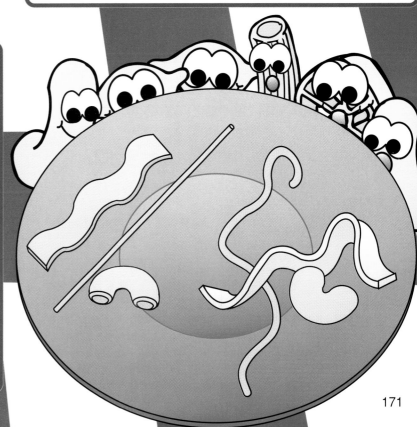

## Pasta Toppers

Put your youngsters' taste buds to the test with this saucy graphing activity! Ahead of time, cook enough elbow macaroni for three small servings per child. Next give each child three 9-ounce paper cups and have him write his name on the side of each one. Then heat a jar of red sauce, a jar of white sauce, and a jar of cheese sauce (yellow or orange in color) until warm. Help each child carefully drizzle a different sauce over each cup of pasta. Provide plastic forks and invite youngsters to sample their pasta combinations. Once everyone has tasted all three sauces, have each child select his favorite, set that cup aside, and throw the other two cups away. Cover a table with a red checkered cloth; then help your students graph their favorite sauces by arranging their chosen cups into three rows (according to sauce preference). Compare the graph to see which sauce is tops!

## A Savory Story

Your pasta lovers will satisfy their emerging appetites for reading by cooking up these personalized books. (You may want students to complete each page in a separate session, rather than all at one time.) To prepare, cut three 4-inch lengths of yellow yarn, two 2-inch lengths of yellow pipe cleaner, and three 1-inch lengths of drinking straw for each child. Provide red glitter glue, a shallow pan of red paint, and separate bowls containing uncooked spaghetti noodles (broken into fourths), elbow macaroni, pasta wheels, pasta shells, and bow-tie pasta. Each child also needs glue, a marker, crayons, a paintbrush, and a construction paper copy of the booklet on pages 173–176.

Have each child cut out her booklet's pages on the bold lines. Next invite her to color the pot rim and sides on every page, except the cover. Then have her complete her booklet as described. When the paint and glue are dry, stack all of the pages in order behind the cover and staple the pages along the left edge. Then invite your little ones to share their booklets with their families.

**Cover:** Trace the question mark with a marker. Color the pot to match the booklet pages.

**Page 1:** Trace the word *hot* with red glitter glue.

**Page 2:** Glue three pieces of yarn inside the pot.

**Page 3:** Glue three drinking straw shapes and two small pipe cleaner rings inside the pot.

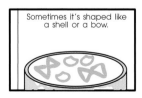

**Page 4:** Draw small shell shapes and bow shapes inside the pot.

**Page 5:** Brush red paint inside the pot.

**Page 6:** Glue pasta inside the pot. Write your name where indicated.

# What Do You Think Is in the Pot?

## It's something to cook up nice and

sss

hot.

1

Sometimes it's shaped like
a skinny string.

2

Sometimes it's shaped like
a tube or a ring.

3

# Sometimes it's shaped like a shell or a bow.

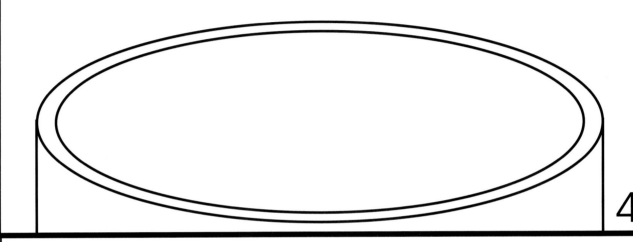

4

# It's often topped with sauce. Now, do you know?

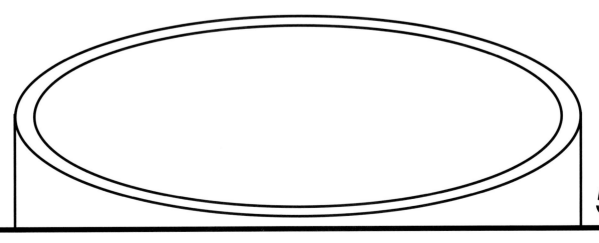

5

# It's pasta!

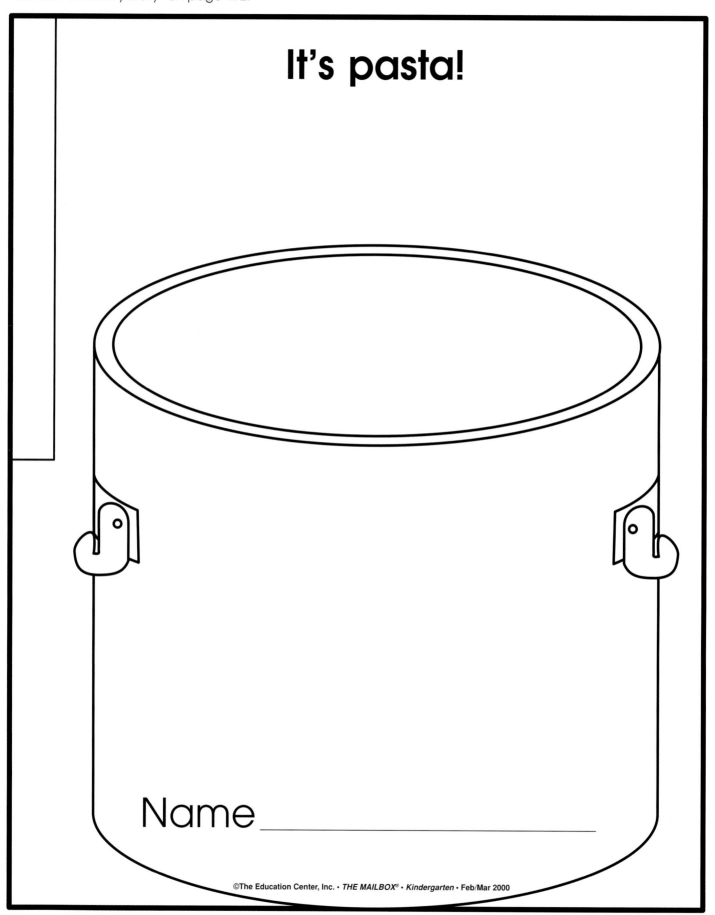

Name _____

# Blustery Day Play!

Windy conditions are headed your way! So breeze into these activities that add a whirl to your classroom curriculum!

## Windy Day Storytime

Set learning into motion with one of these stories. Invite students' participation by having them take a deep breath and give their best windy day blast as you turn each page.

Karen Attanasio
Black Mountain Memorial Library
Dallas, PA

*Catch the Wind!*
Written and Illustrated by Gail Gibbons
Little, Brown and Company

*The Wind Blew*
Written and Illustrated by Pat Hutchins
Aladdin Paperbacks

*Wind*
Written by Ron Bacon
Scholastic Inc.

*Who Took the Farmer's Hat?*
Written by Joan L. Nodset
Illustrated by Fritz Siebel
HarperTrophy

## Little Wind

Get children swishing and swaying with this movement activity. Softly whisper the first verse and have little ones pretend they're a gentle breeze. Then shout the second verse while students pick up speed. Whew! What a whirl!

Little wind, little wind,
Blowing through the trees.
Little wind, little wind,
I feel the gentle breeze.

Big wind, big wind,
Flying kites so high.
Big wind, big wind,
Gusting through the sky.

Brenda Hume—Gr. K, Sangaree Elementary School, Summerville, SC

## Huffing and Puffing!

Children think it's magic when you teach them about the power of wind with light and heavy objects! Each child needs a flexible drinking straw. Each pair of students needs a one-inch Styrofoam® ball, a small feather (three inches or less), a Ping-Pong® ball, a facial tissue, and a half-inch wooden bead.

Begin by dividing students into pairs. Have each child bend her straw, as shown. Next have her put the long end of the straw in her mouth, making sure the bent end faces upward. Then have her hold the Styrofoam ball on the bent straw tip. Direct her to blow through the straw and let go of the ball as she observes how high the ball rises in midair. (Continuous air powers the ball.) Have children repeat this activity using a wooden bead. Then discuss which item is easier to blow. Encourage children to continue until they have tried a Ping-Pong ball, a facial tissue, and a feather. Abracadabra!

Seema Gersten—Gr. K, Harkham Hillel Hebrew Academy, Beverly Hills, CA

## Bubble Solution

Mix:

12 cups water
4 cups Dawn® dishwashing soap
4 Tablespoons sugar

Makes one gallon.

## Windy Playmates

Breathe new life into your science center by heading outdoors with toys that move in the wind. Prepare by putting flags, windsocks, paper airplanes, pinwheels, and wind chimes in a windy, grassy area. Next fill a wading pool with water and add toy sailboats. Finally, fill a bucket with bubble solution and wands. Now invite youngsters to see that wind moves in a certain direction. Here's wishing every day is a windy day!

adapted from an idea by Laura Bentley—Gr. K
Captain John Palliser Elementary School
Calgary, Alberta, Canada

## Breezy Music

Youngsters can enjoy the soothing sounds of wind chimes with this craft. In advance, collect a class supply of clean 16-ounce plastic water bottles (water bottles are more flexible than soda bottles). Use scissors to remove the top and bottom of each bottle; then cut the remaining piece into a spiral shape. Each child also needs eight 1/2-inch craft bells, eight 3-inch pipe cleaner pieces, and one 9-inch pipe cleaner piece.

Help each student complete his wind chime by using a hole puncher to put one hole at the top of the spiral and eight more at varying distances. Next have the child thread the nine-inch piece of pipe cleaner through the top hole and then twist the ends to form a hanger. Direct him to thread each bell onto a different three-inch pipe cleaner piece. Then have him insert each pipe cleaner piece through a hole on the spiral and twist the pipe cleaner's ends to secure it. Hang your youngsters' chimes near a window or outdoors. Shh…Can you hear the music?

Pam Crane

## The Wind Flies Over the Ocean
(sung to the tune of "My Bonnie Lies Over the Ocean")

Improve your little ones' listening skills by having them alternate between standing and sitting every time the word *wind* is sung. Begin by singing the song slowly. Then repeat the song, singing faster.

The wind flies over the ocean.
The wind flies over the sea.
The wind flies over the ocean.
Oh, bring back the wind to me.

Bring back, bring back,
Oh, bring back the wind to me, to me.
Bring back, bring back,
Oh, bring back the wind to me.

## High Fliers

Making an airplane is as easy as 1, 2, 3! Copy page 181 for each little pilot in your class. Have the child write his name on the same side as the printed numbers. Next help him crease his paper along the 1s, as shown. Have the child continue creasing along the 2s and the 3s. Invite him to decorate his plane with stickers. Now your aviators are ready for flight!

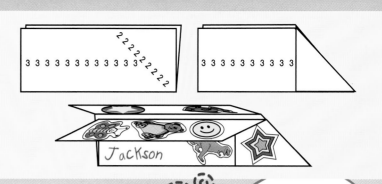

## Soaring With the Wind

How far can planes soar? Have your fliers find out in this math activity. Take the paper airplanes made in "High Fliers," a supply of nonstandard measuring tools such as blocks or drinking straws, and some pencils outdoors. Have a small group of students fly their aircrafts from a designated starting point. Once their planes land, have each child measure his flight distance by placing blocks from the starting point to his plane's landing spot. After he counts the blocks to determine the distance, have him write that number on his plane. Repeat this flying activity until every child has piloted his aircraft.

Suzanne Maio—Gr. K
Myers Elementary School
Elkins Park, PA

## Traffic on the Runway!

Now it's time to put away the landing gear, gather the planes, and graph landing points using this airplane display. Title your bulletin board "Traffic on the Runway!" Staple yarn to the bulletin board, forming a graph similar to the one shown. Make sure the graph's programming corresponds with the range of measurements your pilots used to mark their flight distances during "Soaring With the Wind" on this page.

Start the activity by calling out a number along the bottom of the display. Have each student look at the number he wrote on his plane. If it is the same number, have him tack his aircraft vertically above the number, as shown. Continue until every child's plane is showcased. How far did your plane fly? Check the graph and see!

Suzanne Maio—Gr. K

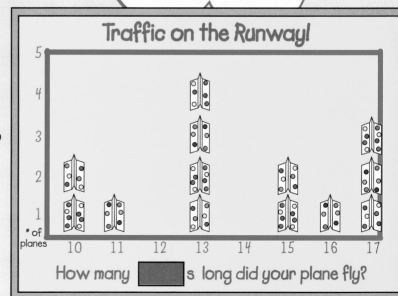

## Roaring Wind Catchers

On a windy day, these lions will roar with the wind while they also sharpen your students' critical-thinking skills! To make one, each child will need a brown paper lunch bag, five 10-inch brown streamers, five 10-inch yellow streamers, one 8-inch yellow streamer, two 12-inch lengths of yarn, scissors, glue, and a brown construction paper copy of the pattern on page 182. Help each child complete her project using the following directions:

1. Cut out the lion's face, ears, and tail along the bold lines.
2. Fold the bag twice to form a cuff.
3. Make a lion's mane by folding the ten-inch streamers in half and then gluing them, in alternating colors, between the bag and the cuff around all four sides as shown.
4. Fold the lion's face and ears along the tabbed edges. Glue the ears to the outside of the bag, and then glue the face's tab under the bag's cuff, as shown.
5. Glue the eight-inch yellow streamer to the bottom of the bag.
6. Glue the tail piece to the end of this streamer.
7. Punch a hole in the middle of each short side of the bag's open end. Tie a 12-inch yarn piece through each hole; then tie the two ends together.

Now your little ones are ready to go outdoors and catch the wind! Once everyone has flown her wind catcher, ask students questions similar to the ones listed here.

1. What happens to our wind catchers when we stand still?
2. What happens to our wind catchers when we run or twirl?
3. From what direction is the wind blowing?
4. How does the wind feel?

adapted from an idea by Alison G. Hovda—Gr. K
St. Patrick's School, Fayetteville, NC

## Wispy Windscapes

Are you looking for a simpler way for your little ones to communicate through the fine arts? Have them paint pictures inspired by nature music containing wind sounds. Gather a class supply of large feathers. Next mount lengths of white bulletin board paper to vertical surfaces at a child's eye level. Then prepare several pans each of blue and gray tempera paint.

While the windy music plays, encourage children to paint in sweeping movements using the feathers. Direct them to vary movements according to the music's speed. Once students finish, have them compare their paintings. Discuss how the paint strokes are thick where they painted fast, and thin where they painted slowly. What priceless masterpieces!

adapted from an idea by Jennifer Strathdee
Palmer Elementary, Baldwinsville, NY

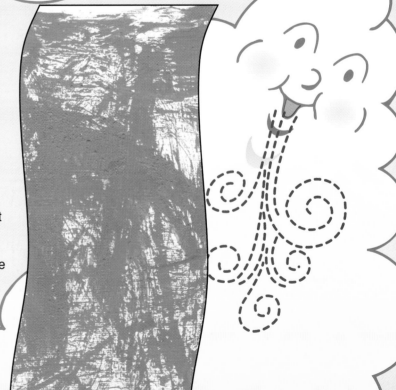

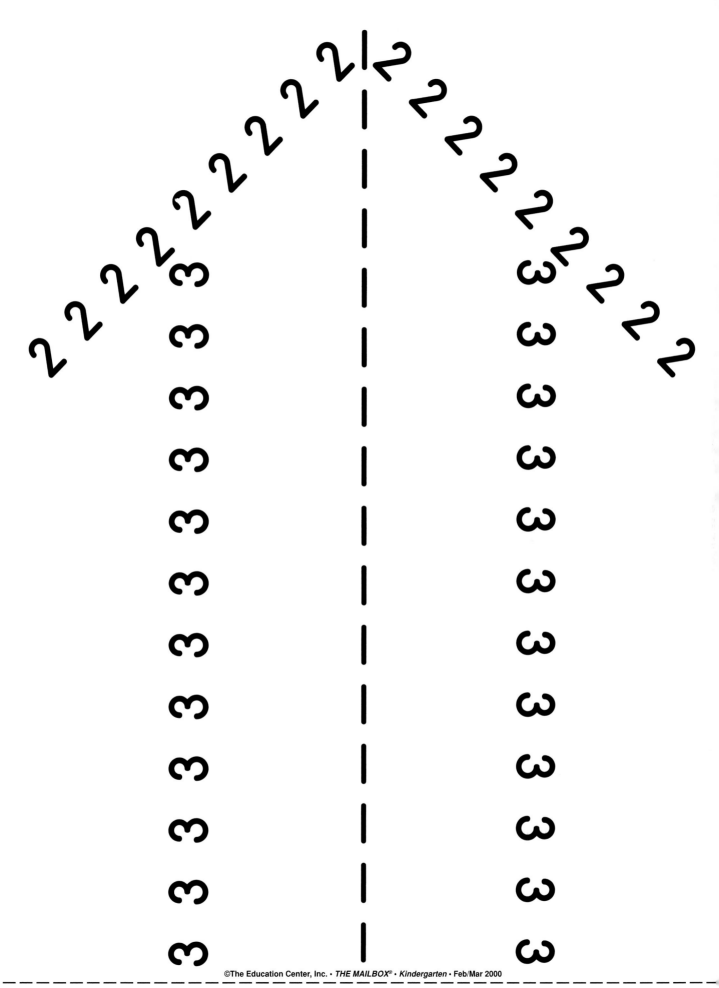

**Note to the teacher:** Use this page with "High Fliers" on page 179.

# Lion Patterns

Use with "Roaring Wind Catchers" on page 180.

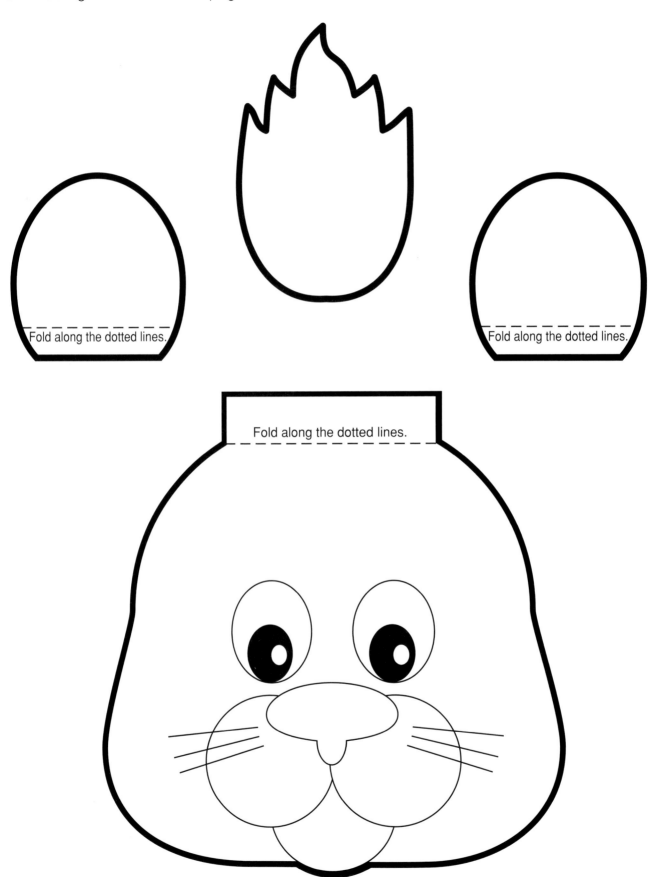

Fold along the dotted lines.

Fold along the dotted lines.

Fold along the dotted lines.

# From Hives to Honey

Buzz, buzz, buzz! Spring is in the air and so are the bees! Get your whole hive humming with these cross-curricular ideas and activities that are as sweet as honey!

*ideas contributed by kindergarten teachers*

## 5 Senses Study

Seeing 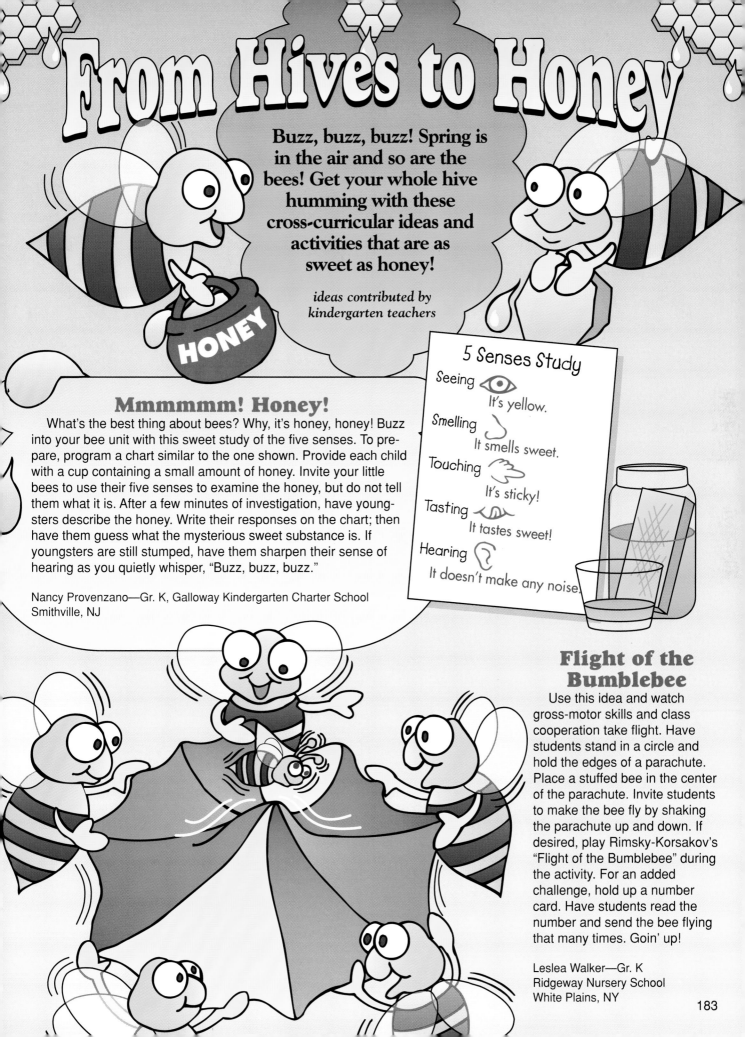 It's yellow.

Smelling — It smells sweet.

Touching — It's sticky!

Tasting — It tastes sweet!

Hearing — It doesn't make any noise.

## Mmmmmm! Honey!

What's the best thing about bees? Why, it's honey, honey! Buzz into your bee unit with this sweet study of the five senses. To prepare, program a chart similar to the one shown. Provide each child with a cup containing a small amount of honey. Invite your little bees to use their five senses to examine the honey, but do not tell them what it is. After a few minutes of investigation, have youngsters describe the honey. Write their responses on the chart; then have them guess what the mysterious sweet substance is. If youngsters are still stumped, have them sharpen their sense of hearing as you quietly whisper, "Buzz, buzz, buzz."

Nancy Provenzano—Gr. K, Galloway Kindergarten Charter School
Smithville, NJ

## Flight of the Bumblebee

Use this idea and watch gross-motor skills and class cooperation take flight. Have students stand in a circle and hold the edges of a parachute. Place a stuffed bee in the center of the parachute. Invite students to make the bee fly by shaking the parachute up and down. If desired, play Rimsky-Korsakov's "Flight of the Bumblebee" during the activity. For an added challenge, hold up a number card. Have students read the number and send the bee flying that many times. Goin' up!

Leslea Walker—Gr. K
Ridgeway Nursery School
White Plains, NY

# What's All the Buzz About?

Timmy — I went to the zoo with my dad.

Sadie — I learned all my ABC's.

Jamal — I have a new baby brother.

**Mrs. Tessier's Hive**

Angie — I can spell cat. C - A - T!

Stephen — I lost a tooth.

## What's All the Buzz About?

Place this display in a hallway and the entire school will soon be buzzing by. To prepare, mask the facial features on the large bee pattern (page 188); then make a class supply of bees. Have each child personalize, color, and cut out his bee. Then help him cut out a small circle in the bee's face as shown. Glue a photograph of the child behind the circle so that his face shows through the opening. Cut a large beehive from bulletin board paper. Then mount the bees and hive on a wall or bulletin board.

Explain the meaning of the saying, "What's all the buzz about?" Then have each student dictate (or write) something new and exciting that is happening at home or at school. Mount his response beside his bee. If desired, frequently change the students' captions on the display as needed. What's all the buzz about? This unique display!

adapted from ideas by: Judi Lesnansky—Title I K–4, New Hope Academy, Youngstown, OH
Robin Jolley—Gr. K, Janie Howard Wilson Elementary, Lake Wales, FL

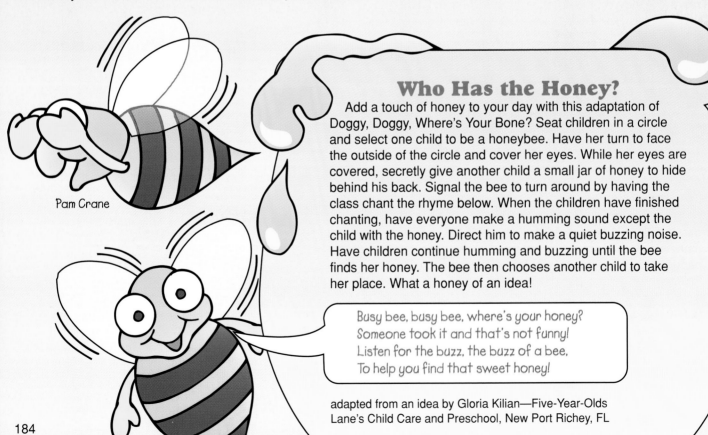

Pam Crane

## Who Has the Honey?

Add a touch of honey to your day with this adaptation of Doggy, Doggy, Where's Your Bone? Seat children in a circle and select one child to be a honeybee. Have her turn to face the outside of the circle and cover her eyes. While her eyes are covered, secretly give another child a small jar of honey to hide behind his back. Signal the bee to turn around by having the class chant the rhyme below. When the children have finished chanting, have everyone make a humming sound except the child with the honey. Direct him to make a quiet buzzing noise. Have children continue humming and buzzing until the bee finds her honey. The bee then chooses another child to take her place. What a honey of an idea!

Busy bee, busy bee, where's your honey?
Someone took it and that's not funny!
Listen for the buzz, the buzz of a bee,
To help you find that sweet honey!

adapted from an idea by Gloria Kilian—Five-Year-Olds
Lane's Child Care and Preschool, New Port Richey, FL

## A⁺ Behavior

This positive management idea will bring out the best in your little bees. To prepare, mask the stripes on the large bee pattern (page 188); then duplicate a bee for each child. Label the wing of each bee with a different child's name. Cut out and laminate the bees. Then mount them on a wall or bulletin board. If desired, decorate an inexpensive clay pot or plastic container to resemble a honey pot. Then fill the pot with treats.

Review with your class examples of positive "bee-havior," such as walking quietly in the hallway or helping one another. When a little one demonstrates good behavior, use a dry-erase marker to draw a stripe on his bee. When a child has earned a predetermined number of stripes, offer him a treat from your honey pot. Use a tissue to wipe the stripes from his bee and "bee-gin" again!

Jan Freshwater—Gr. K, Lake Norman Elementary
Mooresville, NC

# A⁺ "Bee-havior"!

Tim  Angel  Aziz  Tony  Karla  Deanne  Stephen  Cara  Mika  Keesha

## P Is for Pollinate!

This small-group activity will have youngsters buzzing over letter recognition and sound association. To prepare, duplicate the hive pattern on page 190. Color, cut out, and laminate the hive. Then tape it to a plastic bowl. Next make several construction paper copies of the flower pattern on page 188. Tape each flower to the floor near the hive. Then place a piece of Alpha-Bits® cereal on each flower.

Explain to a small group of children that bees collect pollen from flowers and bring it back to the hive to eat. Invite each child, in turn, to act like a bee and then "fly" to a flower. Have her pick up the pollen (cereal), identify the letter, and then bring it back to the hive. If student ability allows, have the child make the letter sound as she flies back to the hive. When all of the pollen has been collected and placed in the hive, reward each of your bees with a handful of fresh Alpha-Bits cereal. Mmmm, this pollen sure is tasty!

Judi Lesnansky—Title I K–4, New Hope Academy, Youngstown, OH

## Pick a Peck of Pollen

If youngsters enjoyed the activity in "P Is for Polli-nate!" try this variation in your math center. To prepare, make a supply of construction paper flowers from the pattern on page 188. (Or use the flowers from "P Is for Pollinate!") If desired, laminate each flower for durability. Place the flowers on a table and then place pollen (bingo chips) in the center of each flower.

To play the game, the first player rolls a die, reads the number, and then collects that many pieces of pollen from the flowers. The game continues in this manner until all of the pollen has been collected. My, what hard-working bees!

Roberta M. Neff, Espy Elementary, Kenton, OH

Ticktock! Ticktock! Reinforce time-telling skills with this center that takes only minutes to prepare. Program a large behive cutout with 12 clocks showing times to the hour. Next use the patterns on page 189 to make 12 bees. Color, laminate, and cut out the bees. Then use a permanent marker to program each one with a time represented on the beehive. Place the bees and hive at a center. Then invite each youngster to buzz over and match each bee with its corresponding clock. It's time to tell time!

Paula Idroli—Gr. K, Katherine D. Malone School
Rockaway, NJ

## Peanut Butter Bees

This nutty snack is sure to make a beeline to little tummies! In advance, prepare a batch of peanut butter play dough. (See recipe below.) Provide each child with a waxed paper square and a tablespoon of dough. Have her roll the dough into an oval shape to make a bee's body. Then have her insert an almond sliver wing into each side as shown. Next direct the child to use black decorating gel to draw stripes on her bee. Finally, have her add two chow mein noodles for antennae. Encourage the child to buzz like a bee before she eats her snack. "Bee-licious!"

Jill Beattie—Four- and Five-Year-Olds
The Apple Place Nursery School
Chambersburg, PA

### Peanut Butter Play Dough
(makes 10 servings)

**Ingredients:**
4 tablespoons peanut butter
4 tablespoons honey
1 cup powdered milk

Mix the peanut butter and honey in a bowl. Gradually add the powdered milk and knead until the dough is no longer sticky.

## Honeybee Lotto

Reinforce letter recognition with this lively lotto game. To prepare, make a class supply of the hive pattern on page 190. Program each hive with a different set of letters. As you call out letters, have youngsters use pieces of Honeycomb® cereal to cover the corresponding letters on their cards. The first child to cover his card wins. For an added challenge, make the letter's sound instead of giving the letter's name. Then have children find and mark the appropriate letter on their cards. What fun!

Jill Beattie, Chambersburg, PA

## "Marble-ous" Bees!

Grab a pan and get your marbles! It's time to make some bees! To make one bee, cut yellow construction paper into the shape of a bee's body. Place the bee shape in a small pan. Next dip a few marbles in black paint and then drop them into the pan. Gently tilt the pan to roll the marbles over the bee, covering it with black stripes. Remove the marbles and set the bee aside to dry. Cut a coffee filter into four sections as shown. Then glue one of the sections onto the bee for a wing. Bend a black pipe cleaner and tape it to the back of the bee's head as shown. Finally, add a black pom-pom nose and a wiggle eye. Bzzz! Bzzz! Bzzz!

Inez Hughes—Gr. K, FL Moffett, Center, TX

## Give Me a B!

Youngsters will swarm to this center that focuses on the letter *B*. To prepare, make an enlarged copy of the hive on page 190 on tan tagboard. Program the hive as shown. Then laminate it and cut it out. Next have youngsters search through magazines and cut out small pictures of objects that begin with the letter *B*. Then have them cut out a variety of other pictures. Set the pictures aside. Next make a supply of construction paper bees from the patterns on page 189. Cut out each bee and glue a magazine picture to its wing. Color and laminate the bees. Then place them in a center along with the hive.

Invite each student to find the bees with *b* pictures and then place them on the "*B*-hive." If desired, make additional hives for each letter represented in the pictures—such as an "*A*-hive" or a "*C*-hive." Then have the student place each bee on its corresponding hive. Ahhh! Hive, sweet hive!

Jennifer Barton—Gr. K, Elizabeth Green School, Newington, CT

## A "Bee-dazzling" Display!

This crafty display is the bee's knees! In advance, collect a supply of toilet paper tubes and paper towel tubes. Cut each tube into inch-long pieces. Glue the tubes' sides together to form a hive. Cover a bulletin board with yellow paper; then use pushpins to mount the hive on the board as shown. Next provide each child with three segments of an egg carton. Have her paint the cups yellow and black to resemble a bee. When the paint is dry, help her poke pipe cleaners through the cups for legs and antennae. Then have the child glue a pair of waxed paper wings to the bee. Finally, mount the bees around the hive.

Becky Barker—Gr. K
Discovery Days, First Baptist Church
Allen, TX

## Large Bee Pattern

Use with "What's All the Buzz About?"
on page 184 and
"A+ Behavior" on page 185.

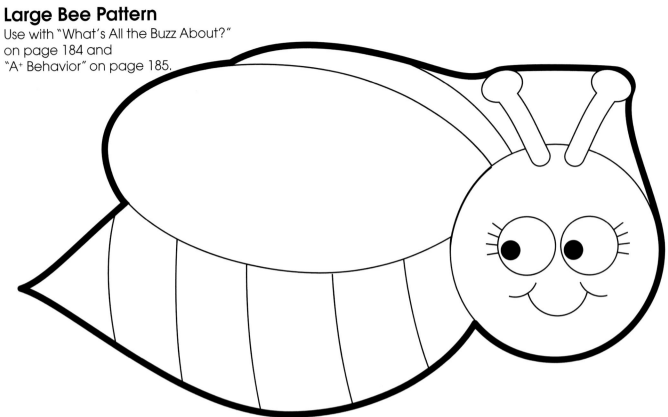

## Flower Pattern

Use with "*P* is for Pollinate!" and "Pick a
Peck of Pollen" on page 185.

# Hive Pattern

Use with *"P* Is for Pollinate!*"* on page 185; *"Honeybee Lotto"* on page 186; and *"Give Me a B!"* on page 187.

# It's a Spring Fling!

Your youngsters will leap into learning with this springtime rhyming unit!

*ideas contributed by Suzanne Moore*

| | |
|---|---|
| bow | pain |
| row | rain |
| grow | chain |
| sow | brain |
| | |
| stones | long |
| bones | song |
| | |
| hand | free |
| land | tree |
| sand | bee |

## Growing Rhymes

Inch by inch, row by row, time to make some rhyming words grow! Share the book *Inch by Inch: The Garden Song* by David Mallett (HarperCollins Publishers, Inc.) with your youngsters. After discussing the book, read it again—this time leaving out some of the rhyming words. Encourage students to supply the missing words. After the reading, print several of the rhyming words from the story on chart paper using different-colored markers to highlight the rhymes, as shown. Challenge each student to name other rhyming words that correspond with the rhyming words listed or that are new. List his responses on the chart. Then display the chart and invite your youngsters to add new words as they complete the activities that follow.

## A Basketful of Rhymes

Young minds will bloom in this rhyming center. In advance, gather pairs of small toys or other miniature objects that rhyme in a springtime basket. (See the list at the right for suggestions.) Next, make a paper flower for each pair of objects, or use sheets from a flower-shaped notepad. Laminate the flowers for durability. Then place the flowers and the basket of objects at a center. To complete the activity, a child spreads out the flowers, finds the rhyming pairs of objects, and places each pair on a separate flower. A-tisket, a-tasket, a springtime rhyming basket!

string—ring
shell—bell
block—rock
car—star
stick—chick
bear—square
bee—tree
yarn—barn

## What a Funny Bunny!

Use this bunny's guessing game to entice students to hop right into rhyming fun. To create Funny Bunny, cut out construction paper facial features and glue them to the lid of a small shoebox. (If desired, use really large wiggle eyes for a wackier effect.) Then cut out construction paper ears and glue them to one end of the shoebox, as shown. Prepare the game by placing an object from "A Basketful of Rhymes" in the box. Then gather your little ones around and invite them to guess the item by saying the chant below. Repeat the game by hiding other objects in the box and substituting both real and nonsense rhyming words for the underlined words. This game guarantees grins and giggles!

Funny Bunny, what do you hide?                                    *Gently shake box.*
Gee, we wonder what's inside!
It rhymes with [sock] and [clock] and [tock].
Maybe it could be a…
Let's see what's in this Funny Bunny.                            *Pause to get students' responses.*
Did someone say [block]? You're right on the money!              *Open box and show the item.*

191

## Bears Everywhere!

These bear cubs are coming out of hibernation just in time to make a rhyme! Gather the supplies needed (see below) for each child. Then assist him in following the instructions to make a mobile. Hang all the mobiles from your classroom ceiling or encourage each youngster to take his mobile home to rhyme with his family. It's "paws-itively" perfect!

**Materials needed for each student:**
— one 9" paper plate
— 3 index cards
— 4 pieces of brown yarn (different lengths)
— 1 copy of page 194
— crayons
— scissors
— glue
— 1 brown pom-pom
— hole puncher

**Instructions:**
1. Color both sides of the paper plate brown.
2. Color and cut out the head and paw patterns.
3. Glue the head and paws to the back of the plate, as shown.
4. Glue on the pom-pom nose.
5. Punch three holes in the plate underneath the edges of the paws.
6. Punch one hole at the top of the plate.
7. Punch one hole at the top of each index card (held vertically).
8. Choose three rhyming words. Illustrate and label each word on a different index card.
9. Tie each index card to a separate hole in the plate using a different length of yarn.
10. Loop the remaining length of yarn through the hole at the top of the plate and then knot it to make a hanger.

## Chick Picks

Now that your little ones have had some experience with rhyming words, play this small-group game to assess students' learning. Choose one student to be the chick. (If desired, glue some yellow craft feathers to a yellow tagboard headband for the chick to wear.) Have her pick a word and say, "Chick picks [star]." Then have each child in the group name a word that rhymes with the chick's chosen word. (Nonsense words are okay, too!). Select another child to be the chick and play again. Continue until each child has had a turn to peep!

## Snap, Clap, and Slap

To clap or to slap, that's the question here! Teach your little ones the chant below. Have them pause to listen to you say the third line. Fill in the line with spring-related words. Then have students answer your question by clapping if the words rhyme or slapping their legs if the words do not rhyme. As your students get the hang of it, encourage volunteers to call out the third line. Spring fever is sure to elevate with this activity!

Slap, slap, and clap, clap, clap!    *Slap legs and clap hands.*
Rhyming words are a snap!    *Snap when you say "snap."*
[Grass], [grass], [grass], does
   [class] rhyme with [grass]?

## The Name Game

Baby animals abound in spring, so why not use their names to reinforce rhyming? To prepare, make a set of five cards, with each card showing an illustration of a different baby farm animal. Begin this activity by reading aloud Sue Nicholson's *A Day at Greenhill Farm* (DK Publishing, Inc.). After the story, see how many baby animals students can recall. Then give each of the picture cards to a different student. Arrange the five students side by side against a wall. Have them hold their cards so that the rest of the class can see the animals. Then invite a volunteer from the remaining students to call out a word (real or nonsense) that rhymes with one of the five animals' names. Instruct the child holding the picture of the rhyming animal to take a step forward and make his animal's sound. Continue in this manner until one of the animals reaches a predetermined distance. Then have youngsters switch roles and play another "moo-ving" round.

## Spring Brings Colorful Things

Cultivate youngsters' rhyming skills with this creative flip booklet. In advance, make a copy of pages 195 and 196 for each child. Then gather a variety of objects that students can make prints with, such as film canisters, cut vegetables, star-shaped beads, Q-tips®, and pom-poms. Provide crayons, shallow pans of paint (including red and blue), green markers, scissors, and access to a stapler.

To make a booklet, each child colors the booklet's cover and writes her name where indicated. Then, on each page, she makes flower prints that correspond to the text. When the paint is dry, the child uses a marker to add leaves and stems. Finally she cuts the booklet pages out, stacks them sequentially behind the cover so that the top edges are even, and staples them together at the top. Practice reading the booklets as a group before sending each child home to share her booklet with her family.

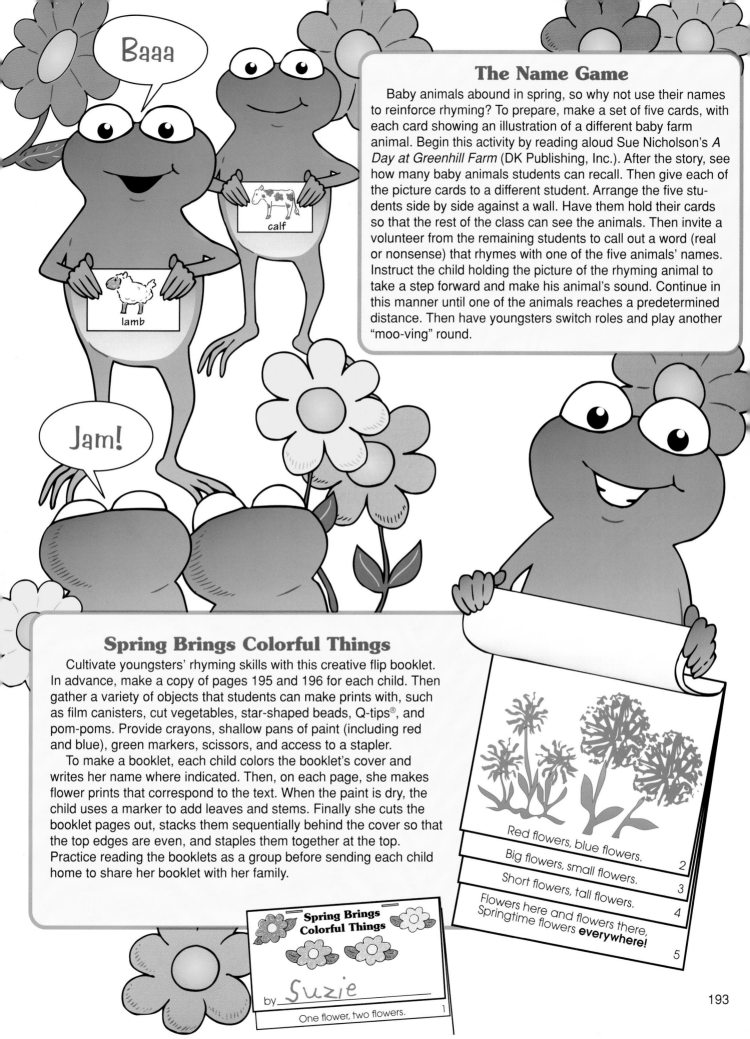

## Bear Patterns

Use with "Bears Everywhere!" on page 192.

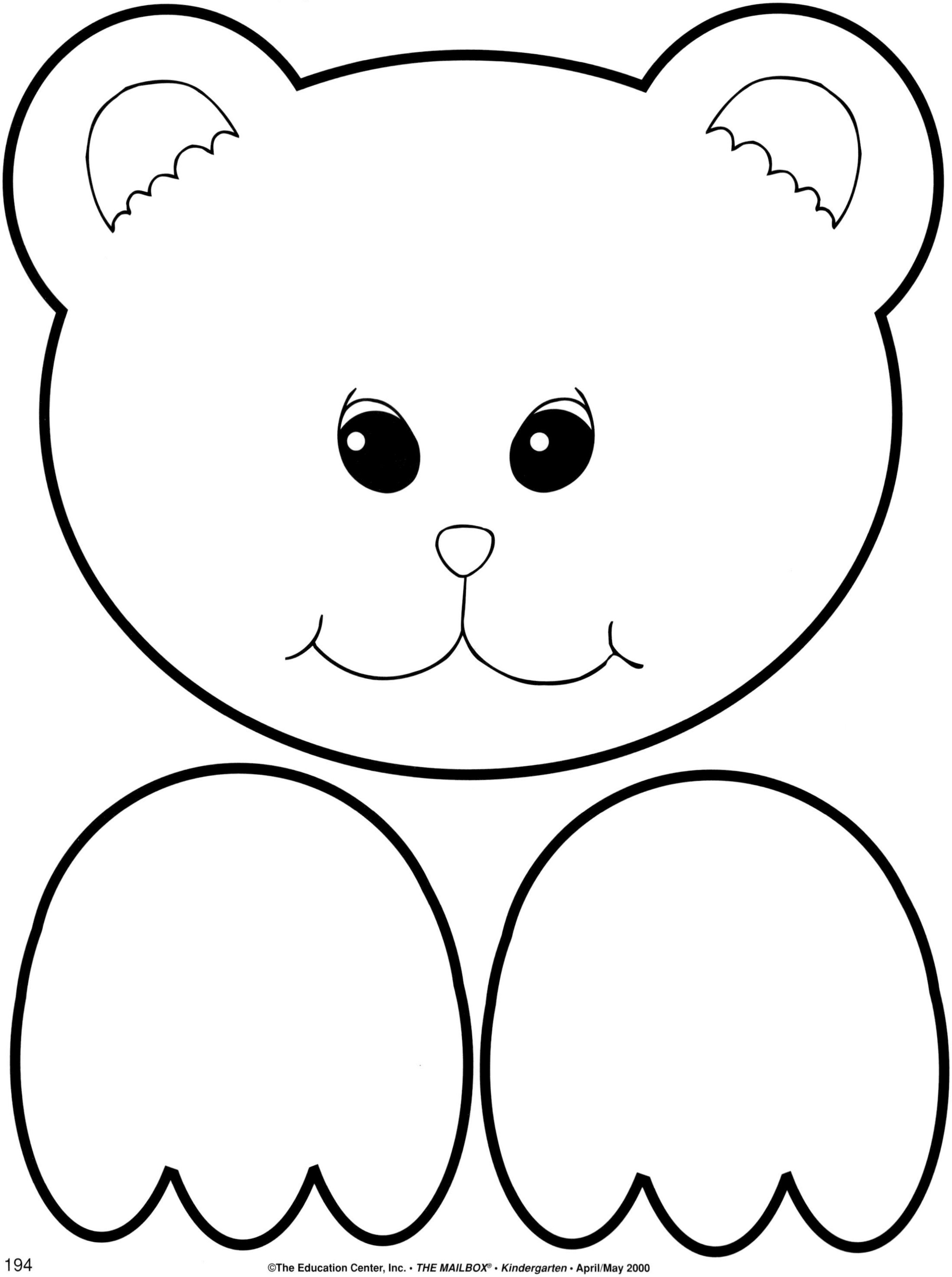

2

Red flowers, blue flowers.

1

One flower, two flowers.

3

Big flowers, small flowers.

**Spring Brings Colorful Things!**

by _____

©The Education Center, Inc. • *THE MAILBOX*® • *Kindergarten* • April/May 2000

195

# Booklet Pages 4 and 5

Use with "Spring Brings Colorful Things" on page 193.

5

Flowers here and flowers there,
Springtime flowers **everywhere!**

4

Short flowers, tall flowers.

# It's Gotta Be a Gator!

What has a tail that's long and rough? What has a body that's big and tough? Why, it's gotta be a gator! With this collection of ideas, facts, and activities, teaching youngsters all about alligators is a *snap!*

*ideas contributed by Lucia Kemp Henry*

## Gator Guessing Game

Introduce alligators to your students with this flannelboard activity that really gets them guessing! To prepare, make tagboard tracers from the tail and body patterns on page 203 and the head and leg patterns on page 204. Trim the glue strips off the tail and body pieces. Then trace the alligator parts onto heavy interfacing (available at your local fabric store). Cut out the interfacing pieces and lay each piece over coarse sandpaper. Next, use a green crayon to rub over the interfacing to create a texture that resembles alligator skin. Use a black crayon to draw a mouth and nostril. Then glue a large wiggle eye to the alligator's head.

To begin the activity, recite the poem below as you place each corresponding alligator part on the flannelboard. Pause after each line and allow students time to *silently* guess the name of the animal. Then, at the end of the poem, prompt students to say "Alligator!" When your little ones are familiar with this activity, place the alligator pieces and flannelboard in a center for youngsters to use independently.

What has a tail that's long and rough?
What has a body that's big and tough?
What has a head with a wide, flat snout,
And short, little legs for crawling about?
It's an—*alligator!*

## Great Gator Facts

- The American alligator is the largest reptile in North America.
- Alligators are *semiaquatic.* They spend time on land and in water.
- Alligators hunt and eat other animals, such as turtles, birds, and fish.
- Alligators have wide, blunt snouts. Crocodiles have long, narrow snouts.
- Young alligators are black with bright yellow spots and stripes. Adult alligators can be green, blue-gray, or black.
- Female alligators can lay as many as 60 eggs.
- Baby alligators are only about ten inches long when they hatch, but grow to be an average of 12 feet long as adults.

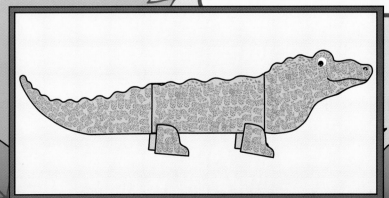

197

# Irresistible Alligator Puppets

Help your little ones learn the parts of an alligator with these perky puppets. Copy the alligator patterns on pages 203 and 204 onto construction paper for each child. Have her color and cut out each pattern piece. Next, have her glue the tail, body, and head together as indicated. Help the child use brads to attach the legs to the body and the jaw to the head. Have her glue a wiggle eye to the head and then staple the eyelid piece above it as shown. To complete the gator puppet, have the child glue a large craft stick to the body just behind the front legs. When the puppets are finished, have your little ones use them with the snappy song below.

## Get Those Gators Moving!

Your youngsters will grin like gators with this alligator song and activity. Have each child use his puppet from "Irresistible Alligator Puppets" to perform the alligator actions in the song below.

*(sung to the tune of "The Wheels on the Bus")*

The alligator's [tail] go(es) [swish, swish, swish];
[Swish, swish, swish; swish, swish, swish].
The alligator's [tail] go(es) [swish, swish, swish]
Down in the swamp!

Repeat the verse, substituting the underlined words with *eye/wink, legs/splash,* and *jaws/snap.*

## Rock and Roll!

Did you know that alligators eat rocks to help digest their food? After swallowing its food whole, an alligator will eat rocks to help break the food into pieces. Use this science experiment to demonstrate why rocks are an important part of an alligator's diet. To prepare, fill two resealable plastic bags with fresh, green leaves. Then put several small rocks in one of the bags. Next, invite students to rub each of the bags between their hands. The leaves inside the bag with rocks will break up more easily than the leaves inside the bag without rocks. Amazing!

Randi Austin—Gr. K
Gasconade C-4
Falcon, MO

## Sizing Up the Alligator

Challenge your students with the question "How big are baby gators?" Then give youngsters the opportunity to explore the answer with this activity. To begin, have students guess the length of a baby alligator and then inform them that baby gators are approximately ten inches long. Give each child a construction paper copy of the baby alligator on page 205. Invite the child to find objects in your classroom that are equal in length to the alligator. Record students' findings on a chart similar to the one shown and display it during your alligator studies. As an extension, line up 15 baby alligators to show the approximate length of a full-grown gator (12 feet). Wow!

Randi Austin—Gr. K
Gasconade C-4
Falcon, MO

A baby alligator
is as long as . . .

a book

a lunchbox

a tissue box

## Sand Table Hatchery

Use this idea to crack into an alligator egg exploration! To prepare, make a tagboard tracer of the baby alligator pattern on page 205. Next, trace a supply of baby alligators onto black craft foam. Cut out the alligators and then divide them into three groups. Use yellow fabric paint or colored glue to mark each group of alligators with its own distinct pattern. When the paint is dry, fold each gator and put it inside a large plastic Easter egg. Bury the eggs in your sand table under a large mound of sand. Then cover the mound with artificial leaves or leaf cutouts.

Invite a small group of students to the sand table. Discuss with your youngsters how a mother alligator lays her eggs under mounds of mud and leaves. Then have students dig into the mound at the sand table and find the eggs. Direct students to crack open the eggs and sort the baby gators by pattern. Later, invite small groups of students to use the materials at the sand table to build their own alligator nests.

## Play a Gator Game

Use this exciting gator game to reinforce number recognition or other basic skills. To begin, seat students in a circle on the floor. Choose one child to be the alligator and have her sit in the middle of the circle. Next, provide half of the seated children with one number flash card each. (Keep an identical set of flash cards.) Play a lively musical selection and direct students to pass the cards around the circle. When the music stops, show students a card from your pile. Have them recite the chant below, filling in the blank with the number shown. Direct the alligator to find the child holding the chosen number and switch places with him. Then repeat the game with the new alligator.

A very hungry alligator is lurking in the swamp.
He/She wants to eat the number [16].
Chomp! Chomp! Chomp!

Judi Rogas—Gr. K
R. E. Tobler Elementary School
Las Vegas, NV

## Sounds Like...

Although alligators' ears are hard to find, they can hear very well—even underwater! Use this small-group activity to sharpen your youngsters' ability to hear letter sounds. To begin, give each child in the group an alphabet or picture card. Then have the children turn away from you. Recite the chant below, filling in the blank with a letter sound. The child with the corresponding card turns around, reveals his card to you, and identifies the letter(s). Then the remaining children turn around to see the card. Repeat the activity until each child has had a turn.

Alligators, alligators,
Can you hear this sound? [\sh\]!
If you think you have it, please turn around.

Judi Rogas—Gr. K

## Later, Gator!

Get your little gators giggling with this rhyming activity! To begin, write the poem below on a sheet of chart paper and then read it with your class. Have students identify the rhyming words and circle them on the chart. Then invite students to recite the poem again and act out the corresponding movements. As an extension, challenge students to add lines to the poem by brainstorming other rhyming actions. Write the new lines on the chart and perform the poem again.

"Kinder-gators" clap.
Alligators snap!

"Kinder-gators" wink.
Alligators blink!

"Kinder-gators" stomp.
Alligators chomp!

"Kinder-gators" giggle.
Alligators wiggle!

The end,          (Take a bow.)
My friend.        (Shake a classmate's hand.)

Randi Austin—Gr. K
Gasconade C-4
Falcon, MO

200

# Get Swamped!

Do your little ones know that alligators are just as comfortable on land as they are in water? Help each child learn about an alligator's habitat by having her create this model swamp. To begin, provide each child with a clean Styrofoam® tray. Direct her to fingerpaint one half of the tray with dark green paint to represent swamp water. Then have her fingerpaint the other half of the tray with brown paint to represent the swamp land. When the paint is dry, have the child create greenery by gluing crumpled pieces of green tissue paper to the land. Provide the child with a reduced copy of the baby alligator pattern on page 205. Direct her to color the pattern and then glue a strip of construction paper to the back as shown. Or have each child create the alligator in "Artsy Alligators" on page 26. Invite the child to place her gator in the swamp and then use the props to tell an alligator tale.

## Alligator Booklets

Use this versatile booklet project to help reinforce alligator concepts or basic skills. Scan the ideas below; then choose the booklet that best suits the needs of your students. To make one booklet, reproduce the cover (page 205) onto green construction paper. Next, cut a matching back cover from green construction paper and then cut booklet pages from white paper. Bind the pages between the two covers, staple them along the left side, and add an appropriate title.

- Have youngsters use their booklets to record their newfound gator knowledge.
- Invite little ones to create an *Aa* booklet. For each page, direct students to cut out a magazine picture or draw a picture of something that begins with the letter *A*. Have them label each picture and then share their booklets with their classmates.
- Program each page of a child's book with a simple addition problem. Provide alligator counters for the child to use to solve the equations. Have him record the sum on each booklet page.

# Alligator Delight

Wrap up your alligator study and thrill your youngsters by having a parent volunteer help you make this amazing alligator cake! To begin, obtain the materials and ingredients on the shopping list below. Mix a batch of red velvet cake batter and pour it into two round eight-inch cake pans. Bake according to the package directions. When the cakes are completely cool, cut them and assemble the pieces according to the diagrams shown. Next, cover the cake with whipped frosting tinted with green food coloring. To create the alligator's eyes, place two large marshmallows on the head and then use frosting to attach a miniature peanut butter cup or Rolo® candy to each one. Use pieces of red licorice for the mouth and Corn Pops® cereal for the nostrils and toenails. Add a row of chocolate chips down the alligator's back; then sprinkle green-tinted coconut over the entire cake. If desired, surround your alligator with blue-tinted coconut to resemble water. Fresh alligator, anyone?

tail

body

3″

5″

tail

snout
(Place long sides together to form snout.)

snout
(Place long sides together to form snout.)

leg

leg

leg

head

5″

Discard.

Discard.

leg

tail

tail

---

**Shopping List for Alligator Delight**

- 2 round eight-inch cake pans
- 1 box of red velvet cake mix
- whipped frosting
- green and blue food coloring
- 1 bag of shredded coconut
- 2 large marshmallows
- 2 miniature peanut butter cups or Rolo® candies
- chocolate chips
- Corn Pops® cereal
- red licorice

Cheryl Jones—Gr. K
Will Rogers Elementary
Houston, TX

# Amazing Alligator Tales

*Alligator Shoes*
Written by Arthur Dorros
Published by E. P. Dutton

*There's an Alligator Under My Bed*
Written by Mercer Mayer
Published by E. P. Dutton

*Gertie and Gumbo*
Written by Matt Novak
Published by Orchard Books

*Alligators All Around*
Written by Maurice Sendak
Published by HarperCollins Children's Books

*For Pete's Sake*
Written by Ellen Stoll Walsh
Published by Harcourt Brace & Company

*The Lady With the Alligator Purse*
Written by Nadine Bernard Westcott
Published by Little, Brown and Company

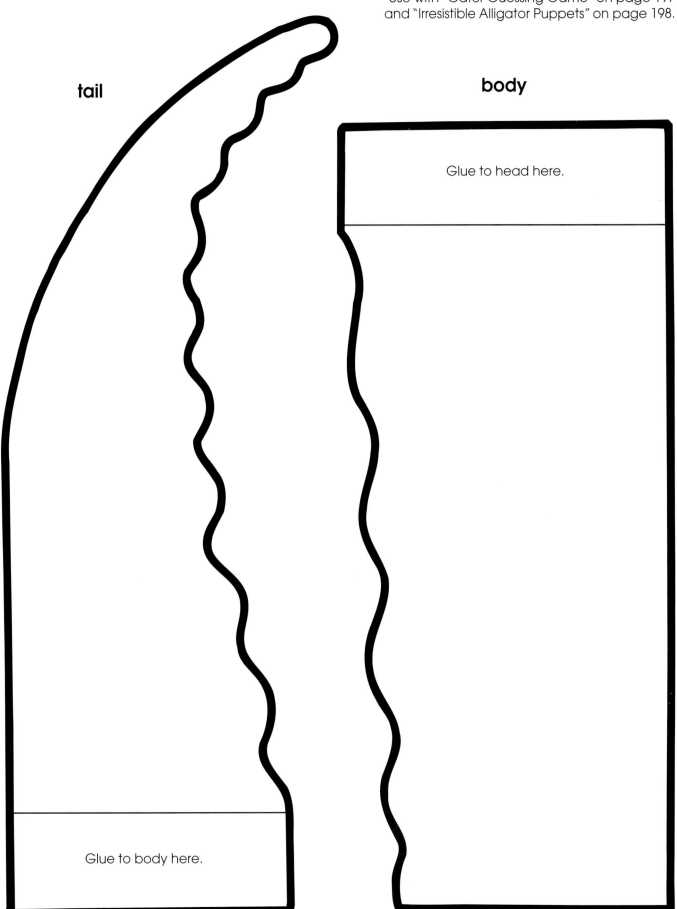

# Alligator Patterns
Use with "Gator Guessing Game" on page 197
and "Irresistible Alligator Puppets" on page 198.

tail

body

Glue to head here.

Glue to body here.

# Alligator Patterns

Use with "Gator Guessing Game" on page 197 and "Irresistible Alligator Puppets" on page 198.

head

eyelid

jaw

legs

©The Education Center, Inc. • THE MAILBOX • Kindergarten • June/July 2000

## Baby Alligator Pattern
Use with "Sizing Up the Alligator"
and "Sand Table Hatchery" on
page 199 and "Get Swamped!"
on page 201.

# HELPING HANDS

## MAKING THE MOST OF CLASSROOM JOBS

Do you have a classroom full of enthusiastic little hands that are raring to help out at a moment's notice? Choose from among the ideas in this unit to help you get the most out of classroom job opportunities.

ideas contributed by kindergarten teachers

- Classroom jobs encourage responsibility.
- Classroom jobs promote organization.
- Classroom jobs promote self-esteem.
- Classroom jobs foster a feeling of ownership.
- Classroom jobs can free up the teacher's time.
- Classroom jobs help children learn effective ways to approach and complete tasks.

## TWO BY TWO

When a task seems a bit overwhelming, teamwork is the ticket to get the job done! Assign selected classroom jobs to teams of two. For example, you might choose two people to accomplish a larger task such as cleaning up your block area. Ask the team members to work together to devise a plan to get the job done. Encourage them to support each other by complimenting one another's good work. Big jobs don't seem quite as big when you approach them two by two!

Julie Maffett
Child Care Association
Cocoa, FL

## ANYBODY KNOW A GOOD PHOTOGRAPHER?

Sure, a whole lot of 'em! Instead of taking time out to be your own photographer, assign the job to your students. At the beginning of the year, use an old camera to teach children how to take photographs. Keep the camera in your dramatic-play area for practice. When you think students have the hang of it, create a press badge and a paper bag vest. Then, at each different event, assign a different child to wear the badge and vest and be the class photographer with a real disposable camera. Tell each child how many pictures she can take and then leave the rest up to artistic interpretation!

Ericka Way—Gr. K
Leslie Fox Keyser
   Elementary
Front Royal, VA

### 9 Ways to Clean Our Room

1. Clean up the floor.
2. Empty the trash.
3. Wipe off the tables.
4. Straighten the papers.
5. Push in the chairs.
6. Erase the board.
7. Put the crayons away.
8. Straighten the cubbies.
9. Wipe out the sink.

## COUNTING ON HELP

Here's an idea for those days when the cleanup is a little too much for individual classroom helpers. Start by choosing a number, such as nine. Then ask the class to brainstorm *nine* ways to clean up the room. Write their responses on a chart. Have a different small group of children volunteer for each different idea listed. Then divide and conquer!

Michele Griffith—Gr. K, Duffy Elementary, West Hartford, CT

## TABLE TOPPERS

If it's on a table, Table Toppers come to the rescue! Each week, assign a team of children to be Table Toppers. Then, when anything pops up that involves a table, you know just where your help is. Table Toppers can set the table, clean messy tables, pass out supplies, etc. If it's on a table, they're tops!

AnnaLisa R. Damminger—Gr. K
Mullica Hill, NJ

## PLAYGROUND PALS

Gathering up your playground equipment is made simple when you have Playground Pals. In advance, label a sheet of paper with the names of your playground toys and a simple drawing of each one (as shown). Laminate the page; then put it on a clipboard. When you're ready to go to the playground, have your chosen Playground Pal use a dry-erase marker to check off each item that is going out. When you come back inside, have that helper check each item in. If anything is missing, your Playground Pal can alert you right away and lead the search.

| Toys | Out | In |
|------|-----|-----|
| ○ | | |
| Y | ✓ | ✓ |
| ▭ | ✓ | ✓ |
| | ✓ | ✓ |
| | ✓ | ✓ |

adapted from an idea by AnnaLisa R. Damminger—Gr. K

## STAFF MEETINGS

How important your little ones will feel when they get to attend staff meetings! If you assign classroom jobs by the week, hold a staff meeting midway through the week. After discussing areas of concern and praise, send your little workers off to complete their term of service with pride!

Vivi Sadel—Gr. K, Finletter School, Philadelphia, PA

# A Tribute to Trees

Use these tree-themed activities to capture the blossoming, budding wonderment of trees as your students honor National Arbor Day by creating this magnificent classroom display!

*by Lucia Kemp Henry*

## Get the Feel for It

Challenge youngsters to feel their way through this tactile activity using their "tree-mendous" problem-solving skills! In advance, place a twig, leaf, walnut, pinecone, and piece of bark into separate brown paper bags. Gather your little investigators and tell them that each bag holds a clue to what they will be studying. Invite a volunteer to close her eyes and place her hand inside a bag. Ask her to describe the shape and texture of the object and then guess what it is. Then have her show the object to the class. Continue in this manner with the remaining bags. Display all five clues and then ask for students' conclusions about the topic of study, leading them to "trees" if necessary. Finish the activity by sharing *Crinkleroot's Guide to Knowing the Trees* by Jim Arnosky (Simon & Schuster Books for Young Readers).

## Hug a Tree Today!

Embark on this hands-on activity that gets your little woodworkers up close to a tree! First give each pair of students two six-inch squares of white paper and a piece of brown crayon. Then take your class outside to mingle with the trees. Ask each child to close his eyes, touch the bark of a tree, and describe to his partner what it *feels* like. Next, ask each child to open his eyes and describe what the bark *looks* like. Then ask one child in each pair to hold a paper square flat on the tree while his partner uses the side of the crayon to create a rubbing. (If you do not have access to real trees, share books with photographs or drawings of tree trunks, and have each child create his own bark design.) Have partners change roles and repeat the crayon-rubbing activity. Ask your youngsters to glue their bark rubbings onto a length of brown bulletin board paper to create a large tree trunk. Later staple the top edge of the tree trunk to a bulletin board so the bottom edge touches the floor. Then tape the lower section of the trunk to the wall. Complete this model tree with the four activities on page 209. What a great way to spruce up your classroom!

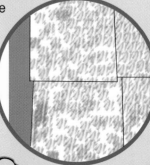

## Getting to the Root of It!

Down, down, down go the roots and up, up, up grows a tree! Show your little ones a picture of tree roots from a reference book, such as *The Tree* by Gallimard Jeunesse and Pascale de Bourgoing (Scholastic Inc.). Ask them to describe what a tree's root system looks like and then point out where the thickest and thinnest roots are located. Discuss how the roots keep the tree from falling over when the wind blows and how they carry water to the tree's trunk and leaves. Then create a root system for your classroom tree. Give each of several children a length of brown crepe paper streamer to tape to the bottom of the tree trunk and onto the floor to represent the larger roots. Provide the remaining children with lengths of thick brown yarn to tape onto the streamers to represent the thinner roots. Remind students to watch where they step so they don't uproot their work!

## "Leaf" It to Us!

Top off this terrific tree with student-made leaves! Collect real leaves for your youngsters to observe. Ask each child to carefully look at a leaf and describe its color and vein pattern. Explain that the leaves make food for the tree. Next, make a construction paper copy of the leaf pattern on page 211 for each child. Have small groups of students sponge-paint their leaves green and then use green-tinted glue to add veins. When the paint and glue are dry, have each child cut out her leaf. Then staple or tape your youngsters' fabulous foliage to the branches of the classroom tree.

## Branching Out

Your budding tree experts will reach for the treetops as they create the branches for their tree model. Step outside with your class to observe the branches of a real tree. Explain that the branches give the tree its shape. Show examples of how the branches twist and turn. Return to the classroom and give each child a 1' x 2' strip of brown bulletin board paper. Demonstrate how to roll the paper into a tube, twist it into a branchlike form, and then tape it closed, as shown. Then help each child roll, twist, and tape his paper. Finally, arrange and staple (or tape) the branches above the trunk. Your classroom tree is shaping up!

## Finishing Touches

If desired, label word cards with the parts of the tree (trunk, roots, branches, leaves) and add them to the display along with the title "Tree-mendous!" Later, encourage your tree experts to tell you about each part of the classroom tree. Then allow your youngsters to stretch out as they dramatize "I Am a Tree!" on page 210. Trees are top-notch!

leaves

## Trees Are Our Friends

Plant some respect for trees with this thoughtful activity. In advance, cut two large tree shapes from bulletin board paper. Label one tree "A tree is…" and the other one "A tree has…" Post the trees near the model tree created in the activities on pages 208 and 209. Read aloud the book *Be a Friend to Trees* by Patricia Lauber (HarperCollins Publishers, Inc.). Show the book's illustrations as you ask each child to suggest a word to complete the phrase "A tree is…" Write each response on the matching tree. Next, use the tree parts from "Get the Feel for It" (page 208) to prompt responses to the phrase "A tree has…" Write youngsters' comments on the corresponding tree. What a forest full of facts your students have cultivated!

A tree is…
green
big
beautiful

A tree has…
leaves
branches
roots

## Let's Tell About a Tree

Reinforce what your tree lovers have discovered about their woodsy friends with this song. Have your students sing the first verse several times, each time finishing the verse with a different word from the "A tree is…" tree (see "Trees Are Our Friends" on this page). Then ask them to sing the second verse in the same manner, using words from the "A tree has…" tree. There's so much to tell about trees!

*(sung to the tune of "The Farmer in the Dell")*

Let's tell about a tree.
Let's tell about a tree.
We know about a tree;
We know a tree *is* [green].

Let's tell about a tree.
Let's tell about a tree.
We know about a tree;
We know a tree *has* [leaves].

## I Am a Tree!

When your youngsters perform this action rhyme, they will really get a feel for what it means to be a tree!

I am a tree. These are my roots.
They help hold me up,
Like a strong pair of boots!

*Stand tall and point to feet.*
*Place feet apart, toes pointed out.*
*Rise up and lower on toes.*

I am a tree. My trunk is right here.
I'm dressed up in bark
In the front and the rear!

*Stand straight; put hands on hips.*
*Pat legs and tummy with hands.*
*Point to chest; point to back.*

I am a tree. My branches are wide.
They grow up and up
And sway side to side!

*Stretch arms out to the side.*
*Stretch arms overhead.*
*Wave arms side to side.*

I am a tree. These are my leaves.
They make cool, green shade
As they blow in the breeze.

*Wiggle fingers.*
*Arch arms over floor in front of body.*
*Wiggle fingers and sway side to side.*

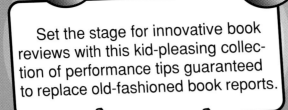

Set the stage for innovative book reviews with this kid-pleasing collection of performance tips guaranteed to replace old-fashioned book reports.

# RAVE

## Casting Call

Combine book reviews with dramatic play, and you have a recipe guaranteed to be fun! After reading a story together, divide the class into small groups. Provide them with several minutes to rehearse, and then invite each group to act out the story in front of the class. For a challenge, assign each group a different part of the story to dramatize, or extend the activity by inviting each group to make up a sequel to the story. Places, please!

Cynthia Fogt—Gr. K
Rummel Creek School
Houston, TX

*Quick! Back through the cave!*

## Buddy Up!

For an esteem-building partnership, involve older students as book buddies in your class. On a regular basis, pair each kindergartner with an older child and have them read stories together. Have each pair select its favorite book and then design a book jacket, using construction paper, crayons, markers, scissors, and glue. When the book jackets are complete, invite each pair to present its creation and a brief story synopsis.

Barbara Corsaro—Gr. K
Maple Road School
West Milford, NJ

## Bag of Tricks

Book reviews are in the bag when you use this parent-involvement idea! Send each child home with a backpack containing a book, a white lunch bag, markers, crayons, and a parent note explaining the activity. Instruct the child to read the book with a parent and then decorate the outside of his bag with pictures that tell about the story. (Encourage creativity!) Then have him place three or four household objects inside the bag that remind him of the story. Assign each child a day to bring his completed project to school to share with the class. Ta-da!

Randi Rote—Gr. K
Wesley Learning Center
Sandy Hook, CT

# REVIEWS

## What a Character!

Get all decked out for a book character day! In advance, choose a favorite author with a variety of different story characters, such as Eric Carle. Read books by that author with your class; then encourage each student to simply dress as her favorite character. (For example, a grouchy ladybug could wear red clothing and antennae.) On the specified day, lead an informal character parade around the room; then invite each child to tell about her costume. Darling, you look marvelous!

AnnaLisa R. Damminger—Gr. K
West Jersey Child Development Center
Voorhees, NJ

## Practice Makes Perfect

Use this tip to help youngsters relax and become accustomed to giving oral presentations such as book reviews. Stock a center with dolls, stuffed animals, puppets, and books. Have a child in this center practice retelling or reviewing his book with the toys as both props and audience. When the child feels confident, have him give his presentation to another child in the center. Then your student will be ready to present to the group. No more stage fright!

Julie Dombroski—Gr. K
St. Dominic Catholic School
Kingsport, TN

## Prop Shop

This center will have your students eagerly crafting book presentations. Designate a center as the prop shop and fill it with paper, crayons, markers, craft supplies, scissors, and glue. Encourage each child to read a book at home with her parents. Then, during center time, have each child visit the prop shop to make a prop, simple character puppet, or scenic background to accompany her story. At a designated group time, invite each student to share her prop shop creation and story with the class.

Jodi Ruby—Gr. K
Minford Primary School
Minford, OH

213

# Picnic, Anyone?

Here's a feast of activities that your little learners are sure to enjoy! So unfold your blanket and start unpacking this cross-curricular spread of picnic pleasures.

*ideas by Michele M. Stoffel Menzel*

## Picnic Hot Spots

Where are the picnic hot spots in your area? Have your kindergartners discover this information with this graphing activity. To prepare, draw a large grid containing six-inch blocks on a length of bulletin board paper. During a group time, brainstorm places to picnic and then list these locations along one side of the grid. Give each child a small index card. Have him draw his favorite picnicking place (or where he would most like to have a picnic). Then make a class graph by having each child tape his picture next to the corresponding location on the grid. So where is the class's favorite hot spot? Check the graph and see!

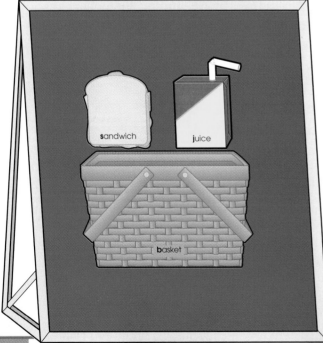

## Picnic Begins With P

Invite your children to the flannelboard and sing this catchy tune to help them develop phonemic awareness. In advance, gather an assortment of typical picnic items (simply illustrated) along with a picnic basket cutout. Label each of the pictures and then highlight the beginning sound of each word. Attach a piece of self-adhesive felt to the back of each piece. Introduce the activity by putting the picnic basket on the board as you sing the verse below. Cue your little ones to sing additional verses by placing different picnic items above the basket. For more practice, have students draw pictures of other items to put "in" the basket. Sing the corresponding verses to match youngsters' illustrations. End the song by filling in the blank with *picnic* as you refer to the basket now filled with picnic items.

*(adapt to the tune of "The Farmer in the Dell")*

[Basket] begins with [\b\].
[Basket] begins with [\b\].
[\b\ \b\ \b\ \b\ \b\ \b\]
[Basket] begins with [\b\].

# Bits of Problem Solving

This quick picnic is perfect for practicing addition and subtraction. Give each child a paper plate and ten Ritz® Bits® minicrackers. Tell an addition story problem (use one of the suggestions below or make up your own). Then have each child use her crackers to determine the answer. Repeat with several more problems, reminding students to start with an empty plate each time. Next, have each picnicker practice subtraction. Direct her to put all ten crackers on her plate. Once again dictate story problems, but this time have each child eat her Ritz Bits to determine the answers. Then brush off the crumbs and get ready for more picnic fun!

**For addition practice:**

[Two students' names] went to the park.
They saw [three students' names] on the playground.
They decided to have a picnic!
How many sandwiches did they need?

[Four students' names] came over to play with [student's name].
[Last student's name]'s mom prepared six lunches.
Was there enough food for everyone?

**For subtraction practice:**

Ten children went to the zoo.
One child had to leave at eleven o'clock and two more
　　children went home at noon.
How many children stayed longer?

[Teacher's name] had seven crackers.
She shared her crackers with [five students' names].
How many crackers did [teacher's name] get to eat?

# Ant Antics

No picnic would be complete without ants! Use these beanie ants to gather up some gross-motor skills. Ahead of time, you will need to make four ant beanbags. To make one, stuff a brown or black sock with dried beans. Use three rubber bands to segment the ant's body and then fold the sock cuff as shown. If desired, use craft glue to attach six felt legs, two felt antennae, and two wiggle eyes. Next, go outdoors and prepare a grassy area for the antics by spreading out a blanket and placing a picnic basket in the center of the blanket.

To play, arrange each of four groups of children in a line at a different side of the blanket. The first child in each group gets three tries to toss the ant inside the basket. (To speed up the activity, you may want to have a designated helper to toss the beanbags back out to the lines.) Continue until everyone has had a turn to toss. To vary this activity, have each child balance an ant on his head, hold an ant between his knees, or hop with an ant balanced on his foot as he travels a predetermined distance to drop the ant in the basket. That's "f-ant-astic!"

# Pick a Center!

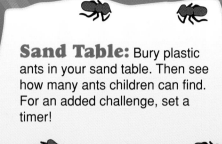

Enjoy this sampler of learning activities that spreads the picnic theme into every area of your classroom.

**Sand Table:** Bury plastic ants in your sand table. Then see how many ants children can find. For an added challenge, set a timer!

**Math:** Fill a picnic basket with an equal number of paper napkins and plastic forks, knives, and spoons. Cut toilet paper tubes to use as napkin rings and add them to the basket. Invite each student to sort the utensils into groups and then make sets consisting of one fork, one knife, and one spoon. To finish, have the child wrap each set in a napkin, secure it with a napkin ring, and place it in the basket.

**Dramatic-Play:** Turn your dramatic-play area into a beach picnic using the props listed below and a small pool filled with moist sand.

- blanket
- picnic basket
- picnic items
- seashells
- cooler
- sunglasses
- beach balls
- large umbrella
- sand toys
- hats
- books/magazines
- sunscreen

**Art Center:** Provide a variety of collage materials (see list below for suggestions) and a paper plate for each child. Invite her to create and glue onto her plate the items that represent her favorite picnic foods. Display the foods on a checkered bulletin board background or use the plates in dramatic play.

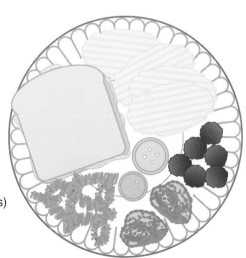

- craft foam (slices of bread, meat)
- ribbed card stock (chips)
- tissue paper (lettuce)
- orange pipe cleaners (cheese curls)
- pom-poms (grapes/blueberries)

- yarn and dried pasta pieces (pasta salad)
- large colorful buttons (gelatin shapes)
- natural-colored or wooden buttons (cookies)
For printing:
- cucumber half and green paint (pickles)

**Music and Movement:** It's not a picnic without the pokey! Teach your students the song at the right. Put a basket full of different picnic items in a center. As pairs of children visit the center, have one child sing the verse, filling it in with the name of an item from the basket. Then have the other child perform the actions in the song. That's what it's all about!

*(sung to the tune of "The Hokey-Pokey")*

You put the [apple] in. You take the [apple] out.
You put the [apple] in and you shake it all about.
You do the picnic pokey and you turn yourself around.
That's what it's all about!

**Fine-Motor:** Prepare batches of play dough using the recipes below. The peanut butter dough is edible; the jelly dough is not.

### Jelly Play Dough

5 tbsp. cream of tartar
³/₄ c. salt
3 c. all-purpose flour
.14-oz. package of unsweetened, grape-flavored drink mix
3 c. water
3 tbsp. vegetable oil
blue and red food coloring

Stir all of the dry ingredients in a large pot. Slowly add the water and oil. Using a large wire whisk, blend the mixture until all of the lumps are gone. Whisk in several drops of blue and red food coloring until the mixture is a medium purple color. (The dough will darken as it cooks.) Cook the mixture over medium heat, stirring constantly with a large spoon until it forms a ball. While the mixture is still warm, knead it on a lightly floured board for several minutes or until the dough has a soft, satiny feel. Store the dough in a sealed container at room temperature for up to a month.

### Peanut Butter Play Dough

2 c. creamy peanut butter
2 c. honey
4¹/₂ c. powdered milk

Mix the honey and peanut butter together in a large bowl. Slowly add the powdered milk and knead the mixture until the dough is of a thick consistency. Store the dough in a sealed container and refrigerate when not in use.

**Gross-Motor:** It's time to play hopscotch using the beanbag ants from "Ant Antics" on page 215. Use a wide-tipped permanent marker to draw the hopscotch grid onto a sturdy skid-resistant tablecloth.

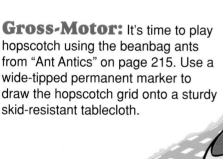

**Reading Area:** Consider including the following picnicking stories in your reading area. If desired, make a recording of yourself reading each story so that students can read along on their own.

*Picnic Farm*
Written by Christine Morton
Published by Holiday House, Inc.

*The Picnic*
Written and Illustrated by Ruth Brown
Published by Dutton Children's Books

*Up the Ladder, Down the Slide*
Written and Illustrated by Betsy Everitt
Harcourt Brace & Company

# Let's Go Outside!

Take your science curriculum outdoors with these ideas that focus on observation, communication, testing, and collecting data.

*ideas by Suzanne Moore*

## Sensing Summer

A good scientist uses many of her senses as she observes. Review the five senses with your youngsters as they complete this outdoor journal. Each child will need five sheets of paper, a 9" x 12" piece of tagboard, a copy of the text strips (page 221), access to a stapler, crayons, scissors, and glue. To make the journal, each child stacks his paper on top of the tagboard and staples them together along the top edge. Next, he titles his journal and personalizes the cover. He then cuts the text strips apart and glues each one to the top of a different page.

When the journals are ready, head outdoors with crayons in hand for some observing and recording! Spend a little time at several locations around the schoolyard. Have each youngster record in his journal what he sees, feels, smells, and hears. Come back into the classroom and invite youngsters to share their data. Has anyone discovered yet that *taste* was not included? Finish up the activity by discussing why scientists have to be careful about tasting. Then brainstorm situations in which it would be okay to taste. For example, maybe a scientist is trying to develop a new ice-cream flavor. Makes sense!

## Just Hangin' Out

Now that your youngsters have some experience with scientific observation, narrow their focus to a smaller outdoor area. To prepare, photocopy the poem on page 221 for each child. Each student will also need a plastic hanger, a large craft stick, four index cards, four different lengths of yarn, tape, scissors, crayons, and access to a hole puncher.

Have students take their hangers and craft sticks outside and spread out. Direct each child to place her hanger on the ground. Then encourage her to focus on the area inside the hanger. What can be seen? Explain that the craft stick can be used to gently move rocks, dirt, or blades of grass. After several minutes of observing, return to the classroom. Once inside, instruct the child to draw on each index card a different item that she observed. Then have her label the pictures. Help her punch a hole in each card and then attach it to the hanger with yarn as shown. Finally, have each child write her name on the poem and cut it out. Then help her fold and tape the top corners of the poem around her hanger. Display the hangers from the ceiling or along a wall. My, what terrific little observers!

# Dirt Traps

With the summer breeze comes summer dust. Making these dirt traps will provide your students with a closer look at just what's floating around out there. To prepare, gather a class supply of plastic lids. Punch a hole in each one. Then cut an 18-inch length of yarn for each child. Students will also need access to a permanent marker and some petroleum jelly. Have each child write his name on one side of a lid and then smear some petroleum jelly on the other side. To finish the dirt trap, instruct the child to tie on a length of yarn.

Have students hang their catchers in various locations around the schoolyard. After several days, direct each child to collect his dirt trap and observe the findings with a magnifying glass. Encourage students to compare to see if everyone collected the same types of items. This might be a great opportunity to discuss the effects of air pollution or the benefit of wind for seed dispersal. No matter what topic this activity initiates, children will no doubt learn that science can be a breeze!

# Buggy Boards

Bugs abound in summer. Try this easy experiment to show your youngsters that some bugs prefer the sun's light and heat, while others seek cooler, darker places. Have a sheet of plywood cut into small sections to equal the number of children in your class. (Or use any kind of scrap wood you have handy.) Give each child a section of the wood. Provide bright-colored permanent markers for each child to use to personalize her piece of wood. When the buggy boards are complete, take your students outside. Invite each child to pick a place in the schoolyard to lay her board. Leave the boards in place overnight. The next day, have each child carefully observe her board to see what's on and around it. Then have her carefully lift one end of her board and take a peek. Encourage youngsters to compare what is found under their boards. Continue checking under the boards for several days. Then invite each child to take her buggy board home to provide a buggy bungalow for some backyard buggies.

219

## Shadow Shenanigans

Take advantage of the sizzling sun to cast a shadow on science. On a sunny morning, divide your students into pairs. Give each pair a piece of chalk and then take the whole class to the sidewalk or blacktop area. Direct one child in each pair to stand very still. Have the other student trace the child's shoe prints and draw a line from the child's feet to the tip of his shadow. Instruct the pair of students to switch roles and repeat the activity. Before leaving, have each child write his name near his shoe prints. Return to the area at noon and at the end of the day. Encourage each child to stand in the same spot as before and have his partner draw another line the length of his shadow. Did the size or position of the shadow change? In the morning and afternoon, shadows are longer because the sun is lower in the sky. At noon, the sun is at its highest point in the sky, so shadows are very short. Shadows change positions because of the earth's rotation—that makes the sun seem to move across the sky.

After this structured shadow experiment, encourage students to have a little fun with their shadows. Challenge each child to hide from his shadow. Then see if he can fit inside a friend's shadow. Finally, encourage the child to make his shadow shake hands with a classmate's shadow without actually touching hands.

## Sandy Science

Got some dry play sand handy? Then you've got a great science activity! Gather a small group of students around a large container of dry sand. Have a few volunteers try to build a tower with the sand. What happens? Explain that it is difficult to build with dry sand because the grains have jagged edges that don't fit together. Now have students brainstorm what can be done to the sand to make the grains stick together. If necessary, lead them to the solution of adding water. Instruct a volunteer to add some water to the sand. Then have more volunteers try to build a tower. Eureka!

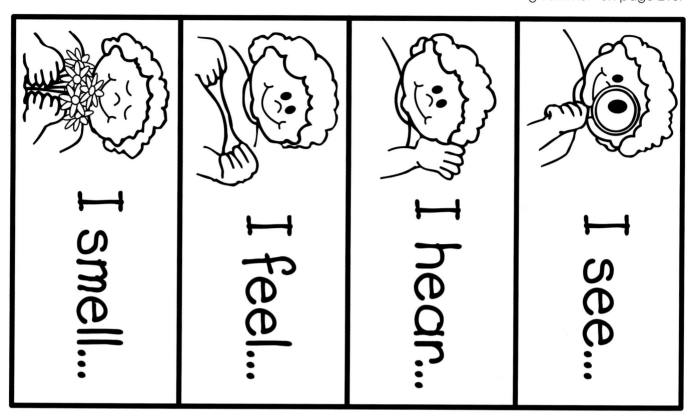

I smell...

I feel...

I hear...

I see...

**Poem**
Use with "Just Hangin' Out" on page 218.

I took this hanger outside
And put it on the ground.
I looked inside the hanger,
And this is what I found!

fold

fold

**Name** _____

# I Do!

Dearly beloved, we are gathered here together for the marriage of Mr. Q and Miss U! These exquisite ideas and activities will help you plan the quintessential wedding that will have youngsters saying "I do!" to learning.

*ideas contributed by Michele Dare, Angie Kutzer, and Kari Murray*

## The Bride Wore White...

Outfit each of your little brides and grooms with these fashionable veils and bow ties. To make a veil, die-cut a *U* from white construction paper. Then have your little bride-to-be decorate the *U* with gold sequins and glitter glue. Next, direct her to glue the *U* onto a sentence strip headband. Then help her staple a piece of white tissue paper or netting to the back of the headband.

To make a bow tie, die-cut a *Q* from black construction paper. Then have each groom glue the *Q* onto a white bow tie cutout as shown. Next, have him use a quarter stamp and ink pad to make coin prints on the tie. Punch two holes at the top of the tie and then tie a length of yarn through each hole. Have each little groom and bride wear their ties and veils during the wedding. (See "Going to the Chapel" on page 223.)

## Great Gift Ideas

Need gift ideas for the happy couple? Create a bridal registry with this cooperative classification activity. To begin, divide your class into small groups. Assign each group a gift category, such as kitchen items, bathroom accessories, or fine china. Then provide each group with a supply of catalogs, construction paper, scissors, crayons, and glue. Direct students in each group to cut out pictures of gifts for their assigned category. Have them glue the pictures to a sheet of construction paper; then have them write the names of the gifts beside the pictures. Have each group present its gift ideas to the class, and then bind all of the registry pages together with a cover.

## Shower Power

Wrap up youngsters' phonics skills with this quaint bridal shower! In advance, send parents a copy of the note on page 224, asking them to send a gift-wrapped item that begins with *Q, U,* or *Qu.* On the day of the shower, seat your youngsters in a circle and place the gifts in the middle. (Be sure to have a few extra gifts for students who are unable to bring one.) Invite each child, in turn, to open one gift (not his own) and identify the beginning sound of the gift. As an extension, place all of the opened gifts in a center and invite students to sort them by beginning sound.

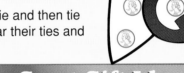

## You Are Cordially Invited...

The big day is just around the corner! Better send out those invitations! To prepare, cut a class supply of satin ribbons, each approximately 27 inches long. Then make a construction paper copy of the invitation and heart pattern on page 224 for each child. Punch holes in each invitation and heart as indicated. Have the child lace the ribbon through the invitation. Then tie on the heart with the ribbon's ends. Encourage your youngsters to take their invitations home and invite their parents to the wedding of *Q* and *U.*

## A "Marry" Melody

*Quick. Quiet. Queen.* What other words begin with *Qu?* Invite youngsters to brainstorm a list of *Qu* words and then use them in the song below. If desired, create corresponding actions for students to perform with each *Qu* word. Then have your little brides and grooms perform the song at the wedding.

*(sung to the tune of "She'll Be Comin' Round the Mountain")*

**Boys:** Oh, today I'm gonna marry Miss U.
**Girls:** Oh, today I'm gonna marry Mr. Q.
**Together:** Oh, we'll have a lot of fun
When our two sounds become one!
And together we can make a word like
[Queen]!

Repeat the verse, substituting the underlined word with other words from the list.

Pam Crane

## Going to the Chapel

Bells are ringing! It's wedding day! To prepare, set up chairs in your classroom or auditorium in vertical rows. Tape white bulletin board paper down the center aisle; then scatter die-cut *Q*s and *U*s onto the paper. Next, have your little grooms don their bow ties, and have your little brides slip on their veils. (See "The Bride Wore White…" on page 222.)

To begin the ceremony, have youngsters perform the song from "A 'Marry' Melody" above. Then have them form a line of boys and a line of girls. Play a traditional wedding march as the two lines walk down the aisle side by side. If possible, arrange for a quartet of older students to play the wedding march. Following the ceremony, host a reception and serve Nestlé® Quik®, quesadillas, and cupcakes arranged to form the letters *Q* and *U.* Congratulations *Q* and *U!* By the power vested in me, I now pronounce you \kwə\.

## Parent Note
Use with "Shower Power" on page 222.

Dear Parents,

We are pleased to announce the upcoming wedding of the letters *Q* and *U*. As part of the festivities, our class will be having a bridal shower for Mr. Q and Miss U. Please help your child find an object in your house that begins with *Q*, *U*, or *Qu*, such as Q-tips® cotton swabs, an umbrella, or a box of Quaker® Oats. (These items will be returned.) Gift wrap the item and send it to school on _____. Thank you!
  (date)

©The Education Center, Inc. • *THE MAILBOX*® • *Kindergarten* • June/July 2000

## Wedding Invitation
Use with "You Are Cordially Invited..." on page 223.

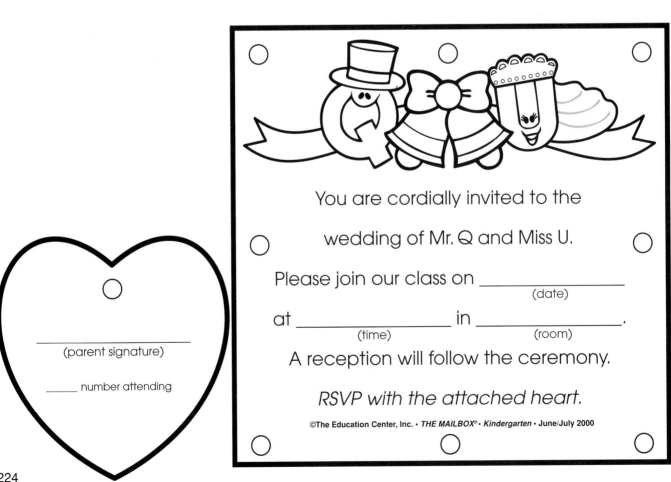

_____
(parent signature)

_____ number attending

You are cordially invited to the

wedding of Mr. Q and Miss U.

Please join our class on _____
  (date)

at _____ in _____.
  (time)          (room)

A reception will follow the ceremony.

*RSVP with the attached heart.*

©The Education Center, Inc. • *THE MAILBOX*® • *Kindergarten* • June/July 2000

# GIVE A CHEER FOR THE END OF THE YEAR!

Looking for ways to keep you and your students motivated during those last few weeks of school? Look no further! These tips, ideas, and activities will keep you and your class on your toes until the very last day.

## CLASS-MADE KEEPSAKES

Good behavior will abound with this management idea! Have weekly drawings for your class-made books and projects! During the last month of school, pass out good behavior tickets to students. Have each child write his name on his ticket and place it in a designated box or container. At the end of each week, draw one or two names from the container; then allow the winning students to choose a class book or project to take home and keep.

Kelly Mouw—Pre-K and Gr. K, McLeod Academy, Marion, IA

Kindergarten, Kindergarten, Who Do You See?

Omar

In this bag you will find some things

That hold the key to what your future brings.

It is with great sadness that I watch you depart

Because you have a special place in my heart.

©The Education Center, Inc. • THE MAILBOX® Kindergarten • June/July 2006

Mrs. Roberts
Miss Ewing

## GRADUATION GOODY BAG

Bid a fond farewell to your youngsters with this idea—a goody bag full of fun and symbolism! To make one bag, duplicate the poem and note on page 227. Glue the poem to the outside of a paper lunch bag and then sign the bag. If desired, invite other teachers who have worked with the student to sign the bag. Next, place the note inside the bag along with the following items: a ruler, a handful of Hershey's® Kisses®, a pencil, a marker, a penny, and an eraser. On the last day of school, present each child with a bag and help her read the note inside. What a great way to say good-bye!

Mary Kibe—Gr. K, Visitation BVM, Norristown, PA

## SUMMER BIRTHDAY CELEBRATION

Little ones with summer birthdays will appreciate this idea! Designate one day during the last week of school for a summer birthday celebration. To prepare, ask parents of summer birthday children to send cupcakes, napkins, drinks, or other birthday goodies for the celebration. On the designated day, read birthday books, graph students' birthdays by month, make birthday cards and party hats (see page 26), and play traditional party games. At the end of the day, sing "Happy Birthday" to each child with a summer birthday, and then serve a birthday party snack. Happy birthday to you!

Lin Attaya—Gr. K
Hodge Elementary, Denton, TX

225

## STUDENT TEACHERS

This brilliant end-of-the-year idea has youngsters at the head of the class—teaching a lesson! To prepare for this activity, have each child begin thinking of his own talents and special interests. If necessary, help students brainstorm lesson ideas, such as blowing a bubble with gum, tying shoes, or preparing a special snack. Send home with each child a parent note explaining the activity and a copy of the planning sheet on page 228. When you have received a response from each child, create a schedule, and let the teaching begin! If desired, send parents a copy of the schedule and invite them to their little ones' lessons.

Lin Attaya—Gr. K
Hodge Elementary
Denton, TX

## BANANA SPLIT BEHAVIOR

Encourage appropriate behavior with this cool display. To prepare, cut out the parts of a banana split—such as an ice-cream dish, a banana, scoops of ice cream, hot fudge, whipped cream, and a cherry—from bulletin board paper. Next, program the ice-cream dish with a poem similar to the one shown and then mount it on a bulletin board or a wall. When your class demonstrates positive behavior, add a piece to the banana split display. When the final ingredient (a cherry) is added, treat your little ones to a banana split party. What a great way to go bananas!

Angelena Pritchard—Gr. K
Fountain Inn Elementary
Fountain Inn, SC

### SUMMER'S HERE! LET'S SPLIT!

Let's build this banana split,
Piece by piece until it's done.
We'll earn each piece with good behavior.
Ice cream, whipped cream—oh, what fun!

## BONUS BOOKS FOR GOOD BEHAVIOR

If you have acquired a large number of bonus points from book clubs, use them to order books as rewards for your students. During the last few weeks of school, present the books to students who demonstrate good behavior. Or hold a drawing on the last day of school for students who have earned a specified number of good behavior points. Good work, little ones!

Taryn Lynn Way—Gr. K
Los Molinos Elementary
Los Molinos, CA

In this bag you
will find some things

That hold the key to
what your future brings.

It is with great sadness
that I watch you depart

Because you have
a special place in my heart.

**Goody Bag Note**
Use with "Graduation Goody Bag" on page 225.

A  to remind you that there are always rules to follow

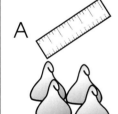 to remind you that you are loved

A  to remind you that there are still many things to learn

A 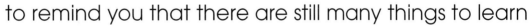 to remind you to leave a good mark wherever you go

A  to remind you to use good sense

An  to remind you that it's all right to make mistakes

Name _____

# MY TIME TO TEACH

🍎 My lesson is…

👦👧 I want my classmates to learn…

⚾🎨 Materials I will bring from home…

✂️ Materials I will need from school…

## Please add any further information on the back of this sheet.

**Note to the teacher:** Use this page with "Student Teachers" on page 226.

# AUTHOR UNITS

# Bruce McMillan

Bruce McMillan is an award-winning photo-illustrator with the unique ability to capture vibrant colors and basic concepts to create picture-perfect children's books. McMillan uses his camera to capture sensational views as well as the hearts and minds of children everywhere. So zoom in on this collection of Bruce McMillan books. Your youngsters will discover—in a flash—the unique delights of McMillan's gift!

*by Mackie Rhodes*

## Counting Wildflowers
*Published by Mulberry Books*

Count on the magnificent photos in this book to reinforce counting and color skills. After sharing this book with your class, invite students to create a painted version of the book. To prepare, arrange the book, paints, a supply of art paper, and a supply of correspondingly colored sticky dots in your art center. Ask each child to paint a floral scene of up to 20 of the same kind of flower. When the picture is dry, have him attach the matching number of sticky dots on his paper. Then have each child use a black marker to write the corresponding numeral on his paper. Bind all the pages together along with a title page. Then invite each child to share his page with the group. Just beautiful—Bruce McMillan would be proud!

## Gletta the Foal
*Published by Cavendish Children's Books*

Gletta, a cute and curious foal, learns that not everything she hears can be seen. After sharing this story, invite students to speculate about the source of the sound. Then challenge their listening skills with this sound-location game. To begin, appoint four students to be soundmakers. Give each soundmaker a set of rhythm sticks; then station each one in a different area of the room. Invite another child to assume the role of Gletta. Have her sit in a chair with her eyes covered. To play, silently signal one soundmaker to tap her sticks together. Then ask Gletta to uncover her eyes and gallop to the location of the sound. Did she correctly locate the sound? Invite different children to be soundmakers and Gletta; then repeat the game. Listen carefully!

## Growing Colors
*Published by Lothrop, Lee & Shepard Books*

In this book filled with luscious-looking fruits and vegetables, color recognition is the focus of McMillan's vibrant photos and clever layouts. After reading this delicious delight, reinforce youngsters' thinking, classification, and color skills with this large- or small-group activity. To prepare, put an assortment of colorful construction paper circles in a basket. Blindfold a child volunteer. Then have him remove a circle from the basket and hold it up for his classmates to see. Invite the rest of the group to call out foods of the same color until the blindfolded child guesses the color that he is holding. Repeat the activity with a different volunteer for each round. Hmmm—it's the color of peas…and broccoli…and lettuce…and pears…and the outside of a watermelon…and lime lollipops…and pickles…

## Mouse Views:
## What the Class Pet Saw
*Published by Holiday House, Inc.*

When a classroom mouse house is left open, the class mouse finds himself on the sight-seeing tour of his life! After sharing this story, invite each child to take a mouse-view tour of your classroom. To prepare, make a construction paper set of mouse patterns for each child. Have each child cut out her patterns and glue the ears on the head. Instruct her to use art supplies to complete the mouse's face. Help each child glue her mouse onto a tagboard headband. Then invite each child to wear her headband while pretending to be a mouse. Have her explore different areas of the classroom from a mouse's vantage point. Then ask each child to write about (or dictate) and illustrate an interesting mouse view. Invite each child to share her special view with the class; then help her post her picture and mouse for display. What did you see, little mouse?

## Nights of the Pufflings
*Published by Houghton Mifflin Company*

On a small Icelandic island, young children participate in an unusual late summer tradition—a puffling rescue mission! Read the story; then invite students to practice their gross-motor skills and following directions with this play version of a puffling rescue. You'll need two boxes, a sock for each child, lots of plastic grocery bags, and a few sheets of blue butcher paper cut to resemble the ocean. To make a puffling, stuff plastic bags into a sock; then knot the sock cuff. Randomly toss the pufflings onto a grassy area outdoors. Arrange the boxes and the ocean at one end of the outdoor area. Then divide your class into two teams. Instruct each team to line up behind its assigned box. At your signal, have each team member, in turn, run to pick up a puffling and deliver it to his team's box. When all the birds are gathered, have each team member toss one of the pufflings into the ocean from a designated distance. (See page 28 of the book for the correct puffling toss!) To set up for the next rescue mission, simply toss the pufflings onto the field again.

**Note:** Since passersby are bound to be curious about this activity, encourage your children to be ready to share about their author study and the story of the pufflings on the Icelandic island!

## More by McMillan

*Eating Fractions*
Published by Scholastic Inc.

*Grandfather's Trolley*
Published by Candlewick Press

*Jelly Beans for Sale*
Published by Scholastic Inc.

*One, Two, One Pair!*
Published by Scholastic Inc.

*Play Day: A Book of Terse Verse*
Published by Holiday House, Inc.

*Sense Suspense: A Guessing Game for the Five Senses*
Published by Scholastic Inc.

# Notable Laura Numeroff

If you give a child a book by Laura Numeroff—he's going to want another one! Best known for *If You Give a Mouse a Cookie* and its sequels, Laura Numeroff has written more than 20 children's books. Her first children's book was published at the same time she finished college, but her writing ambitions actually started at the age of nine. Walking dogs, waitressing, running a carousel, and working at a radio station have offered Ms. Numeroff the opportunity to create stories from real-life experiences. From the wildest ideas imaginable to sweet truths from home, Laura Numeroff is a creative writer and her books are thoroughly enjoyable.

—*ideas contributed by Carole Dibble and Kathy Lee*

## *What Mommies Do Best/What Daddies Do Best*
### Illustrated by Lynn Munsinger
### Published by Simon & Schuster Books for Young Readers

Moms *do* give piggyback rides and dads *can* sew on buttons! This story invites children to relate to their own parents (and caregivers) and to be proud of the many things their parents can do. After sharing the story, invite students to tell about their favorite times spent with parents or other care-givers. Then help each child make his own version of the story to share with these special people in his life. Make a book for each child by stapling five sheets of construction paper together on the left side. Also, provide a supply of markers or crayons, old magazines, scissors, and glue.

Direct each child to choose two special caregivers and then think of three things each person does well. Write the title for the first half of the book on the front cover. Then, for the next three pages, have the child draw or cut out illustrations showing the chosen activities. Write his dictation on each page. On the last page, write "But most of all, [caregiver's name] gives me lots and lots of love!" and have the child illustrate the page. To finish the book, flip it over to the back cover so that the binding is still on the left side. Write the second title on the cover and then help the child complete the pages as before. Encourage each child to take his unique book home to read to his family.

## *Dogs Don't Wear Sneakers*
### Illustrated by Joe Mathieu
### Published by Simon & Schuster Books for Young Readers

In this whimsical rhyming book, animals look hilarious as they do all sorts of people activities. It's all a matter of a child's dreaming and imagination! Before sharing this story with your youngsters, cut out an assortment of magazine illustrations that show animals in realistic and imaginative situations. Divide a sheet of chart paper into two columns. Label one half "Real" and the other half "Pretend." After reading the story aloud, discuss with your students the difference between *real* and *pretend.* Have students give examples of what a dog can and can not do. Then have each child pick a picture from your collection and tape it to the correct column on the chart. If your youngsters

want even more of this zaniness, follow up with a reading of the sequel *Chimps Don't Wear Glasses.*

## Monster Munchies
Illustrated by Nate Evans
Published by Random House, Inc.

Beware! The hungry monsters in this story are eating everything in sight—maybe even you! Your little ones will get a kick out of this rhyming and rollicking text. Follow up a reading of the story by having each youngster draw a picture of his favorite snack. Ask him how he (or an adult) makes the snack and then write his dictated recipe on the page. Compile students' drawings into a class book titled "Kid Munchies." Read the book aloud and then send it home with a different student each night for families to enjoy. Is anybody hungry?

Spaghetti
String made out of spaghetti
Cheese
Put it in the oven and then put it for twenty minutes. Then you take it out and eat it.

Christopher

## Two for Stew
Co-written with Barney Saltzberg
Illustrated by Salvatore Murdocca
Published by Simon & Schuster
Books for Young Readers

Picture this! You go into a restaurant and can't wait to order because you know exactly what you want. But when you order, the waiter informs you that they are out of your heart's desire! This charming book will have your students laughing as they follow a madame and her poodle on their mission for stew. Extend the story by having your youngsters make their own stew for two.

In advance, ask parents to send in several cans of peas, sliced carrots, and sliced potatoes. On the day of the activity, make a batch of brown gravy and keep it warm in a Crock-Pot® cooker. (You may want to wrap a towel around the pot to protect little hands.) Pour each vegetable into a different bowl. Add a large serving spoon to each bowl and a ladle to the gravy.

Divide your group into pairs. Have each pair take turns being the server and the customer. To make stew, the server takes the customer's order (which veggies to include), adds a spoonful of each requested item into a foam cup, and then tops it off with some gravy and a stir. May I take your order?

## Sometimes I Wonder if Poodles Like Noodles
Illustrated by Tim Bowers
Published by Simon & Schuster Books for Young Readers

This delightful collection of poems, written from a young girl's perspective, is perfect for wondering young minds. The subjects vary from friends and family to the beach and bedtime. There's even a Halloween poem, perfect for this time of year!

Reading the poem "Bath Time" is sure to initiate a lively discussion of youngsters' own bath time fun. Explain the word *routine* to your little ones and invite volunteers to tell you their bath time routines. Then have each child bring in her own special bath toy (labeled with her name). Fill your water table with sudsy water and use the toys for water play. Which ones sink? Which ones float? If desired, include baby dolls from the dramatic play area for children to bathe. (Be sure to have towels nearby to dry off *all* the babes.) Don't forget to compare wrinkly hands!

## For More Reading Fun
*The Chicken Sisters*
Illustrated by Sharleen Collicott
Published by HarperCollins Publishers, Inc.

*Why a Disguise?*
Illustrated by David McPhail
Published by Simon & Schuster Books for
Young Readers

Order books online.
www.themailbox.com

233

# Anybody Want a Cookie?

Or a muffin? Or a pancake? Bring Laura Numeroff's best-selling series into your classroom and use these related ideas to serve up some learning fun.

*—ideas contributed by Susan A. DeRiso and Carole Dibble*

## If You Give a Mouse a Cookie
## If You Give a Moose a Muffin
## If You Give a Pig a Pancake

(The books in this series are illustrated by Felicia Bond and published by HarperCollins Publishers, Inc.)

### Introducing...

Sing this little ditty to introduce any of the *If You Give a...* books. Simply modify the verse with the character and items that pertain to the story.

*(sung to the tune of "If You're Happy and You Know It")*

If you give a [mouse] a [cookie],
Get some [milk]!
If you give a [mouse] a [cookie],
Get some [milk]!
If you give a [mouse] a [cookie], [he] will always want much more.
[He's] a [mouse] like you have never seen before!

### It's in the Bag

Creative thinking and verbal expression are in the bag with this lively language game. To prepare, gather items from the classroom—such as a piece of string, a block, a clothespin, and a doll— so that each child can have a different object. Place all of the items in a bag and arrange your children in a circle.

To play the game, the first player pulls out an object and says the following, "If you give [student's name] a(n) [object]..." Then he gives the person seated to his right the object and that child finishes the sentence by telling what she would do. She then picks a new object from the bag and continues this pattern with the person seated on her right. Let's hear it for hands-on, cooperative storytelling!

### If and Then

*If you give a dog a leash, then he'll want to take a walk.* —Cedric

*If you play in the rain, then you'll get wet.* —Marie

*If you hit your little brother, then your mom will get mad.* —Kyle

### If and Then

Use the three books in this series as a lead-in to discussing cause and effect with your youngsters. Talk about the if/then pattern of the books' texts. Then invite your youngsters to brainstorm a list of cause and effect statements. How many can they come up with? Write each statement and its contributor on chart paper. (If desired, transfer these statements into your newsletter for parents to enjoy.) For independent practice, provide a set of picture cards that show different causes. Have each student choose a card and draw its corresponding effect. Write any dictation the child wants to include. Display the cards and drawings together on a bulletin board titled " 'Effect-ive' Learning."

Order books online.
www.themailbox.com

## If You Give a Moose a Muffin

If you give a child a muffin, he's going to want to practice math—especially if it's a "moose-berry" muffin! Furnish some blueberry minimuffins for snacking while youngsters practice their counting and number recognition skills. Program each of six paper muffin liners with a different numeral or dot set. Place the liners in a muffin tin and provide a bowl of "moose-berries" (blue beads or pom-poms). Have each youngster put the correct number of berries in the corresponding liners.

## If You Give a Mouse a Cookie

Students will be delighted to give these mice some cookies while practicing rhyming skills. Construct several mice (similar to the ones shown) using construction paper, wiggle eyes, black pom-poms, a black marker, scissors, and glue. Use an X-acto® knife to cut around the sides and bottom of each mouse's teeth. Program each mouse's ears with pictures of rhyming words (use clip art or art from worksheets). Make sure each mouse represents a different rhyming family. Cut out a supply of cookies from construction paper. Then program each cookie with a different rhyming picture that corresponds with one of the mice. To complete this activity, a child feeds each mouse the correct rhyming cookie. Reward efforts with…what else? Cookies!

## If You Give a Pig a Pancake

How do you lure your little piggies into learning about the letter *P?* With pancakes, of course! Read the list below and gather the necessary materials. As an extension to the story, fill a plastic squeeze bottle with pancake batter and have each child practice forming the letter *P* onto the griddle. Cook the pancake and place it on the child's plate. Then invite her to visit the topping bar stocked with edibles that begin with *P* (see the list below). After a few grunts and snorts, it's time to p-p-pig out on p-p-pancakes!

**Items Needed:**
griddle
cooking oil
spatula
pancake batter
plastic squeeze bottle
one plate per child
one fork per child

**any/all of the following toppings:**
pineapple
peanut butter
pears
peaches
pecans
peanuts
preserves
powdered sugar

# The Magnificent Jill Murphy

Jill Murphy has been an author and an illustrator for as long as she can remember. She credits her parents for her talents: her father passed on his artistic abilities, and her mother encouraged her to observe and write from age 3. Upon recalling her school days, Jill Murphy claims that she drove her teachers to distraction with her constant writing and drawing. Her persistence has brought such a gift to children's literature. Her fun, fictitious characters have true-to-life experiences. Her humorous, heartfelt writings have universal appeal. Jill Murphy weaves her unique style of writing and illustrating into stories that tenderly touch both heart and home. Thank you, Jill Murphy, for sharing your magnificent gift with us!

*by Mackie Rhodes*

## A Piece of Cake
### Published by Candlewick Press

Getting in shape is no piece of cake! But it takes a piece of cake to help Mrs. Large and her family realize that it's OK to be fat—because elephants are *meant* to be fat. Use this story to open a discussion with youngsters about the characteristics that make them just the way they are meant to be, such as hair color, eye color, skin tone, and height. Afterward, invite students to participate in this fun exercise. To prepare, cut out a class supply of construction paper cake slices. Program each cutout with a numeral from 1 to 10; then laminate each of them. Lay the cutouts on the floor in a large circle.

To play, turn on some lively music and instruct students to skip, dance, or hop around the circle. Stop the music and have each child stand beside a cake slice. Call out an exercise, such as jumping jacks or knee bends, and have the child perform the number of repetitions indicated on her cake slice. Continue play in this same manner until your students are feeling fit!

## Five Minutes' Peace
### Published by Paper Star

Just five minutes of peace. That's all Mrs. Large wants before she faces the demands of the day. But wherever she goes, she's trailed by the characteristic chaos of her three curious kids. After sharing the story, explain that occasionally everyone needs a little time for peace and quiet. Then ask each of your students to describe a peaceful activity he likes to do alone. Next invite each child to choose a quiet pastime such as assembling puzzles, reading, or drawing. Set a timer for five minutes and encourage each child to engage in his pastime until the bell rings. Consider repeating this idea as needed to help students refocus after other highly stimulating activities. Ah-h-h, peace!

## A Quiet Night In
Published by Candlewick Press

It's Mr. Large's birthday, and Mom and Dad have plans to quietly celebrate alone. While reading a bedtime story to the kids, *both* pooped parents drift off to sleep, leaving the three young elephants wide awake and eager to enjoy Dad's birthday dinner. Read this story aloud; then ask youngsters to share their experiences planning special surprises. Afterward, tell students that you need their help to plan a super special surprise—a class birthday party for themselves! Invite each child to create her own place card and chair decoration from craft items. On the appointed day, have her prepare her place at the table. Then serve each child a plateful of birthday goodies, sing a heartfelt round of "Happy Birthday to You," and enjoy a room full of beaming smiles.

## Peace at Last
Published by Dial Books for Young Readers

It's late and his family is asleep, but tired Mr. Bear is kept awake by night noises. After searching all around the house for a quiet place to sleep, he finally finds peace in his own bed—just as the alarm announces wake-up time! After reading this story, challenge students to sharpen their listening skills. Begin by explaining that noises are more noticeable when you are quiet and still. Then dim the lights and have youngsters pretend they are in bed getting ready to sleep.

Instruct students to carefully listen to the sounds around them. After several minutes, ask them to name the sounds they heard, and list their responses on chart paper. Then invite each child to add sounds she might hear at night while trying to sleep, such as animals, planes, or traffic. Extend the activity by asking each child to illustrate some of the sound sources mentioned. Then encourage her to demonstrate the sound created by each pictured item as she shares her drawings with the class.

## What Next, Baby Bear!
Published by Dial Books for Young Readers

It's a perfect evening for a trip to the moon, so Baby Bear dons his space helmet and packs his rocket with all the essentials. Then he travels up the chimney and out into space for an imaginary adventure that brings him back home just in time for his bath. After reading this story, invite youngsters to send their imaginations traveling through space. Provide each child with a sheet of black construction paper and a piece of white chalk. Ask him to illustrate his imaginary space view to resemble the white-on-black pages in the book. Invite each child to tell about his picture during group time; then display the pictures with the title "Out in Space."

**More Books by Jill Murphy**

***All in One Piece***
Published by Paper Star

**The Last Noo-Noo**
Published by Candlewick Press

237

# Cleverly Crafted by Mem Fox

What is it like to be as clever as a Fox? Mem Fox knows! This beloved Australian author has cleverly crafted a number of endearing tales that educate and entertain. Capture the imaginations of your students with these Fox tales and follow-up activities.

*by Mackie Rhodes*

## Possum Magic

Illustrated by Julie Vivas
Published by Harcourt Brace & Company

Grandma Poss's bush magic is wonderful—especially the magic that makes Hush invisible! But then Hush realizes that she can't see what she looks like. So she and Grandma Poss journey across Australia in search of the magic that will make Hush visible once again. After reading the story, use this center idea to give your youngsters an invisible ink experience. To prepare, stock your writing center with a set of Crayola® Color Changeables™ markers. Invite each child to visit the center and use the color change wand from the set to draw an invisible picture. Then direct him to make his picture visible by coloring over the drawing with a changeable marker. Encourage the child to continue to color over his drawing with a variety of markers and then observe the changes in his drawing. Now that's some possum magic!

## Koala Lou

Illustrated by Pamela Lofts
Published by Harcourt Brace & Company

Motivated by love for her mother, Koala Lou enters the Bush Olympics. As she trains, she eagerly anticipates winning and hearing her mother say, "Koala Lou, I DO love you!" Then the big day arrives— and Koala Lou comes in second. But in her disappointment, she discovers that she's still first in her mother's heart. After sharing this tale, have your students discuss the different ways their mothers or other caregivers show their love for them. Then have each child brainstorm something that she can do to express her love for this person. Program a heart cutout similar to the ones shown, complete the sentence with the child's dictation and then have her sign her name. Encourage each youngster to present her heart to a special grown-up and fulfill the promise written on it.

## Whoever You Are

Illustrated by Leslie Staub
Published by Harcourt Brace & Company

Beautiful, bold illustrations unite with a powerful message to help readers see that people all over the world are alike inside. Read the story; then use this activity to help youngsters understand that we all experience the same emotions. Provide each child with a large heart cutout. Send the heart home along with a note inviting parents to help their child cut out pictures of things that make him happy, sad, scared, and angry. After the child glues the pictures onto his heart, direct parents to label each picture with the corresponding emotion. Finally, have the child write his name on the back of the heart and bring it back to school. Collect the students' hearts; then, during circle time, show each child's heart without revealing whose it is. Discuss the pictures and emotions on the cutout and have the class guess which student made the heart. As an extension, mount each child's photograph onto a bulletin board; then staple his heart over the photo, as shown. Invite students to revisit the hearts, recall who made each one and then lift the heart to reveal the photograph.

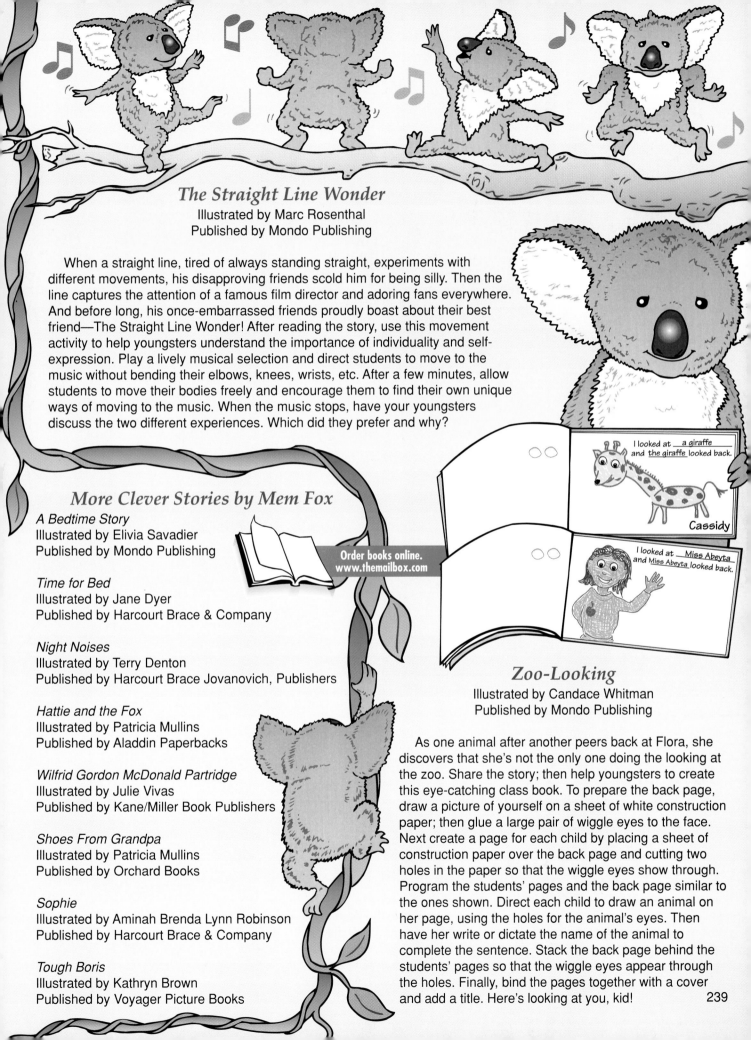

## The Straight Line Wonder
### Illustrated by Marc Rosenthal
### Published by Mondo Publishing

When a straight line, tired of always standing straight, experiments with different movements, his disapproving friends scold him for being silly. Then the line captures the attention of a famous film director and adoring fans everywhere. And before long, his once-embarrassed friends proudly boast about their best friend—The Straight Line Wonder! After reading the story, use this movement activity to help youngsters understand the importance of individuality and self-expression. Play a lively musical selection and direct students to move to the music without bending their elbows, knees, wrists, etc. After a few minutes, allow students to move their bodies freely and encourage them to find their own unique ways of moving to the music. When the music stops, have your youngsters discuss the two different experiences. Which did they prefer and why?

## More Clever Stories by Mem Fox

*A Bedtime Story*
Illustrated by Elivia Savadier
Published by Mondo Publishing

*Time for Bed*
Illustrated by Jane Dyer
Published by Harcourt Brace & Company

*Night Noises*
Illustrated by Terry Denton
Published by Harcourt Brace Jovanovich, Publishers

*Hattie and the Fox*
Illustrated by Patricia Mullins
Published by Aladdin Paperbacks

*Wilfrid Gordon McDonald Partridge*
Illustrated by Julie Vivas
Published by Kane/Miller Book Publishers

*Shoes From Grandpa*
Illustrated by Patricia Mullins
Published by Orchard Books

*Sophie*
Illustrated by Aminah Brenda Lynn Robinson
Published by Harcourt Brace & Company

*Tough Boris*
Illustrated by Kathryn Brown
Published by Voyager Picture Books

Order books online.
www.themailbox.com

I looked at ___a giraffe___
and ___the giraffe___ looked back.

Cassidy

I looked at ___Miss Abeyta___
and ___Miss Abeyta___ looked back.

## Zoo-Looking
### Illustrated by Candace Whitman
### Published by Mondo Publishing

As one animal after another peers back at Flora, she discovers that she's not the only one doing the looking at the zoo. Share the story; then help youngsters to create this eye-catching class book. To prepare the back page, draw a picture of yourself on a sheet of white construction paper; then glue a large pair of wiggle eyes to the face. Next create a page for each child by placing a sheet of construction paper over the back page and cutting two holes in the paper so that the wiggle eyes show through. Program the students' pages and the back page similar to the ones shown. Direct each child to draw an animal on her page, using the holes for the animal's eyes. Then have her write or dictate the name of the animal to complete the sentence. Stack the back page behind the students' pages so that the wiggle eyes appear through the holes. Finally, bind the pages together with a cover and add a title. Here's looking at you, kid!

239

# The Most Talented Bernard Most

He's a witty author and a creative illustrator. He's a gifted, dinosaur lover and an animal enthusiast. He's a known for his entertaining, educational books featuring award-winning professional. He's Bernard Most, best the works of Bernard Most with this collection of informa- dinosaurs and other animals. Introduce your children to tive, thought-provoking books and related activities. They'll soon agree that Bernard Most is *most* talented and that his books are *most* excellent fun!

*by Mackie Rhodes*

| Cock-a-doodle-*doo* | Cock-a-doodle-*moo* |
|---|---|

## Cock-a-doodle-moo!
### Published by Harcourt Brace & Company

*Laughter brightens the morning when a cow helps a voiceless rooster wake the farm tenants.*

After sharing the story, awaken your youngsters' smiles and counting skills with this "moo-velous" graphing activity. To prepare, label 20 rooster-shaped cutouts "cock-a-doodle-doo" and 20 cow-shaped cutouts "cock-a-doodle-moo." Shuffle the cutouts and place them facedown in a basket. Next divide a piece of chart paper in half vertically. Label one side "cock-a-doodle-doo" and the other "cock-a-doodle-moo." If desired, highlight the *doo* and the *moo* on each cutout and the chart as shown for easier decoding.

During group time, pick a child to draw a cutout from the basket. Have the remaining students pretend to be asleep. The child tapes his cutout to the appropriate column on the graph and either whispers "cock-a-doodle-doo" (the group remains sleeping) or loudly says "cock-a-doodle-moo" (the children wake up smiling). Continue the game in this manner until everyone has had a turn to pick a cutout. Then have children compare the graph's results.

## Z-Z-Zoink!
### Published by Harcourt Brace & Company

*Poor pig can't sleep because of loud snoring—his own snoring, that is! And neither can the rest of the farm animals. Who will let the pig sleep with them? Find out when you read this story aloud. After discovering the answer, invite youngsters to the block center to play this twist of a favorite memory game.*

This game is great practice for awakening children's visual memory skills. Have children work in pairs to build two animal pens from blocks; then place several farm animals inside the first pen. To play, one child takes three animals from the first pen and places them inside the second pen. The other child closes his eyes while his partner removes an animal from the second pen and says "Z-Z-Zoink!" The other child opens his eyes and guesses which animal has left the pen. Then the children switch roles and continue playing until interest wanes. Here a pig, there a pig!

## Dinosaur Cousins?

Published by Harcourt Brace
Jovanovich, Publishers

*This selection from the Most collection shows how closely related animals and dinosaurs seem to be in appearance and behavior. Are they cousins?*

Follow up a reading (see note below) of *Dinosaur Cousins?* with a discussion about popular family pets. Have other dinosaur books available for children to use as references and challenge them to find "cousins" for their pets (or other common animals) by comparing similar characteristics.

Extend the activity with a classroom family photo album containing child-illustrated pictures of pets paired with their dinosaur "relatives." Provide each child with two sheets of white construction paper. Have him illustrate a pet on one sheet and the dinosaur it resembles on the other sheet. Assist him in labeling each picture with the appropriate animal name. When each child's illustrations are complete, hole-punch the pet page along the right edge and the dinosaur page along the left edge. Stack the students' pages and bind them together between two construction paper covers so that when the book is opened, each child's set of pictures are side by side as shown. During a group reading, have each child share his pages from the picture album. Hmm, they look like cousins to me!

(Note: You may want to read only a few pages of this book to shorten the story according to your students' interest level.)

*Jeremy's bird*

*Avimimus Dinosaur*

## The Littlest Dinosaurs

Published by Harcourt Brace Jovanovich, Publishers

*In* The Littlest Dinosaurs, *Bernard Most thrills youngsters as he shows them that not every dinosaur is big. This humorous book focuses on dinosaurs that were small enough to measure with objects students easily recognize.*

Encourage family involvement by having parents relate measurement to children's everyday lives. Send home a copy of *The Littlest Dinosaurs,* a one-time-use camera, and a parent note explaining the activity. After reading the story together, have each parent photograph his child with one of the objects shown in the book and then return the camera to school. After the film is developed, display the photos. Then have students compare the photos to the book's illustrations to see who is bigger, the same size, or smaller than the dinosaurs mentioned in the story.

## If the Dinosaurs Came Back

Published by Harcourt Brace & Company

*After reading this lighthearted story, your little ones will wish that dinosaurs could return to the modern world to help them work and play.*

If the dinosaurs came back they could get my kitty out of the tree.
– Amanda

Place several colors of play dough in your art center along with a speech-bubble cutout for each child. Then pose the question, "How might dinosaurs help us at our jobs and in our play?" As each child visits the center, encourage her to create a dinosaur from play dough. When her sculpture is complete, write her name and her response to the question on a speech bubble. Display these projects so that children can share their dinosaurs with classmates and visitors.

## More From Bernard Most

*A Dinosaur Named After Me*
Published by Harcourt Brace Jovanovich, Publishers

*A Pair of Protoceratops* (See page 73 for an activity using this book.)
Published by Harcourt Brace & Company

*A Trio of Triceratops*
Published by Harcourt Brace & Company

*Happy Holidaysaurus!*
Published by Harcourt Brace Jovanovich, Publishers

*My Very Own Octopus*
Published by Harcourt Brace Jovanovich, Publishers

*Where to Look for a Dinosaur*
Published by Harcourt Brace Jovanovich, Publishers

*Zoodles*
Published by Harcourt Brace Jovanovich, Publishers

*Order books online.* www.themailbox.com

# Robert Kraus, Little Mouse, & More!

Meet Robert Kraus! He's the creator of that lovable little mouse and many other memorable characters. With gentle wit and humor, Robert Kraus coaxes young readers to identify with his characters and rejoice in the satisfactory—and often comical—story endings. Collect these Robert Kraus tales; then invite your youngsters to get to know (and love!) Robert Kraus, the little mouse, and more!

*ideas by Mackie Rhodes*

*(All books are illustrated by Jose Aruego & Ariane Dewey unless otherwise noted.)*

## Come Out and Play, Little Mouse
### Published by Mulberry Books

*Monday through Friday, little mouse resists the big bad cat's invitation to play. But on Saturday, his younger brother lacks the wisdom to do the same. Thank goodness for big brothers—and Sundays!*

After sharing this story, invite small groups to play a hide-and-seek game that reinforces the days of the week. To prepare, make seven construction paper copies of the mouse pattern on page 244. Color in details; then label each mouse with a different day of the week. Laminate the cutouts. To play, appoint one child from a group of eight (or fewer) students to be the Hider. Have the other students (Seekers) cover their eyes while the Hider hides the mouse cutouts around the room. Then encourage the Seekers to look for the mice and sequence them by the days of the week. When all the mice are arranged, have the Hider say, "Come out and play, little mouse." Have the Seekers chorally respond, "Not on Monday, Tuesday, Wednesday, Thursday, Friday, Saturday, *or* Sunday!" (The Hider's response? "Rats!") Appoint a different child to be the Hider and invite the group to play another round of this mousy hide-and-seek game.

## Where Are You Going, Little Mouse?
### Published by Greenwillow Books

*When the sad little mouse leaves home in search of a family that loves him, he soon discovers that he was loved all along!*

Before sharing this story, bring in a supply of Hershey's® Hugs® and Kisses® candies. Copy the rhyme on page 244 for the entire class, and cut out each one. Then duplicate the mouse pattern (page 244) onto a half sheet of construction paper for each child. After sharing the story, invite each child to create a mouse who is running *toward* home with a bag full of love.

To begin, invite each child to color and decorate her mouse. Then instruct her to glue a craft stick over the mouse's shoulder as shown. Have her wrap a few Hugs and Kisses candies in a piece of plastic wrap and tie it with ribbon. Help her punch a hole in the rhyme and tie it to one end of the ribbon. Finally, have her tape the candy bag near the end of the craft stick. Invite each child to "run away" to her home to present her family with this token of love.

Monday

Wednesday

Friday

242

## Whose Mouse Are You?

Illustrated by Jose Aruego
Published by Macmillan Publishing Company, Inc.

*To whom does little mouse belong? No one! Or so he thinks at the beginning of this book. But read on for a heartwarming conclusion!*

Before sharing this book, make a class supply of the mouse pattern (page 244) on construction paper. Also, program a page as shown; then make several copies for each child.

After sharing the story, help strengthen each child's family ties by inviting him to create a special book. To begin, ask him to illustrate each of his family members (or special friends) on a separate programmed page. Have him write or dictate to complete the sentence starter (similar to the language pattern in the book). Next, instruct him to color, decorate, and cut out the mouse pattern. Help each child punch a hole in the mouse and attach an 18-inch yarn tail. To make the book cover, use craft glue to secure a 4" x 5½" clear plastic pocket onto a sheet of construction paper (laminating film works well for this). Stack the pages behind the cover, punch a hole in the upper left corner, and tie the pages together with the end of the mouse's tail. Tuck the mouse into the pocket; then write the book title on the cover. When a child reads his book, have him remove the mouse from the pocket and place it on each page as he reads. Families will squeak with delight over this keepsake book!

## Herman the Helper

Published by Aladdin Paperbacks

*From the very first reading of this delightful book, your little ones will love Herman, a colorfully charming and subtly funny octopus helper.*

After sharing this book, use the following display to help build the trait of helpfulness in your youngsters. To begin, cut out a large, simple octopus shape from bulletin board paper. Draw on facial features; then attach the octopus to a board titled "Be a Helpful Herman!" When a child demonstrates helpfulness, invite her to cut out a construction paper shape that was featured in the story, such as a balloon, an *octagon,* or a shell. Write the child's name and helpful deed on the cutout; then tape a length of yarn to the back of it. Attach the free end of the yarn to an arm so that it appears as if the octopus is holding it. Let's fill all of Herman's hands with helpers!

**Note:** Depending on your children's abilities, you might like to precut a supply of just one shape, such as a balloon.

## Meet More Friends by Robert Kraus

*How Spider Saved Easter*
*How Spider Saved Thanksgiving*
*How Spider Saved Valentine's Day*
Illustrated by Robert Kraus
Published by Scholastic Inc.

*Leo the Late Bloomer*
Illustrated by Jose Aruego
Published by Windmill Books

*Little Louie the Baby Bloomer*
Published by HarperCollins Publishers, Inc.

*Strudwick: A Sheep in Wolf's Clothing*
Illustrated by Robert Kraus
Published by Viking

*Mort the Sport*
Illustrated by John Himmelman
Published by Orchard Books

Newest Release

Order books online. www.themailbox.com

# Patterns

## mouse

Use with *Come Out and Play, Little Mouse* and *Where Are You Going, Little Mouse?* on page 242 and *Whose Mouse Are You?* on page 243.

## rhyme

Use with *Where Are You Going, Little Mouse?* on page 242.

Dear Family,
My bag is packed with love for you,
And I know you love me, too!

Dear Family,
My bag is packed with love for you,
And I know you love me, too!

Dear Family,
My bag is packed with love for you,
And I know you love me, too!

Dear Family,
My bag is packed with love for you,
And I know you love me, too!

# WONDERS NEVER CEASE— SCIENCE ACTIVITIES

# Wonders Never Cease
## Simple Science for Young Children
# Making Changes

Have you heard it said that nobody likes change? Well, your classroom scientists will be the exception to that rule! Use the ideas in this unit, along with scientific-process skills, to explore change.

*ideas by Suzanne Moore*

**Objective:** Students will observe, record, and make predictions about changes.

**Vocabulary:** cause

## Read All About It

To introduce the topic of *changes*, share your choice of the books listed below. Ask children what changed in the book(s). Then encourage students to brainstorm a list of other changes they notice in their everyday lives. Write their ideas on chart paper. For added fun, write each item mentioned with a Changeables™ marker (made by Crayola®). Then offer the color changer marker to a child and ask him to trace over the original work. What happens? Change!

### Changes in Our Lives

- weather
- the sky
- clouds
- our ages
- the clock
- ice
- the trees
- water—gets hot and cold
- puppies
- the grass
- a cake if you bake it

*Changes, Changes*
By Pat Hutchins
(Aladdin Paperbacks)

*From Cow to Ice Cream\**
By Bertram T. Knight
(Children's Press)

*Strega Nona's Magic Lessons*
By Tomie dePaola
(Harcourt Brace & Company)

*\*Also in the Changes series: From Wax to Crayon, From Wheat to Pasta, and From Metal to Music.*

## The Building Blocks of Change

Provide a supply of blocks in front of your class. Select a small group of children to join you in the front. Have the remainder of the class close their eyes and begin counting aloud to 30. As the class counts, ask the children in the small group to work together to change the blocks in whatever way they'd like. When the class reaches 30, have the other children open their eyes and observe the blocks. Then ask the questions from "Three Questions." Repeat the process until every child has had a chance to be the *cause* of change.

### Three Questions
1. Do you see a difference?
2. What changed?
3. What caused the change?

Pam Crane

## Did You Know?

In a *physical change,* the original substance remains the same or can be recovered.

## Think About It

Prompt your youngsters to discuss the following questions in relation to the activity in "The Building Blocks of Change" on page 246.

1. Can the original substance (the blocks) be recovered?
2. What kind of change took place?

## Change Back!

Try this simple activity to illustrate another type of physical change. Give each child a paper cup half-filled with clean sand. Instruct each child to add a little water to his cup and use a spoon to gently mix it up. Ask and discuss the three questions from page 246. Then ask children if and how the original substance can be recovered (changed back). Encourage children to record their predictions and then try out their ideas (such as letting the mixture sit out overnight or spreading it out on a paper towel). What happens? Do they think this change was a *physical change?* Why?

## Foam on the Roam

You'll have everyone's attention with this small-group idea designed for scientific observation and loads of learning fun. In advance, cover a table with newspaper. Pour about a cup of vinegar into a bowl. Then give each child in the small group a clear plastic cup. Have each child scoop a tablespoon of baking soda into her cup. Ask each child what she thinks will happen if she adds vinegar to the baking soda. Then invite her to add one tablespoon of vinegar at a time to her cup. What happens? Ask and discuss the questions from page 246. Then ask the questions from "Think About It" on this page.

## Did You Know?

When two or more substances mix together and form a new substance, this is called a *chemical change.* You can't easily get the original substance back again.

# Wonders Never Cease
## Simple Science for Young Children

# Let the Water Out!

Parched for some simple science fun? These hands-on activities about dehydration are bubbling over with science discovery opportunities.

*ideas by Suzanne Moore*

**Objective:** Students will predict, observe, and record changes in foods that do and do not have water in them.

**Vocabulary:** dehydration

## Is It Soup Yet?

Soup's on! Or is it? In this activity, your little ones will discover for themselves the very important missing ingredient. Gather your children around; then empty four or five packets of dried soup mix into a large pot. (Adjust the number of packets needed according to the number of children in your class.) Then pass the pot around with a ladle in it. Ask your students if they'd like some soup. When you're met with their quizzical looks of disbelief, prompt youngsters to explain that the powder isn't soup yet. Guide them to determine the need for water. Then prepare the soup according to the package directions. As children sample the prepared soup, discuss the differences between the soup with and without water. *Now* it's soup!

**Did You Know?**
The powdered soup mix was *dehydrated*. That means that all the water was taken out of it.

| Defrosted | Dried |
| --- | --- |
| feels mushy | feels hard |
| green | white |
| bigger | smaller |
| same shape | same shape |
| It's drippy. | no water |

## Bean vs. Bean

Bean goes up against bean to give your students firsthand experience with dehydration concepts. You will need a bag of dried lima beans, a bag of frozen lima beans (thawed), a lima bean chart similar to the one shown, magnifying lenses, and a plastic plate for each child. Give each child a plate and ask her to take a few of each type of lima bean. Then encourage her to carefully examine each type of bean. Do the beans look the same? Feel the same? How are they alike and different? Are they ready to eat? Write student responses on the lima bean chart and discuss the results. Guide students to determine that the dried beans do not have water in them.

## Put That Back!

Ask your students if they think they can somehow get the water back into the dried lima beans. After discussing their ideas, immerse a handful of dried lima beans in a cup of water. Let them sit overnight and look for the results in the morning!

# Go Bananas!

Add a little graphing practice to your dehydration explorations with this banana activity. In advance, cut out a yellow banana for each child. Draw a two-column graph on chart paper. Title one column "fresh" and the other column "dehydrated." Then display a bunch of bananas and a bag of unlabeled banana chips. Ask your students to visually compare them, guiding students to state that the banana chips have been dehydrated. Then give each small group of children a couple bananas, banana chips, and plastic knives. Ask each group member to use his senses to examine the bananas. Then give each child a banana cutout. Have him write his name on the cutout and post it on the chart to indicate which type of banana he likes best.

| fresh | dehydrated |
|-------|------------|
| Sue | |
| Kim | Paul |
| Eric | Beth |
| Keith | Griffin |

# Just "Weight" and See

Mmmm—who doesn't love a big juicy bunch of grapes! Give each child a grape or two, prompting youngsters to note how juicy each grape is. What makes the juice? What would happen if the water was dried out of the grapes? Raisins!

After this introduction, arrange in a center a bunch of grapes, some raisins, a balance scale, one-inch blocks, and a class supply of the recording sheet on page 250. Encourage children to freely explore the weights of the grapes and raisins. Then guide them to complete page 250. Why do the raisins weigh so much less?

### Did You Know?

Raisins are made from seedless grapes. When the grapes are ripe, workers pick them and let them dry on clean paper trays next to the grapevines. The sun dries the grapes in about two to three weeks. It takes more than four pounds of grapes to make one pound of raisins!

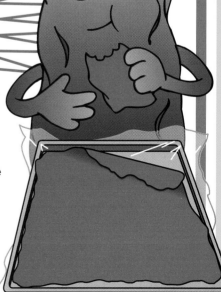

# Apple Leather

Culminate your study of dehydration with this sweet and chewy snack. Line a baking sheet with plastic wrap. Tint two cups of smooth applesauce with red coloring; then spread it thinly on the wrap. Ask your children to predict what will happen if you put the applesauce in a warm oven for several hours. Jot down their ideas; then find out! Bake the applesauce at 150° for six to eight hours. Remove the sheet when the applesauce looks like leather. While it cools, invite students to take a peek and discuss what they observe. When it is cool, peel the wrap off the leather. Roll it up; then cut it into bite-sized pieces. Tasty samples of science!

# Grapes and Raisins

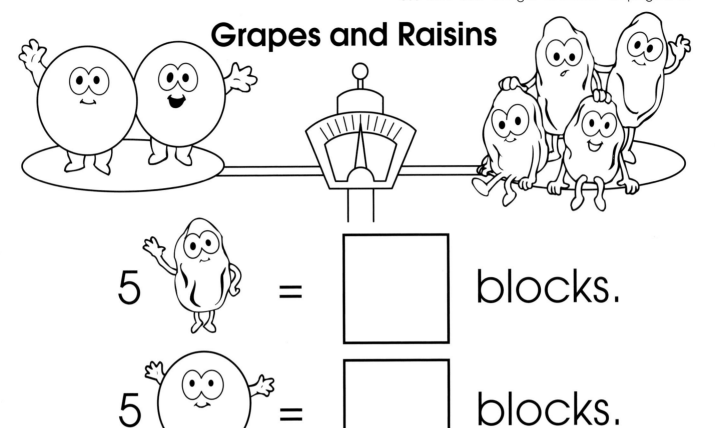

5 = ☐ blocks.

5 = ☐ blocks.

3 = ☐

10 = ☐

**Think:** Why do grapes weigh more than raisins?

# Wonders Never Cease
## Simple Science for Young Children

# Potato Power!

Dish up these "spud-tacular" activities and help your youngsters discover the wonders of potatoes.

*ideas by Alisa T. Daniel and Dr. Suzanne Moore*

**Objective:** Students will use scientific methods to explore the properties and characteristics of potatoes.

**Getting Ready:** To prepare for these studies, make a class supply of the parent note on page 253. Have each student color, cut out, and personalize his note. Then have him glue it to a paper lunch bag. Several days before you begin this unit, send a bag home with each child.

## One Potato, Two Potato

Introduce your class to potatoes with this activity that has youngsters observing, measuring, and collecting data. Have students sit in a circle on the floor with the potatoes they brought from home. (Be sure to keep a few extra spuds handy to replace any lost or forgotten potatoes.) Invite youngsters to examine the potatoes, describe them, and compare the different kinds. Inform children that a potato is a *tuber,* a short root that can sprout new plants from its *eyes.* Show students the eye of a potato; then have them find the eyes on their own potatoes. Next provide each child with a handful of Unifix® cubes and a copy of the data sheet on page 254. Direct her to examine her potato and complete the sheet. As an extension, stock a center with Unifix cubes, a supply of data sheets, and a variety of potatoes. Invite students to visit the center, examine the spuds, and record their findings on the sheets.

## Potato Pageant

Your youngsters will be primping their potatoes with this fun activity that sharpens observation and critical-thinking skills. To prepare for the Potato Pageant, make a class supply of blue construction paper ribbons. Then provide each child with a construction paper label similar to the one shown. Instruct the student to write her name across the label and then tape it to her potato. To begin the Potato Pageant, have each child show her potato to the class; then help students evaluate the potato and choose a winning category, such as "Largest Potato," "Smallest Potato," "Best Color," or "Cleanest Potato." Program a blue ribbon accordingly and present it to the proud potato owner!

**Did You Know?**
There are over 5,000 varieties of potatoes, all with different shapes, sizes, and colors.

# The Eyes Have It!

Use this experiment to demonstrate how a potato can nourish itself into a new plant. To begin, have students examine their potatoes and find the eyes. Label each child's potato or use the labels from "Potato Pageant" (on page 251). Place the potatoes in a warm, dark area. After about a week, the eyes will sprout roots and leaves. Remove the potatoes from the area and have each child examine her potato again. Discuss the changes that have occurred and guide students to the conclusion that the sprouts emerged from the eyes. Explain that the eyes of the potato are actually the seeds. The seeds received both nutrients and water from the potato, then sprouted into a plant. Wow! I don't believe my eyes!

**Did You Know?**
The eyes of a potato are actually the seeds! A potato contains all the nutrients and water needed for a seed to sprout. No planting necessary!

# Lightly Starched

Starch is the nutrient in a potato that feeds the new sprouts. How do we know that potatoes have starch? Use this simple experiment to help youngsters identify the starch in a potato. Provide each child with a sheet of black construction paper and a piece of a freshly cut, peeled potato. Direct him to use the potato to draw a picture on his paper. (Be sure to instruct youngsters to use a slight amount of pressure on the potato when drawing.) After a few minutes, the child's drawing will begin to appear in a white chalklike substance. Lead children to the conclusion that the chalklike substance is the starch from the potato!

# Tap Into a Tuber

In addition to containing nutrients for a new sprout, a potato also harbors its own water supply for a thirsty little seedling. Use this class experiment to extract a little water from a potato. To begin, use a spoon to dig a shallow hole in a potato. Place the potato in a bowl with the hole facing up. Fill the hole with salt; then cover the bowl with plastic wrap. Examine the potato after a day or two. The bowl will have a small amount of water in it. Where did that water come from? It came from the potato! To continue extracting water from the potato, pour out the water, spoon out the used salt, and then repeat the experiment.

**Did You Know?**
A potato is 80% water and 20% solid matter. The solid material is made up of about 85% starch and most of the rest is protein. Potatoes also contain many vitamins and minerals, such as iron, calcium, and vitamin C.

(Child's name)

**We love 'em mashed!
We love 'em fried!
People love 'em nationwide!**

**We love 'em baked
And as a snack!
Please send a potato
In this sack!**

Please send one potato of any
size or variety by

(Date)

Thank you!

(Teacher signature)

©1999 The Education Center, Inc.

---

(Child's name)

**We love 'em mashed!
We love 'em fried!
People love 'em nationwide!**

**We love 'em baked
And as a snack!
Please send a potato
In this sack!**

Please send one potato of any
size or variety by

(Date)

Thank you!

(Teacher signature)

©1999 The Education Center, Inc.

_____'s Potato

Draw and color.

My potato is

small

medium

large

Here is my potato.

I predict that my 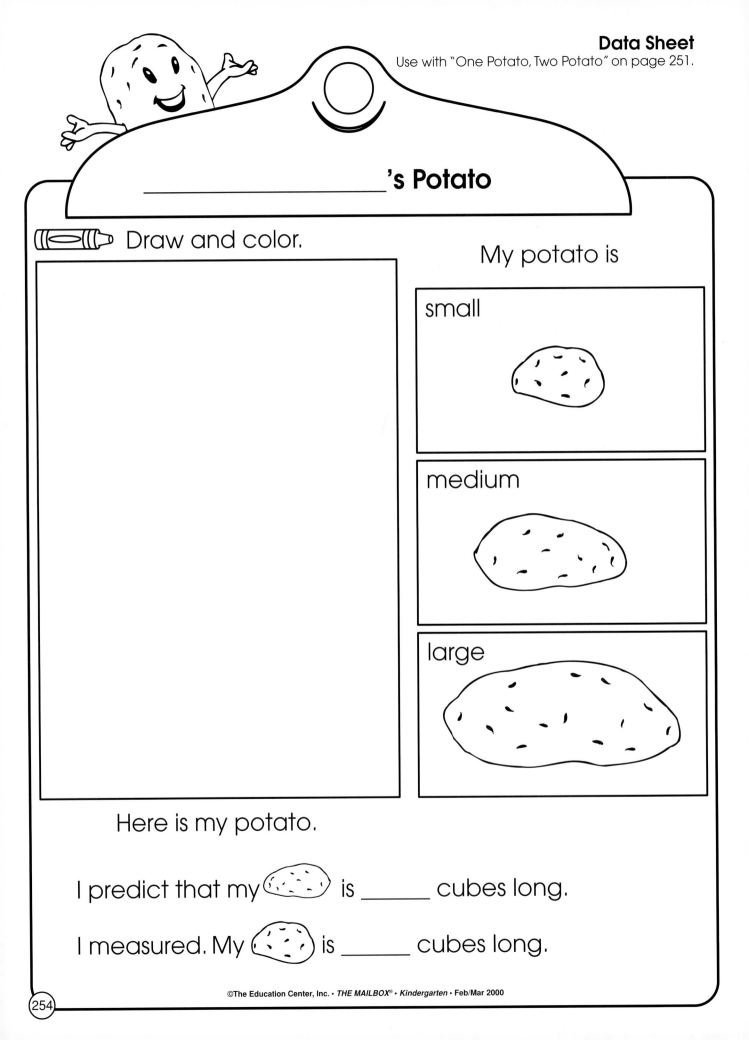 is _____ cubes long.

I measured. My 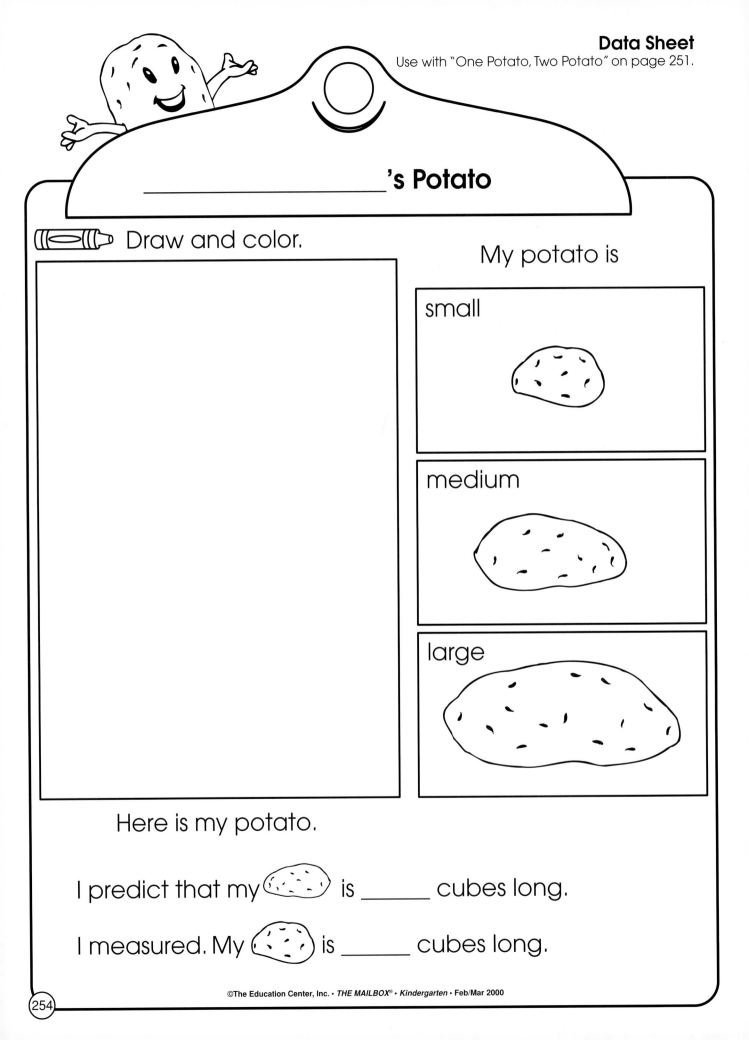 is _____ cubes long.

_____
(Child's name)

**We love 'em mashed!
We love 'em fried!
People love 'em nationwide!**

**We love 'em baked
And as a snack!
Please send a potato
In this sack!**

Please send one potato of any
size or variety by

_____
(Date)

Thank you!

_____
(Teacher signature)

©1999 The Education Center, Inc.

_____
(Child's name)

**We love 'em mashed!
We love 'em fried!
People love 'em nationwide!**

**We love 'em baked
And as a snack!
Please send a potato
In this sack!**

Please send one potato of any
size or variety by

_____
(Date)

Thank you!

_____
(Teacher signature)

©1999 The Education Center, Inc.

_____'s Potato

Draw and color.

My potato is

small

medium

large

Here is my potato.

I predict that my 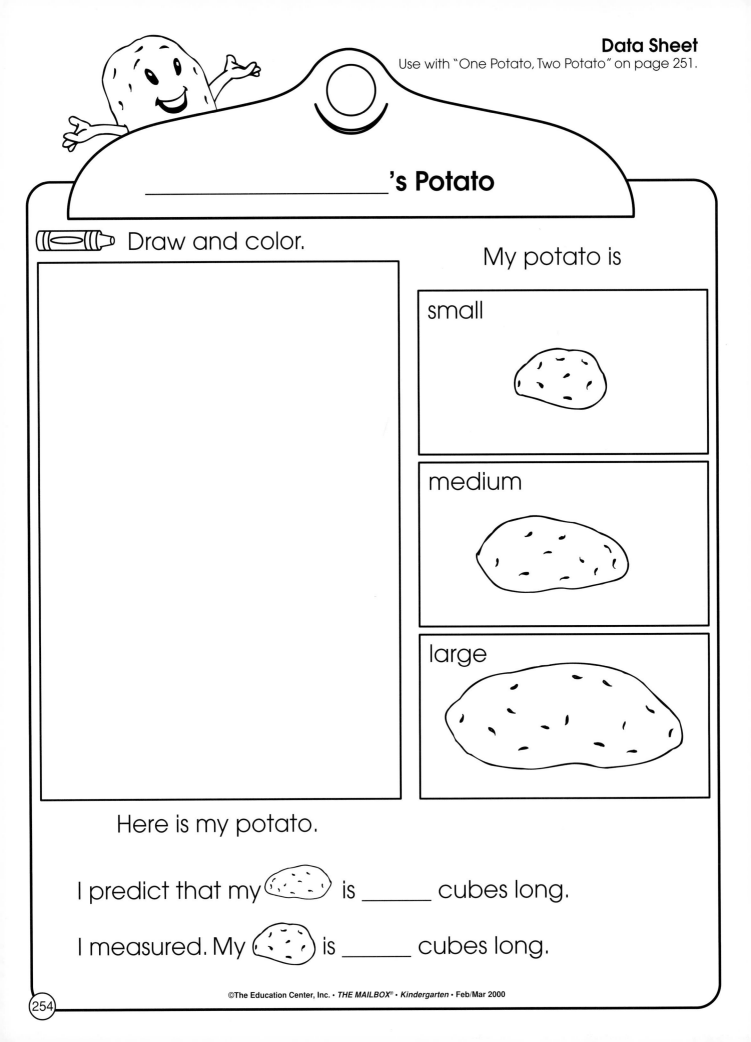 is _____ cubes long.

I measured. My is _____ cubes long.

# Wonders Never Cease

## Simple Science for Young Children

# Exploring Paper

Here's a pack of paper explorations hot off the press!

*ideas contributed by Suzanne Moore*

**Objective:** Students will explore the different properties of paper.

**Getting Ready:** To prepare for these studies, duplicate the parent note on page 258 for each child in your class. Several days before you begin this unit, send home a note with each child.

Dear Parent,
We are exploring all types of paper at school. Please help your child find a paper product from home and send it to school by _____ (date). We will use these products in a class display. Thank you for supporting your child's learning!
_____ (teacher)

## Paper, Paper Everywhere!

Begin your paper exploration with this circle-time activity and display idea. Gather youngsters together with the paper products they brought from home. Read *Paper, Paper Everywhere* by Gail Gibbons. Then have youngsters share their paper products with the class. Write the name of each product on a sheet of chart paper. Next mount a large paper tablecloth on a bulletin board. Then mount the chart on the tablecloth. Staple the students' paper products around the chart and then add a title. Display the board throughout your paper studies. As students discover other paper products, be sure to add them to the display. Paper *is* everywhere!

Paper, Paper!

cup
plate
hat
bag

| Paper | Predictions | Observations and Findings |
|---|---|---|
| Waxed Paper | | |
| Paper Towel | | |
| Toilet Paper | | |
| Construction Paper | | |
| Index Card | | |

## A Spoonful of Water

Will all types of paper soak up water? Set up this small-group activity and find out! In advance, gather a variety of types of paper—such as waxed paper, paper towels, toilet paper, construction paper, and index cards. Next program a chart similar to the one shown; then glue corresponding paper samples in the appropriate boxes.

Invite a small group of students to examine the various types of paper and predict which ones will absorb water. Write their predictions on the chart. Next have a child choose one type of paper. Place the paper on a tray and use an eyedropper to squeeze water onto the paper. Invite your students to carefully observe the paper and water. Did the paper absorb the water? Record students' findings and observations on the chart. When all of the paper samples have been tested, discuss youngsters' observations and findings.

### Did You Know?

Most writing paper contains a water-resistant substance to prevent ink from spreading across the page.

# Paper Blossoms

Writing papers resist water, but not all papers are water-resistant. Use this small-group activity to demonstrate how quickly some papers absorb water. To prepare, make a supply of construction paper flowers and cut them out. (See pattern on page 258.) Then make and cut out another supply of flowers on copier paper. Fold the petals of each flower as shown. Fill a plastic tub or bowl with water. Have youngsters examine the different flowers and predict what will happen when they are placed in the water. Then place a construction paper flower and a copier paper flower in the water as shown. The construction paper flower will open up quickly. The other flower will open slowly, if at all.

1.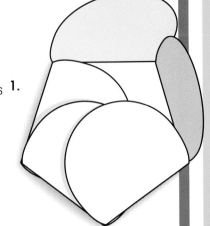

What happened? Most construction paper is not water-resistant. The paper absorbed the water, causing the petals to open. Copier paper is designed to resist water. Therefore, that flower opened slowly.

2. 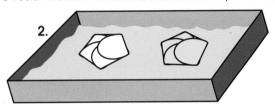   3.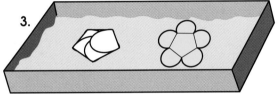

# Ahhh-choo!

Need a tissue? Facial tissues, toilet paper, and paper towels are some examples of highly absorbent paper. How do they absorb? Use this activity to uncover the secret ingredient! In advance, gather two small cups, a box of tissues, and a pencil. Fill one cup with water one-fourth inch below the rim. Then fill the second cup with tissues and count the number needed. Next have students predict how many tissues will fit inside the cup of water. Place one tissue in the cup and use the pencil to press the tissue to the bottom. Direct students to notice any air bubbles in the water. Continue adding tissues to the cup in this manner. When the cup is full, discuss the number of tissues needed to fill it. Students may be surprised to find that *more* tissues could fit inside the cup of water! How is that possible? Highly absorbent papers, like tissues, contain a lot of air. Pushing the tissue down in the water frees the air. Without air, there is a lot less tissue and more room in the cup! So what's the secret ingredient in highly absorbent paper? Air!

# Paper Power!

Use this activity to demonstrate how to make a sheet of paper stronger. To prepare, gather a set of blocks, a small paper cup, a sheet of construction paper, and a supply of pennies. Use the blocks and paper to form a bridge. Then place the cup in the middle of the paper. Have students predict how many pennies the paper will hold. Invite your little ones to count as you place pennies in the cup one at a time. Continue until the paper falls under the weight. Compare students' predictions to the actual results.

Next accordion-fold the same sheet of construction paper and place it back on the blocks as shown. Set the cup in the middle of the paper. Have students predict how many pennies the folded paper will hold and then repeat the experiment. The folded paper will hold more pennies! Why? The folds in the paper make it stiffer, allowing it to hold more weight.

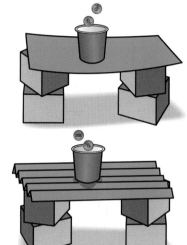

### Did You Know?
The accordion folds in corrugated cardboard boxes are designed to increase the strength of the box.

# Paper Matching

Stimulate youngsters' sense of touch with this unique matching game. To prepare, gather a variety of papers, such as corrugated cardboard, sandpaper, waxed paper, and paper towels. Next glue matching samples of paper onto pairs of index cards. Place the cards at a center along with a blindfold. To play, a child dons the blindfold and shuffles the cards. She then uses her sense of touch to find matching pairs. To check her work, the child removes the blindfold and looks at the cards.

# I Saw the Light

Shed light on classification skills with this center! To prepare, stock the area with a few flashlights and a variety of paper, such as tissue paper, heavy cardboard, and construction paper in a variety of colors. Invite each child to visit the area and examine the papers. Have her predict which ones will allow light to shine through. Direct her to point a flashlight toward the ceiling, place a piece of paper over the light, and then turn it on. Can she see the light through the paper? Or does the paper block the light? Direct the child to sort the papers by their ability to block light. After all of the papers are sorted, invite the child to discuss her findings with you.

## Parent Note
Use with "Getting Ready" on page 255.

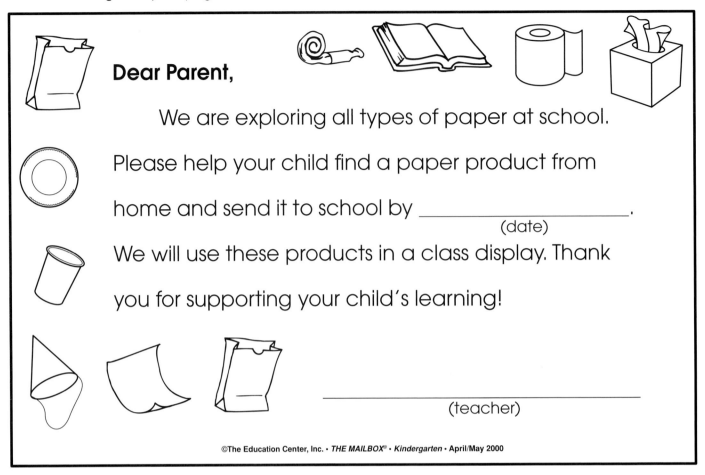

**Dear Parent,**

We are exploring all types of paper at school.

Please help your child find a paper product from

home and send it to school by _____.
(date)

We will use these products in a class display. Thank

you for supporting your child's learning!

_____
(teacher)

©The Education Center, Inc. • *THE MAILBOX® • Kindergarten •* April/May 2000

## Flower Pattern
Use with "Paper Blossoms" on page 256.

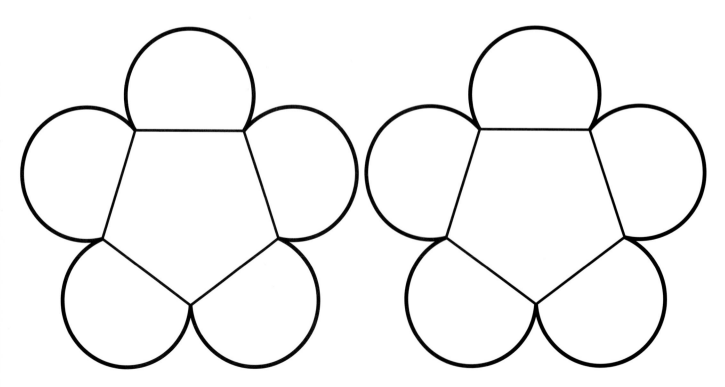

©The Education Center, Inc. • *THE MAILBOX® • Kindergarten •* April/May 2000

# Mix Masters

Give youngsters a taste of what it's like to be a chemist with these easy and safe experiments focusing on mixtures and solutions.

*ideas contributed by Suzanne Moore*

**Objectives:**
1. Students will learn that a *mixture* is formed when two or more substances are combined and no reaction occurs.
2. Students will learn that a *solution* is a type of mixture.
3. Students will learn that mixtures can be separated.

---

### Scientific Snack Mix

(makes 22 half-cup servings)
2 c. O-shaped cereal
12 oz. dry-roasted peanuts
2$^1/_2$ c. raisins (15-oz. box)
2 c. M&M's® candies

---

### Scientific Snacking

Shake up student interest in mixtures with this idea that mingles a tasty learning experience with observation and communication skills. To prepare, make a class supply of the sorting sheet on page 262. Then gather the ingredients for "Scientific Snack Mix" (shown), one gallon-sized resealable plastic bag, and one $^1/_2$-cup measuring cup. During circle time, have students predict what will happen when all of the snack mix ingredients are combined.

To make the mix, pour all of the ingredients into the plastic bag and seal it. Pass the bag around the group and encourage each child to help mix the ingredients by gently shaking the bag. Next, use the measuring cup to serve each child a half cup of the mix on his sorting sheet. Explain that the snack is a *mixture,* a combination of two or more things that, when combined, can still be separated into its original parts. To demonstrate this concept, have the child sort his mixture by ingredients and then mix them back together to create the new snack. After sorting and mixing, invite little ones to munch on the scientific mixture. Mmmm! Tasty!

---

### Salt-and-Pepper Mix-Up

Get your little scientists set for more mixing fun with this small-group project. To prepare, fill a small bowl with salt and a small bowl with pepper. Have students examine the salt and pepper and then predict what will happen when they are shaken together. Next, provide each child with a snack-sized resealable plastic bag; then have her place two spoonfuls each of salt and pepper into the bag. Help the child seal the bag; then direct her to vigorously shake the bag and mix the salt and pepper. Next, provide each child with a plastic magnifying glass and have her use it to examine the salt and pepper through the bag. Lead students to discover that bits of pepper can be seen through the salt. Guide your youngsters to conclude that the salt and pepper created a mixture. (If desired, save the salt-and-pepper mixtures to use in "Salt-and-Pepper Separation: The Sequel" on page 261.)

**Did You Know?**
When two materials mix thoroughly and evenly, a *homogeneous* mixture is created.

## A Scientific Solution

Use this small-group activity to introduce youngsters to the scientific concept of a *solution,* a special mixture that forms when one part *dissolves* in the other. To begin, provide each child in the group with a small clear plastic cup and a plastic spoon. Half-fill each cup with water; then have students predict what will happen if salt is added to the water. Next, invite each child to place one spoonful of salt into her cup. Direct the child to stir the water and salt thoroughly, remove the spoon, and observe the contents in the cup. Encourage youngsters to share their observations; then explain that the salt is still in the water, but it cannot be seen. The salt broke into tiny pieces in the water, or *dissolved,* and formed a solution.

| How Many Spoons of Salt? | |
|---|---|
| Predictions | Results |
| Alex        9 | ‖‖ | |
| Chuck    100 | |
| Lakesha   17 | |
| Tim         10 | |
| Stephen   30 | |
| Angie       50 | |

## How Much Salt?

Can an unlimited amount of salt be dissolved in water? Find out with this stirring science project. To prepare, fill a small clear plastic cup with water. Then have each student predict how many spoonfuls of salt will dissolve in the water. Record student predictions on a chart similar to the one shown. Next, add a spoonful of salt to the water and stir until the salt has completely dissolved. Then make a tally mark in the appropriate column on the chart. Continue adding salt and tallying until the salt no longer dissolves in the water. Explain that the water can dissolve only a certain amount of salt. When no more salt can be dissolved in the water, the solution is *saturated.* Finally, compare students' predictions to the actual number of spoonfuls needed to *saturate* the solution.

# Salt-and-Pepper Separation

Use this small-group activity to demonstrate a wild and woolly way to unmix a mixture! To begin, mix a small amount of salt and pepper on a sheet of paper. Show students a plastic comb and a piece of wool clothing. Have students brainstorm ways to use the comb and wool to separate the pepper from the salt. Next, quickly rub the comb over the wool several times and then hold the comb closely over the salt and pepper. The pepper will jump and stick to the comb! Amazing!

### This Is Why
Rubbing the comb against the wool created static electricity. The static electricity pulled the lightweight pepper bits to the comb, while the heavier pieces of salt remained on the paper.

# Salt-and-Pepper Separation: The Sequel

Use this activity to demonstrate another way to separate salt and pepper. To begin, provide each child with a salt-and-pepper mixture from "Salt-and-Pepper Mix-Up" on page 259. Invite your youngsters to examine their mixtures and predict what will happen when water is added to the salt and pepper. Next, provide each child with a small clear plastic cup and a craft stick. Help your little ones pour the salt and pepper into their cups; then half-fill their cups with water. Next, have students use their craft sticks to stir the water. Then have them remove the sticks and observe the contents in their cups. Your little ones will notice the pepper floating in the water. But where is the salt? Explain that the salt separated from the pepper and dissolved in the water. What a super separation!

# Mix and Munch

Top off your mixture studies by having youngsters mix up this sweet treat! To prepare, place each of the ingredients listed to the right in a separate bowl. Set the bowls at a center; then place the corresponding measuring cup or spoon beside each bowl. Add a class supply of plastic bowls and spoons to the center. Then invite each child to the center and have him follow the recipe to create a mouthwatering mixture.

### Cool and Sweet Fruit Mix
(makes 1 serving)

**Ingredients:**
$1/4$ c. bananas, peeled and sliced
$1/3$ c. canned fruit cocktail, drained
1 tbsp. mini marshmallows
$1/2$ tsp. orange juice concentrate

Place the ingredients in a bowl. Use a spoon to mix the ingredients together and then eat!

# Sort and Snack

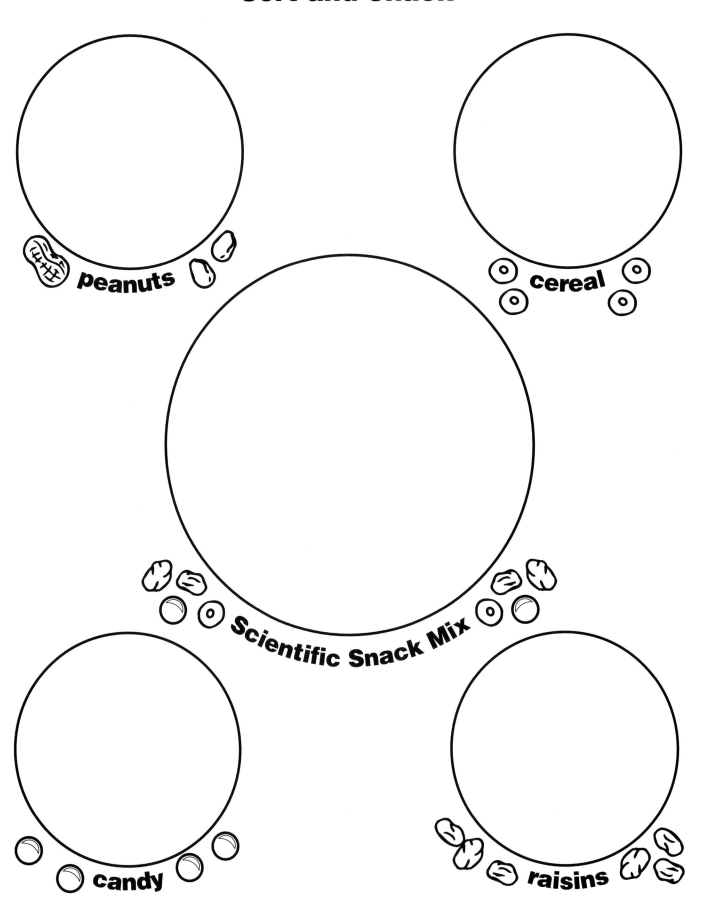

peanuts

cereal

Scientific Snack Mix

candy

raisins

**Note to the teacher:** Make a class supply of this sheet to use with "Scientific Snacking" on page 259.

# KINDERGARTEN CAFÉ

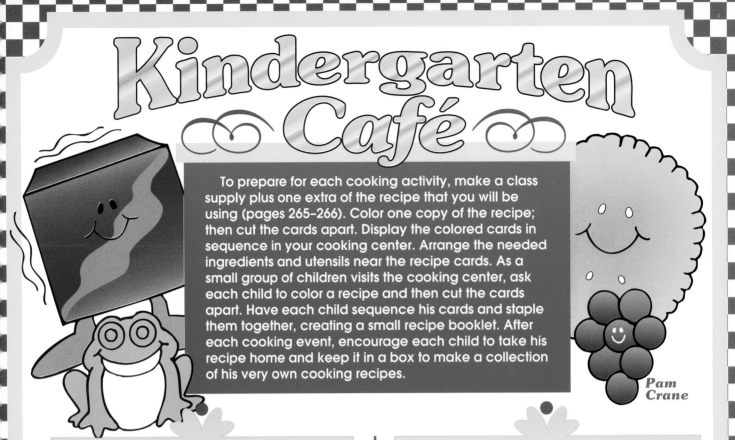

# Kindergarten Café

To prepare for each cooking activity, make a class supply plus one extra of the recipe that you will be using (pages 265–266). Color one copy of the recipe; then cut the cards apart. Display the colored cards in sequence in your cooking center. Arrange the needed ingredients and utensils near the recipe cards. As a small group of children visits the cooking center, ask each child to color a recipe and then cut the cards apart. Have each child sequence his cards and staple them together, creating a small recipe booklet. After each cooking event, encourage each child to take his recipe home and keep it in a box to make a collection of his very own cooking recipes.

Pam Crane

## Boo Blocks

**Ingredients for one:**
5 grape Jell-O® blocks
5 minimarshmallows (to represent ghosts)
5 orange Jell-O blocks
1 Gummy frog or insect

**Utensils and supplies:**
1 plastic cup per child
1 plastic spoon per child
2 serving spoons

**Teacher preparation:**
• Prepare grape- and orange-flavored Jell-O using the Jigglers® recipe. When the gelatin is firm, cut it into blocks. (The recipe on the box makes about 70 one-inch blocks.)
• Put each color of blocks in a separate bowl.
• Arrange the supplies and ingredients for easy student access.

Kim Bryhn
Kim's Day Care
Ettrick, WI

## Crunchy Cornucopias

**Ingredients for one:**
1 Ritz® cracker
peanut butter
1 Bugles® corn snack
6 fruit-shaped pieces of Trix® cereal

**Utensils and supplies:**
1 napkin per child
1 plastic knife

**Teacher preparation:**
• Arrange the supplies and ingredients for easy student access.

adapted from an idea by Jill Rich—Gr. K
West Elementary
Valley Center, KS

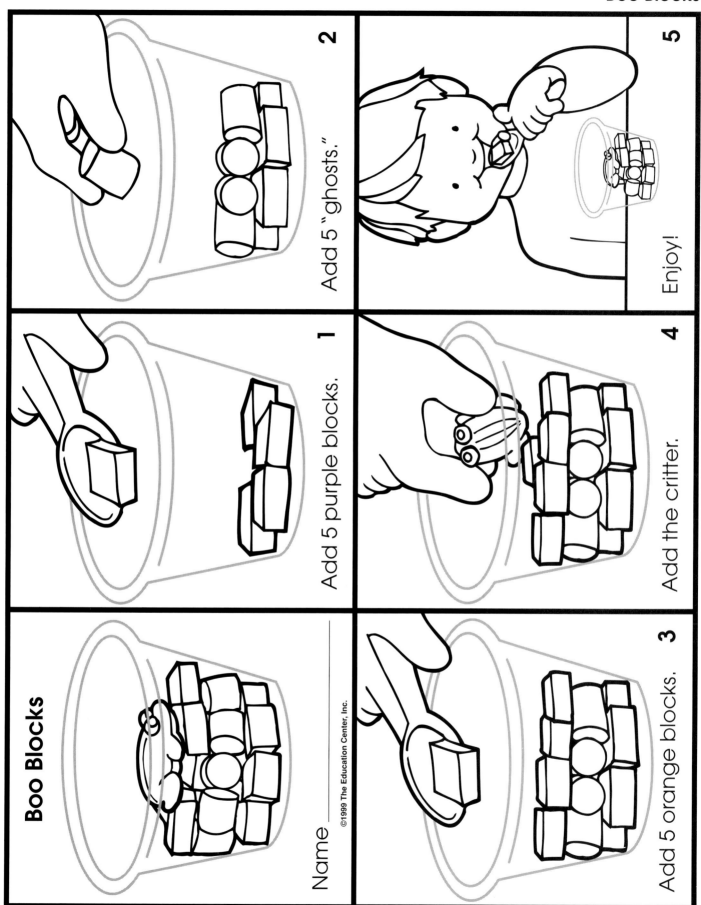

**2**

Add 5 "ghosts."

**5**

Enjoy!

**1**

Add 5 purple blocks.

**4**

Add the critter.

**Boo Blocks**

Name _____

**3**

Add 5 orange blocks.

**Recipe Cards**
**Crunchy Cornucopias**

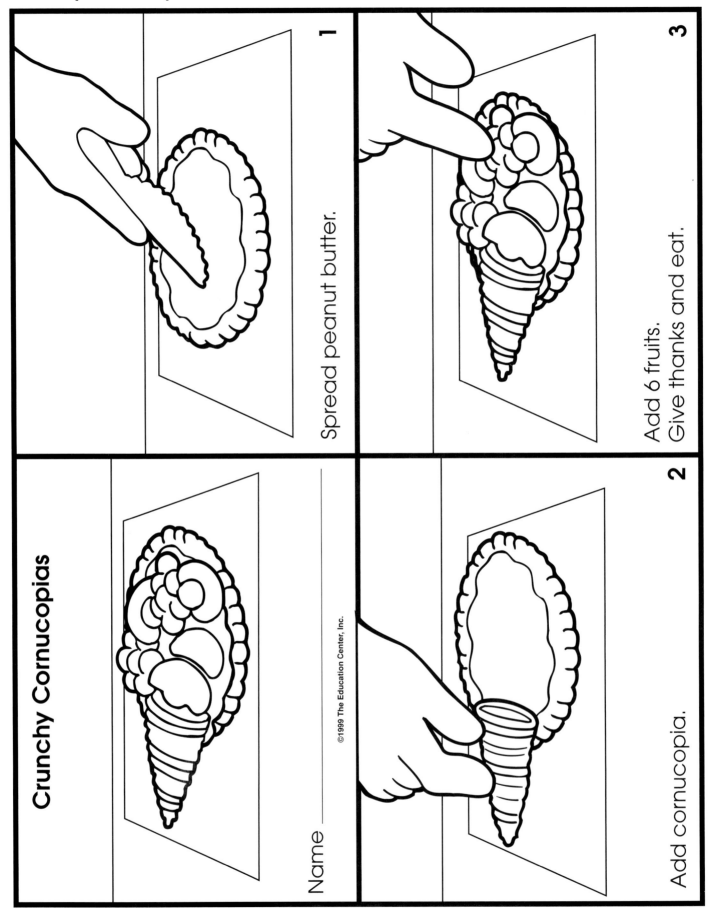

**1**

Spread peanut butter.

**3**

Add 6 fruits.
Give thanks and eat.

**Crunchy Cornucopias**

Name _____

©1999 The Education Center, Inc.

**2**

Add cornucopia.

# Kindergarten Café

To prepare for each cooking activity, duplicate a class supply plus one extra of the recipe (pages 268–269). Color one copy of the recipe; then cut the cards apart. Display the sequenced colored cards in your cooking center. Arrange the ingredients and utensils near the recipe cards. As a small group of children visits the cooking center, ask each child to color a recipe and cut the cards apart. Have him sequence his cards and staple them together, creating a recipe booklet. After each cooking event, encourage the child to take his recipe home and keep it in a box to make a collection of his very own cooking recipes.

*Pam Crane*

## Snazzy Snowman

### Ingredients for one:
| | |
|---|---|
| 3 round crackers | 1 carrot sliver |
| cream cheese | 2 pretzel sticks |
| 4 raisins | colored sugar |

### Utensils and supplies:
1 small plate per child    1 plastic knife

### Teacher preparation:
- Cut a 1¹/₂-inch carrot sliver for each child.
- Arrange the supplies and ingredients for easy student access.

Karen Knipe—Gr. K
Cape Horn Christian Academy
South Williamsport, PA

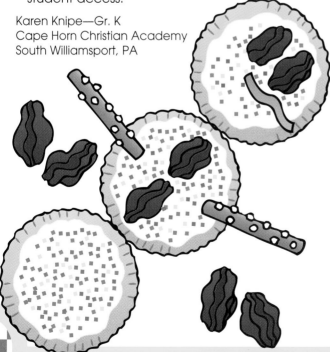

## Penguin Treat

### Ingredients for one:
| | |
|---|---|
| 1¹/₂ Oreo® cookies | 3 pieces of candy corn |
| 2 colored candies | white frosting |
| | (to attach body parts) |

### Utensils and supplies:
1 napkin per child
1 plastic knife (if frosting is not in a tube)

### Teacher preparation:
- For each child, break an Oreo® cookie half (preferably without the white filling) into two pieces.
- Arrange the supplies and ingredients for easy student access.

Susan A. DeRiso—Gr. K
Barrington, RI

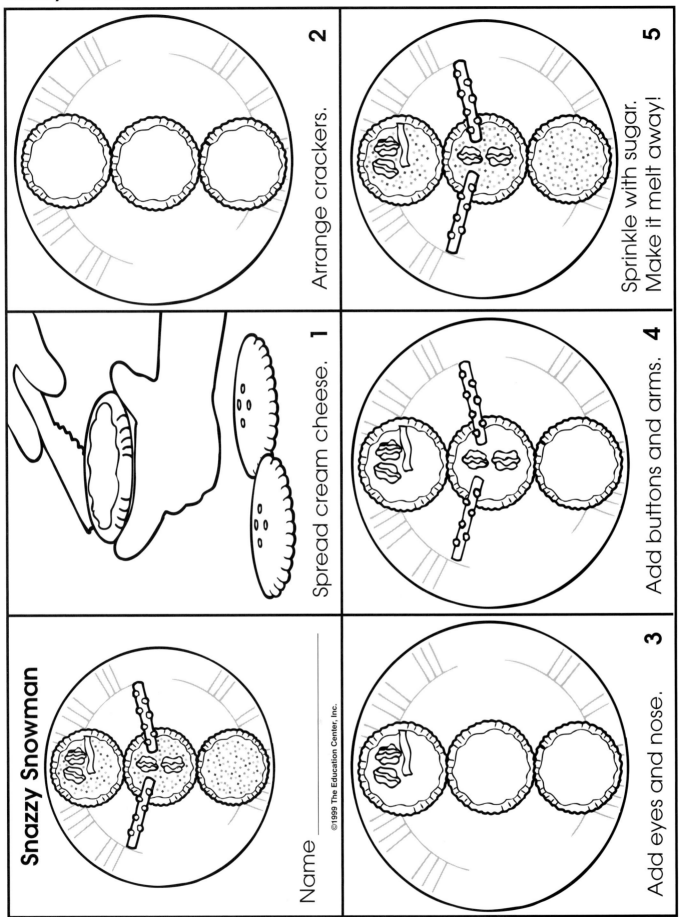

2

Arrange crackers.

5

Sprinkle with sugar.
Make it melt away!

1

Spread cream cheese.

4

Add buttons and arms.

**Snazzy Snowman**

Name _____

©1999 The Education Center, Inc.

3

Add eyes and nose.

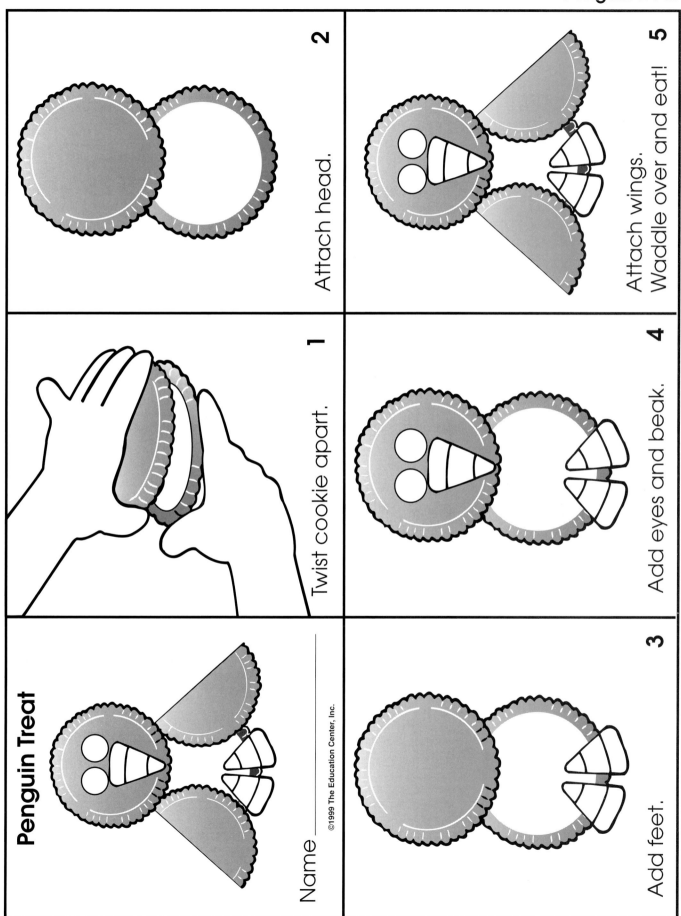

**2**

Attach head.

**5**

Attach wings.
Waddle over and eat!

**Penguin Treat**

**1**

Twist cookie apart.

**4**

Add eyes and beak.

Name _____

©1999 The Education Center, Inc.

**3**

Add feet.

# Kindergarten Café

To prepare for each cooking activity, make a class supply plus one extra of the recipe (pages 271–272). Color one copy of the recipe; then cut the cards apart. Display the sequenced colored cards in your cooking center. Arrange the ingredients and utensils near the recipe cards. As a small group of children visits the cooking center, ask each child to color a recipe and cut the cards apart. Have him sequence his cards and staple them together, creating a recipe booklet. After each cooking event, encourage the child to take his recipe home and keep it in a box to make a collection of his very own cooking recipes.

## Mama Mia's Pizza

**Ingredients for one:**
1 English muffin
pizza sauce
1 slice of mozzarella cheese

**Utensils and supplies:**
toaster oven
1 heart-shaped cookie cutter
1 spoon

**Teacher preparation:**
- Arrange the supplies and ingredients for easy student access.
- If needed, assist with unwrapping cheese slices.
- Plan for adult supervision at the toaster oven.

## Rainbow and Treasure Treat

**Ingredients for one:**
1 graham cracker                yellow decorating
marshmallow creme              sugar
1/2 of a chocolate cookie       M&M's® candies

**Utensils and supplies:**
1 napkin per child
1 plastic knife

**Teacher preparation:**
- Break chocolate cookies in half.
- Arrange the supplies and ingredients for easy student access.

Karen Knipe—Gr. K
Cape Horn Christian Academy
South Williamsport, PA

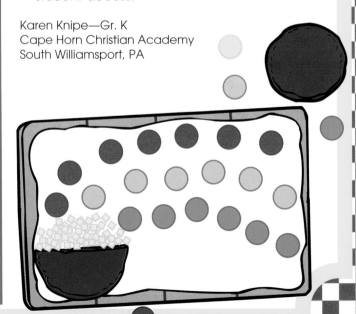

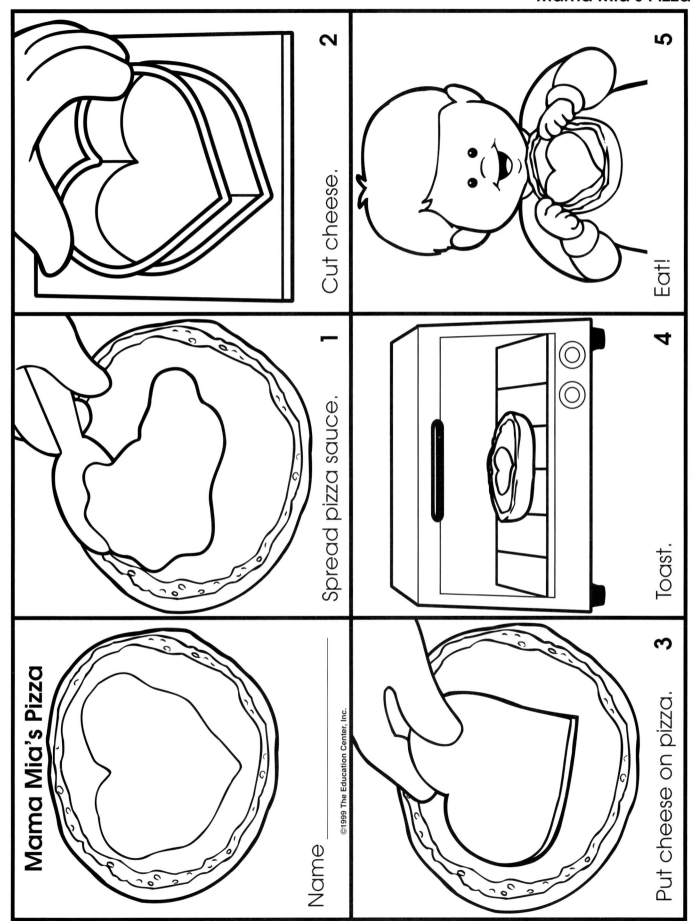

2

Cut cheese.

5

Eat!

1

Spread pizza sauce.

4

Toast.

**Mama Mia's Pizza**

Name _____

©1999 The Education Center, Inc.

3

Put cheese on pizza.

# Recipe Cards
## Rainbow and Treasure Treat

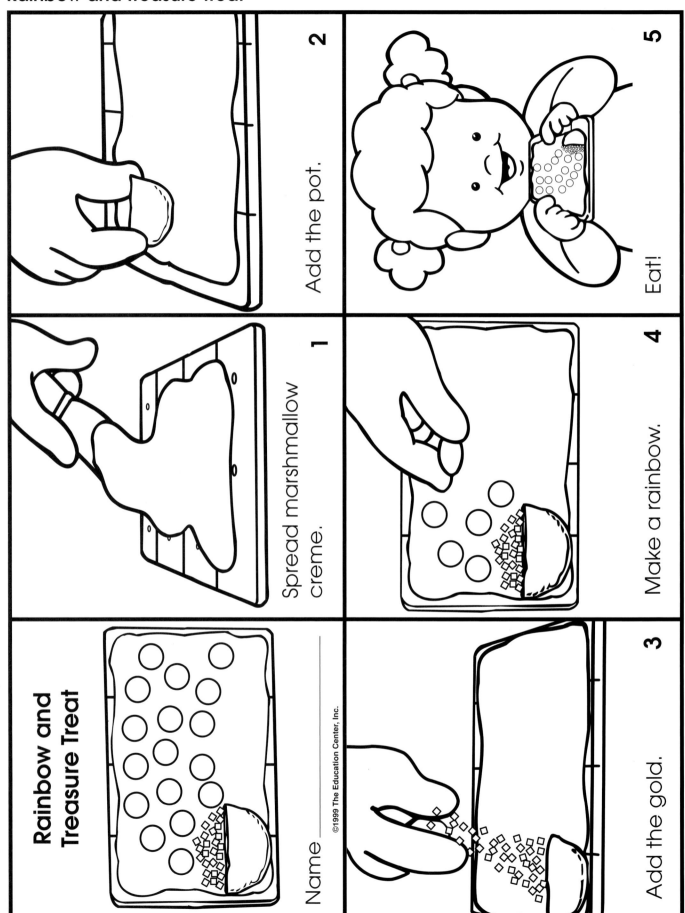

**2**

Add the pot.

**5**

Eat!

**1**

Spread marshmallow creme.

**4**

Make a rainbow.

Name _____

Rainbow and Treasure Treat

**3**

Add the gold.

©1999 The Education Center, Inc.

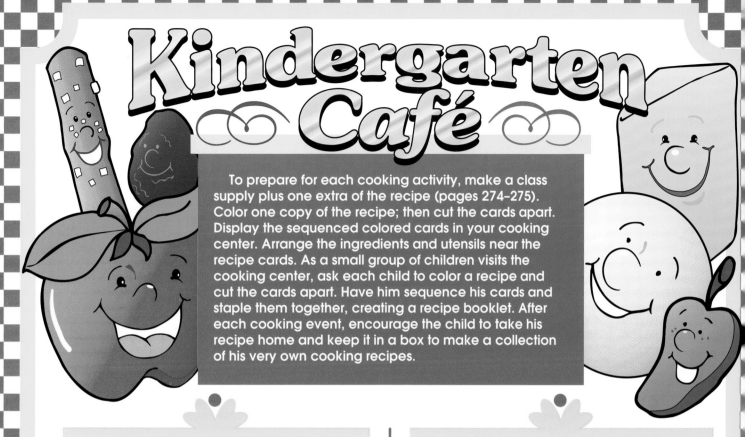

# Kindergarten Café

To prepare for each cooking activity, make a class supply plus one extra of the recipe (pages 274–275). Color one copy of the recipe; then cut the cards apart. Display the sequenced colored cards in your cooking center. Arrange the ingredients and utensils near the recipe cards. As a small group of children visits the cooking center, ask each child to color a recipe and cut the cards apart. Have him sequence his cards and staple them together, creating a recipe booklet. After each cooking event, encourage the child to take his recipe home and keep it in a box to make a collection of his very own cooking recipes.

## Luscious Ladybug

**Ingredients for one:**
$^{1}/_{2}$ red apple
lemon juice or lemon-lime soda
1 chocolate malted milk ball
peanut butter
7 raisins
6 pretzel sticks

**Utensils and supplies:**
1 plastic knife per child
napkins

**Teacher Preparation:**
Cut apples in half. Rub the cut sides with lemon juice or lemon-lime soda to prevent browning. Arrange the supplies and ingredients for easy student access.

Jennifer Barton—Gr. K
Elizabeth Green School
Newington, CT

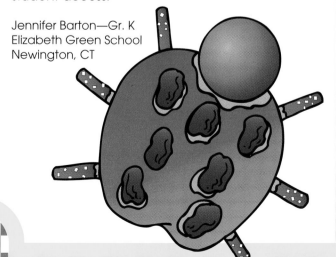

## Cinco de Mayo Snack

**Ingredients for one:**
1 flour tortilla
shredded cheese
mild salsa

**Utensils and supplies:**
1 star-shaped cookie cutter (a metal one works best)
toaster oven
1 spoon
1 paper plate per child
napkins

**Teacher Preparation:**
Arrange the supplies and utensils for easy student access. Provide for adult supervision when using the toaster oven.

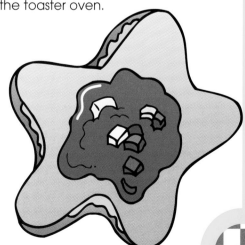

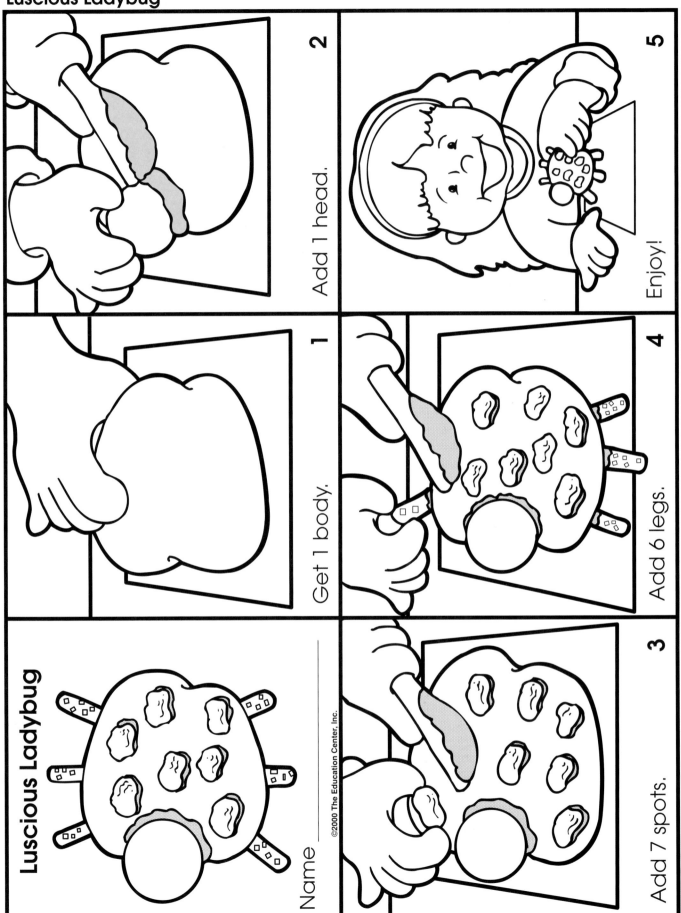

**Luscious Ladybug**

Name _____

2

Add 1 head.

1

Get 1 body.

5

Enjoy!

4

Add 6 legs.

3

Add 7 spots.

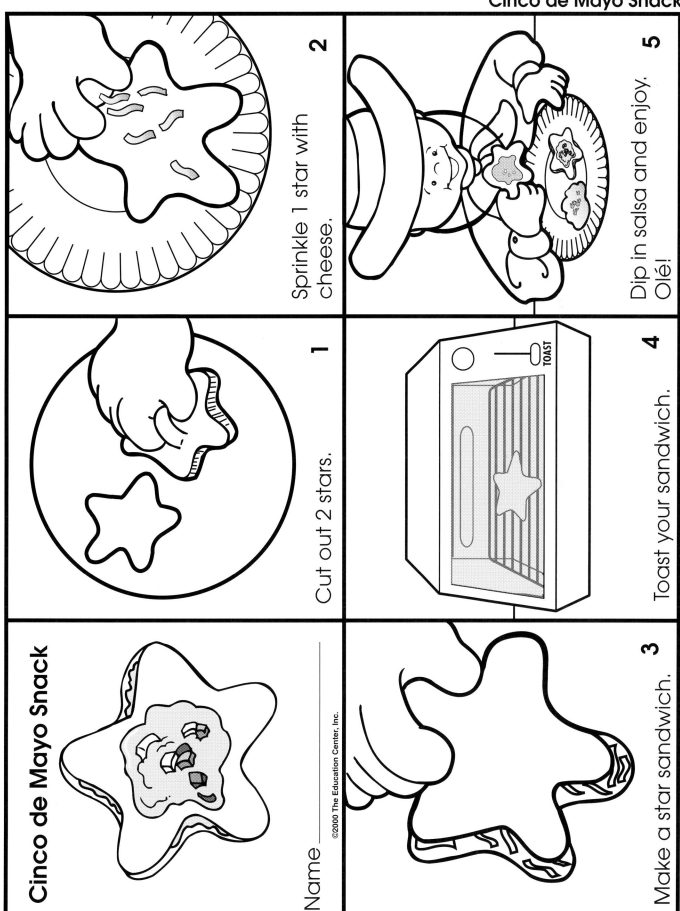

**2**

Sprinkle 1 star with cheese.

**5**

Dip in salsa and enjoy. Olé!

**1**

Cut out 2 stars.

**4**

Toast your sandwich.

# Cinco de Mayo Snack

Name _____

**3**

Make a star sandwich.

# Kindergarten Café

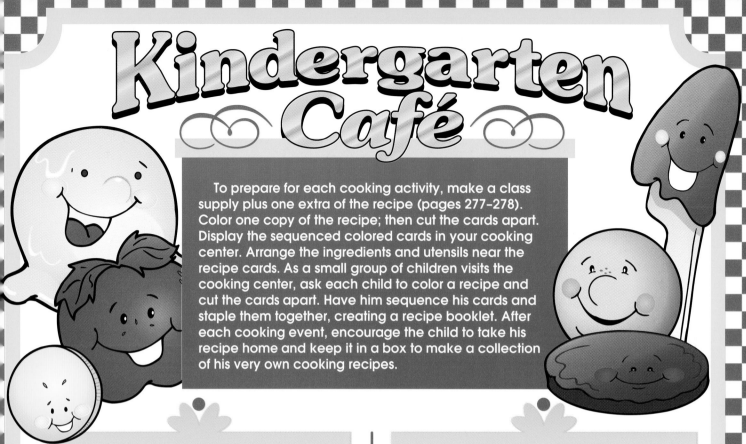

To prepare for each cooking activity, make a class supply plus one extra of the recipe (pages 277–278). Color one copy of the recipe; then cut the cards apart. Display the sequenced colored cards in your cooking center. Arrange the ingredients and utensils near the recipe cards. As a small group of children visits the cooking center, ask each child to color a recipe and cut the cards apart. Have him sequence his cards and staple them together, creating a recipe booklet. After each cooking event, encourage the child to take his recipe home and keep it in a box to make a collection of his very own cooking recipes.

## Chocolatey Fruity Smoothie

**Ingredients for one:**
2 slices of banana
3 strawberries
1 scoop of vanilla ice cream
1/2 c. milk
1 squirt of chocolate syrup

**Utensils and supplies:**
ice-cream scoop
blender
1/2-c. measuring cup
one cup per child
one straw per child

**Teacher preparation:**
- Peel and slice bananas.
- Wash strawberries and remove caps.
- Arrange the supplies and ingredients for easy student access.
- Plan for adult supervision with the blender.

Michelle Myers
Pre-K and Gr. K
Tutor Time Learning Center
Bradenton, FL

## Burger Cookie

**Ingredients for one:**
2 vanilla wafers (buns)
1 chocolate mint patty (burger)
green-tinted coconut (lettuce)
yellow-tinted frosting (mustard)
red-tinted frosting (ketchup)

**Utensils and supplies:**
1 napkin per child
2 plastic knives

**Teacher preparation:**
- Use food coloring to tint coconut and frosting.
- Arrange the supplies and ingredients for easy student access.

Susan Bunyan—Gr. K
Linn Elementary
Dodge City, KS

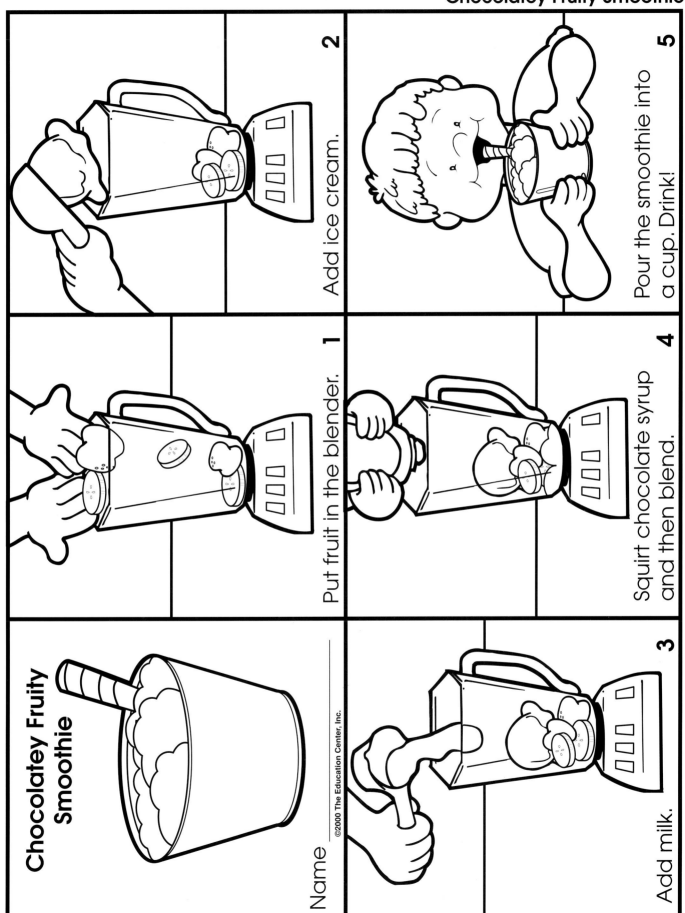

**2** Add ice cream.

**5** Pour the smoothie into a cup. Drink!

**1** Put fruit in the blender.

**4** Squirt chocolate syrup and then blend.

**Chocolatey Fruity Smoothie**

Name

©2000 The Education Center, Inc.

**3** Add milk.

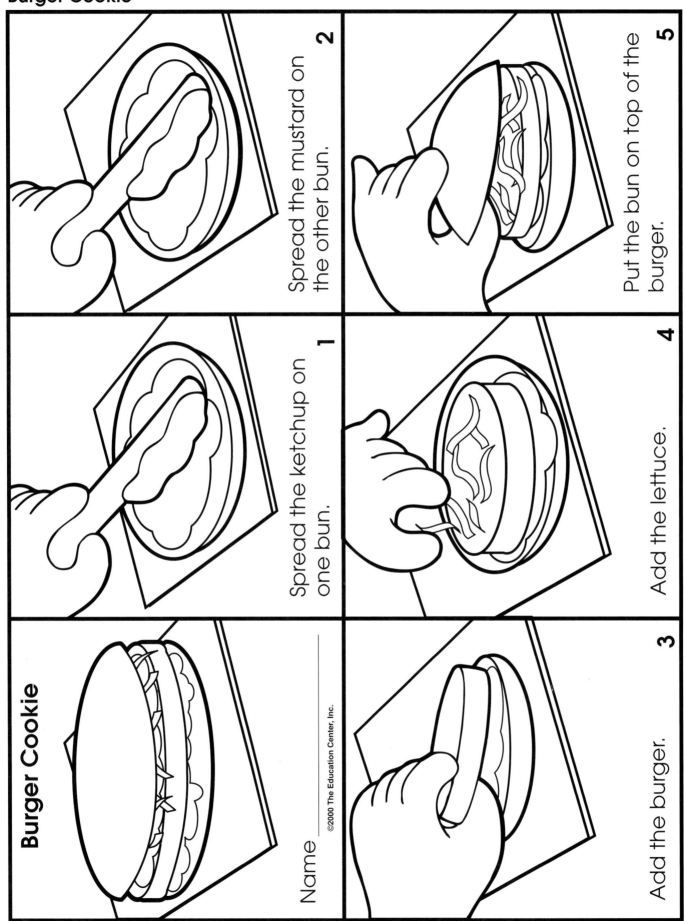

**Burger Cookie**

Name _____

1. Spread the ketchup on one bun.

2. Spread the mustard on the other bun.

3. Add the burger.

4. Add the lettuce.

5. Put the bun on top of the burger.

# Fingerplays, Poems, Songs, & Rhymes

## Columbus Day March

Left, right, left, right! Your youngsters will enjoy marching to the beat while singing this catchy verse about Christopher Columbus. For added fun, start out singing the song slowly and then pick up speed with each repetition.

*(sung to the tune of "The Ants Go Marching")*

Columbus sailed the ocean blue—hurrah, hurrah!
He sailed in 1492—hurrah, hurrah!
Columbus sailed the ocean blue.
He sailed in 1492.
He had hoped to reach the east,
    sailing west.
Oh, he tried his best,
On–his–quest!

adapted from an idea by
June M. Ray—Librarian
Henry A. Malley Memorial Library
Broadus, MT

## Thanksgiving Colors

Are you ready for *the* meal of the year? Here's a poem that builds excitement and reviews color words, as well. Use the poem's pattern as a springboard for creating additional verses with other typical (or not so typical) Thanksgiving dishes. Gobble, gobble!

Orange is the pumpkin.
Yellow is the corn.
Brown is the turkey,
With stuffing to adorn.

Red are the cranberries.
Green are the beans.
Five delicious colors—
In a feast of my dreams.

Happy Thanksgiving!

adapted from an idea by
Jeanene Engelhardt—Gr. K
Workman Avenue School
Covina, CA

## Watch Out!

It's that time of year—ghosts and ghouls are lurking and searching for that big scare. Teach your little goblins this song and the accompanying motions. It's sure to turn those "ghasps" into "ghrins"!

*(sung to the tune of "Santa Claus Is Coming to Town")*

You'd better watch out! You'd better beware!
You'd better believe you're in for a scare!
Halloween is coming tonight!

*Point and shake finger.*
*Shiver.*
*Look wide-eyed.*

Pumpkins aglow with snaggletoothed grins.
Skeletons jump right out of their skins.
Halloween is coming tonight!

*Point to teeth.*
*Jump with arms out.*
*Look wide-eyed.*

Spooky, cackling witches are stirring up their brew.
Mean-faced, green-faced Frankensteins are coming after you!
BOO!

*Stir with fists.*
*Walk stiff-legged.*
*Throw up hands.*

*Repeat first stanza to end the song.*

Diane ZuHone Shore—Gr. K
Marietta, GA

# Fingerplays, Poems, Songs, & Rhymes

## Surprise!
Delight little ones with this fun poem that bursts with springtime enthusiasm. When your students are familiar with the poem, have them recite it as they creatively act it out. Or, introduce the sign language for *butterfly* (see the illustration to the right). Then encourage children to dramatize the poem with their hands, ending with the butterfly sign.

I am a little caterpillar.
In my cocoon, I go to sleep.
And I won't move about for days.
You won't hear a single peep.
But I know I'll surprise you soon.
And do you know just why?
When the time is right for me,
I'll be a butterfly!

adapted from an idea by Patricia McIntyre—Gr. K
Beechwood on the Bay, Quincy, MA

*Oh, when my mom tucks me in bed...*

## Oh, When My Mom...
Moms and children will all feel special when you sing this Mother's Day song. Each time you repeat the song, ask a different child to supply a phrase to fill in the blank.

*(sung to the tune of "When the Saints Go Marching In")*

Oh, when my mom [gives me a hug],
Oh, when my mom [gives me a hug],
Oh, I know that I am special,
When my mom [gives me a hug].

Trish Draper—Gr. K, Millarville Community School
Millarville, Alberta, Canada

## A Planting Plan
Get all hands moving with this little ditty that reinforces the whole planting procedure.

*(sung to the tune of "The Hokey Pokey")*

You scoop the soil in.
You pick the rocks out.
You poke the seed in,
And you pat it all about.
You add a little water
And you wait for it to sprout.
That's what it's all about!

Debra Kujawski—Gr. K, Southold UFSO, Southold, NY

# Fingerplays, Poems, Songs, & Rhymes

## The Itsy-Bitsy Band

This delightfully simple version of "The Itsy-Bitsy Spider" is perfect for an end-of-the-year program. Give each child one of the specified rhythm instruments and have him play on cue as the class sings this classic song. To help little ones practice, print the poem on chart paper and draw the instruments next to each line.

The itsy-bitsy spider climbed up the waterspout.  
Down came the rain and washed the spider out.  
Out came the sun and dried up all the rain,  
And the itsy-bitsy spider climbed up the spout again.

*Tap rhythm sticks.*  
*Play rainstick; then clap cymbals on "out."*  
*Shake jingle bells.*  
*Tap rhythm sticks.*

Stacey Mitchell—Gr. K  
Valley View Elementary School  
Los Angeles, CA

## Terrific Transitions

Need a new transition for those last few weeks of school? Try this tune! Simply insert the activity that's coming up and the desired action to make other verses.

*(sung to the tune of "If You're Happy and You Know It")*

If you're [ready to go outside], [pick up your toys].  
If you're [ready to go outside], [pick up your toys].  
If you're [ready to go outside],  
If you're [ready to go outside],  
If you're [ready to go outside], [pick up your toys].

If desired, sing the verse a second time, requesting another action on your students' part:

If you're [ready to go outside], [please line up].  
If you're [ready to go outside], [please line up].  
If you're [ready to go outside],  
If you're [ready to go outside],  
If you're [ready to go outside], [please line up].

Bonnie Elizabeth Vontz—Gr. K  
Cheshire Country Day School  
Milldale, CT

## Grand Ol' Dad

If you're planning a grand celebration for Father's Day, include this spirited song!

*(sung to the tune of "Grand Old Flag")*

You're a grand ol' dad!  
You're a great guy, dear dad!  
And forever in my heart you'll stay.  
I love you so! Oh, don't you know?  
I wish you Happy Father's Day!

Oh, my heart beats true,  
Yes, I really love you!  
And forever in my heart you'll stay.  
I love you so! Oh, don't you know?  
You're really a grand ol' dad!

adapted from an idea by Pam Fostano and  
 Lisa Friesen—Gr. K  
West Avenue School  
Hilton, NY

# Getting Your Ducks in a Row— Management Tips

# Getting Your Ducks in a Row
## Management Tips for the Classroom

### Half-Pints of Paint

If your classroom sink is constantly filled with paint cups that need washing, then this tip is for you! Open the top of an empty half-pint milk carton; then fill the carton with paint. Keep the paint fresh for weeks by using a clothespin to close the carton when not in use. When the carton is empty, simply toss it in the trash can. You'll never wash paint cups again!

Carole Tobisch—Gr. K, Denmark Early Childhood Center
Denmark, WI

### Flag 'em In

Here's a high-flying alternative to blowing a whistle at the end of recess: Wave a special class flag! As each student notices the flag, she tells another child until all are lined up and ready to go. Add motivation to this process by allowing the first child to arrive to hold the flag. For more flag-watching incentive, have students help create the class flag by using fabric paint to make student handprints on a sheet of fabric. Sew a pocket narrow enough to securely hold a dowel in place; then slip the cloth over the dowel. Betsy Ross would be impressed!

Cheryl Kiser—Gr. K
Jackson Elementary
Boise, ID

### Family Trees

Use this "tree-mendously" helpful display when first learning to recognize all your new students' parents and primary caregivers! On the first day of school or during open house, take a photograph of each student with her significant adults. Mount each photograph onto a tree cutout; then label each tree with the family's name. Arrange the trees on a bulletin board titled "Our Family Trees." Your little ones will love looking at the display, and you will have a handy tool to help you quickly identify parents during those hectic first few days!

Sharon Davis—Gr. K
Lafayette Elementary
Oxford, MS

The Davis Tree

### Crowded Cubby Relief

Create cubby space and save valuable learning time with this clever idea! Use paper grocery bags to create seat packs for students to store their supplies. To make a pack, fold over the top of a grocery bag as shown; then slip the fold over the back of a child's chair. With their supplies at their seats, students will spend less time gathering items and will have more time for learning. The seat packs make great mailboxes and can also be used in a center to hold materials. Replace torn seat packs on your next visit to the grocery store. Paper or plastic? Paper, please!

Elizabeth P. Ridgley and Matthew Periera—Gr. K teacher and student, Haverhill Baptist Day School, Haverhill, FL

### Cleanup Call

Keep your students focused on the task of cleaning up with this cute call-and-response song. Signal cleanup time by singing the first line of the song. Continue singing until the room is clean and you're ready for your next activity.

**Clean Up**
*(sung to the tune of "The Banana Boat Song/Day-O")*

Teacher: Clean up!
Students: Clee-ee-ee-ee-ean up!
Teacher: Clean up your space and check out the floor!
Students: Clean up our space and check out the floor!
Clean up our space and check out the floor!

Deb Scala—Gr. K, Mt. Tabor Elementary, Mt. Tabor, NJ

### Dismissal Made Easy

Simplify dismissal during the first week of school with this organizational tip. In advance, prepare different sets of nametags to identify car riders, bus riders, walkers, and children attending after-school care. Estimate the number of children you will have in each category; then prepare that many blank nametags. As each new student arrives, have her attending adult write the child's name on the corresponding tag. Direct parents to return the tags to school with their child for the first week of school. A few minutes before dismissal, place each child's nametag around her neck; then group students by modes of transportation. Then, when the final bell rings, you can easily see how each of your little ones will get home.

Pam Shaffer—Gr. K
College Park Elementary
LaPorte, TX

Bus Rider
Kathy
Bus 76
AFTER-SCHOOL
Sadie

# Getting Your Ducks in a Row
## Management Tips for the Classroom

## It's Hooping Time!

Try this idea the next time you have students working on projects with lots of pieces. Store a class set of Hula-Hoop® rings within children's reach. When you say, "It's hooping time," each child gets a hoop and puts it on the floor. Have him sit inside his hoop to complete his project. What a great way to cut through the hoopla of keeping projects neat and tidy!

Laura L. Baynard—Gr. K
Cedar Hill Elementary
Lawrenceville, GA

## Transition Tune

Get students to tune in when it's time to change activities with this catchy song.

*(sung to the tune of "Frère Jacques")*

| | |
|---|---|
| Are you listening? Are you listening? | *Teacher sings.* |
| Yes, I am! Yes, I am! | *Children sing.* |
| Now it's time to [clean up]. | *Teacher sings.* |
| Now it's time to [clean up]. | *Children sing.* |
| Here we go! | *Teacher sings.* |
| Here we go! | *Children sing.* |

Repeat the song, substituting *line up, eat lunch,* and *go home* for the underlined phrase.

adapted from an idea by Garla Morin—Gr. K
Pretty Eagle Catholic School
Hardin, MT

## Now You See It; Now You Don't!

Did you know that you can erase permanent marker when it's on a laminated surface? Just use a white vinyl eraser and wipe those marks away. Finally, a simple solution to help you reuse calendars, memos, and displays!

Chava Shapiro
Beth Rochel School
Monsey, NY

## A Prescription for Memory

Remember a child's prescription needs with an alarm clock! All you need to do is set the alarm for the time the student needs the medication. Once the alarm sounds, send the child to receive her medicine. Now that's a perfect Rx!

Lois Gordon—Gr. K
Hillandale Elementary
East Flat Rock, NC

## Ideas in the Bag

Here's an easy way to store those great ideas you've jotted down on paper scraps. Staple or tape the sides of a quart-size zippered plastic bag to the inside of a file folder. Then slip the paper pieces inside the bag and zip it shut. When you get ready to plan, just unzip those ideas!

Ashlei B. Lockhart—Gr. K
Dunleith Elementary School
Marietta, GA

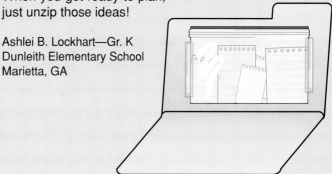

## Stickin' to It!

Are you looking for a tangible behavior plan for *every* student in your class? Then try this suggestion. Divide each child's daily incentive chart into sections that will allow her to experience success. (Chart divisions will vary from child to child.) After finishing designated time segments, allow children to put stickers inside their boxes. This constant feedback is the ticket to delightful behavior!

Chava Shapiro

285

# Getting Your Ducks in a Row
## Management Tips for the Classroom

### Poetic Organization

Where, oh, where can that poem be? Finding just the right holiday poem or seasonal song is a snap with this organizational tip. In a three-ring binder, place a divider for each month of the school year. Or label file folders in the same manner. Place a copy of each song or poem in the appropriate file. When you need a song to capture the spirit of the season, simply pull one out of the file!

Ericka Lynn Way—Gr. K
Leslie Fox Keyser Elementary
Front Royal, VA

### Substitute Helpers

Here's a creative solution to absent classroom helpers. Substitute helpers! Assign one child to be a substitute helper for the week. Then have that child fill in for any absent helpers. What a super idea!

Barbara Cohen—Gr. K, Horace Mann School, Cherry Hill, NJ

### Garbage Bag Binding

Don't toss those garbage bag ties! Use them to bind your class books. After laminating the pages of each book, punch holes in the pages. Then slip a tie through each hole to form a ring and twist to fasten. Pages can easily be added or removed by untwisting the ties. "Tie-rrific!"

Tricia Cooke—Gr. K
YMCA Kindergarten
Northboro, MA

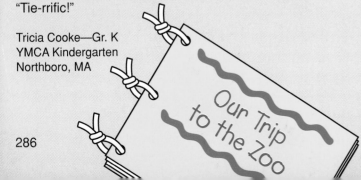

Our Trip to the Zoo

### Mini Magnetic Boards

Cook up some magnetic fun with this idea! Use burner covers as individual magnetic boards. Place the covers at a center along with magnetic letters or numbers. Then have students use the letters and numbers on the inside of the cover. If desired, use self-adhesive felt to cover the outside of the burner cover and reduce noise. Now that's a hot idea!

Carolyn Parson—Gr. K
Union Valley School
Hutchinson, KS

### Just a Dot

Teach youngsters this catchy rhyme to help them remember exactly how much glue will do.

Just a dot.
Not a lot.
Only a spot
Of glue
Will do!

Julia Mashburn—Gr. K, Black's Mill Elementary, Dawsonville, GA

### Just-Right Journals

Need a way to brighten up your youngsters' journals? Use napkins! Brightly colored party napkins make lively journal covers. To make a cover, glue a napkin to a large sheet of construction paper; then laminate it. Cut the cover to the desired size; then bind it together with the journal pages. If desired, use seasonal and holiday napkins to make journals that correlate with your current themes. Write on!

Faye M. Barker—Grs. K–1
Estes Hills Elementary
Chapel Hill, NC

# LITERACY LINKS

# Literacy Links

### *D* Is for Dalmatian

Fire Prevention Week in October is the perfect time to teach your youngsters all about fire safety, dalmatian fire dogs, and the letter *d*. Have your little ones make these dalmatian dog ears to help reinforce letter recognition, writing skills, and letter-sound association. From white felt, cut a pair of five-inch-long dog ears for each child. Then have her use a black marker to draw spots on each ear. Provide the child with a two-inch-wide tagboard headband, and direct her to write upper- and lowercase *d*'s on it. Next staple each ear to the strip and fold it over as shown. Adjust and staple the strip to fit the child's head; then use face paint to color the tip of her nose black. These headbands would be great to wear during your annual field trip to the fire station. "Howl" cute!

Flo Spradlin—Gr. K, Central Elementary, Pascagoula, MS

### Placemat Picture Match

Set the table for literacy with this nifty center idea! In advance, purchase several seasonal or holiday placemats with a variety of pictures. For each picture depicted on the mat, write its name or its beginning letter on a small tagboard card. If desired, add a simple picture cue beside the word. Set the word cards with the placemats and challenge your students to match the words to the pictures. Change the placemats and cards throughout the year to correspond with different seasons, holidays, and themes. Now that's a center for all seasons!

Susan Schneider—Gr. K, Durham Elementary, Purling, NY

### Great Wall of Rhyming

Encourage rhyme and reading in your classroom with this color-coded display! Brainstorm with students a list of words that rhyme. Then, using different-colored paper for each rhyming family, draw a simple sketch of each word. Next write the word on each illustration. Sort the papers by color; then mount them on a wall in your classroom. Encourage your youngsters to write sentences using words from the display. Or invite students to create and label their own illustrations for the words. During center time, provide your little ones with a pointer and have pairs take turns reading the words to each other. What an off-the-wall idea!

Barbara Bauer—Gr. K, Follow Through School, Buffalo, NY

## Fun With Fonts

The variety of fonts in print can be confusing for little ones just learning their letters. Help ease the confusion and reinforce letter recognition with this alphabet booklet idea. Use a computer to type a letter in three different fonts as shown. Add a title; then print the page for each child. Cut each page into fourths and then staple the four pieces together to make a book. Next print a variety of small pictures that begin with the featured letter, or use pictures cut from magazines. Invite each student to choose three pictures for her book; then have her glue one on each page. Encourage your little ones to share their books with each other before they take them home. What a "font-astic" idea!

Cindy Sweeney, Homan Elementary School, Schererville, IN

## Alphabet Cans

Your youngsters are sure to have some phonics fun with this "sound" idea! Have students bring 26 one-pound coffee cans to school. Cover the cans with solid-colored Con-Tact® paper; then label each one with a different letter of the alphabet. As you study each letter, have students bring in small, inexpensive items that begin with that letter. Direct your youngsters to place the items in the corresponding can; then review the items during your letter study. To help reinforce letter sounds, place the can in a center and invite youngsters to examine and say the name of each item. Or place several cans in the center and challenge students to sort the items by beginning sounds.

Pat Bollinger—Gr. K, Marble Hill, MO

## See Them Learning!

Here's an alphabet innovation of *Brown Bear, Brown Bear, What Do You See?* that is sure to please your youngsters. As you study each letter, have students brainstorm a list of words that begin with that letter; then include the words in a chant similar to the one shown. In rebus form, write the chant on a sheet of chart paper or on sentence strips to be placed in a pocket chart. Have students recite the chant as you point to the words and pictures. For additional alphabet reinforcement, remove the pictures from the chart and challenge students to match each picture with the corresponding word.

Rita V. Fulp—Gr. K
Christenberry Elementary
Knoxville, TN

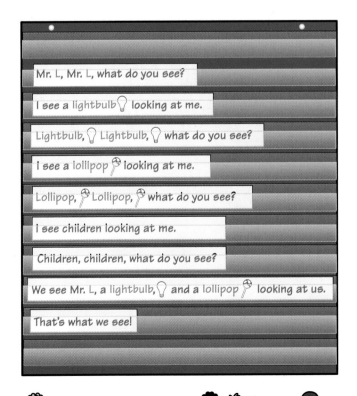

289

# Literacy Links

## Good Point!

Use these pint-sized pointers to motivate and point little ones toward literacy. To make one pointer, simply place a seasonal pencil topper on the end of an unsharpened pencil. If needed, demonstrate how to use these nifty tools. Then set the pointers in your reading area and invite youngsters to use them as they read aloud. Point well made!

Mary Kulpa—Gr. K, St. Mary's School, Bloomington, IL

## V Is for Violets, Vines, and Valentines

Roses are red. Violets are blue. Here's an activity just for you! Use this craft idea to help reinforce sound recognition for the letter *V*. In advance, cut a class supply of vase shapes from inexpensive velvet. Provide each child with a vase, a sheet of violet construction paper, and several small squares of purple tissue paper. After reviewing the letter *V*, direct the student to glue her vase onto the construction paper and draw vines coming out of it. Next have her crumple the tissue paper squares to resemble violets and then glue them onto the vines. For added holiday fun, have the child glue heart-shaped valentines on the vase. Title each child's paper as shown; then have her identify all of the things on the paper that begin with the letter *V*. Vvvv-ery nice work!

Tracey Jean Quezada—Gr. K, Presentation of Mary Academy, Hudson, NH

## Valentine Card Hunt

Hunting for a fun idea that encourages reading? Use this small-group activity that has youngsters hunting for a secret valentine message. To prepare, write each word of the message on the back of a different small valentine card. Hide the cards around your room; then invite the group to find them. When all of the cards have been found, challenge students to read each word and then sequence the cards to form a sentence. A-hunting we will go!

Kathy Lotito—Gr. K, St. John Lutheran, Wrightstown, WI

## Rhyme Time

Help develop youngsters' phonemic awareness with this box of rhymes. Cover a sturdy cardboard box with Con-Tact® paper. Then place inside the box pairs of items with rhyming names, such as a *sock* and a *block,* a *hat* and a stuffed *cat,* or a *dish* and a toy *fish.* Throughout the year, invite students to add rhyming objects to the box. Then encourage your youngsters to use the box to match and sort the objects. Now there's an activity with rhyme and reason!

Fern Satin—Grs. K–2 Special Education
Mamaroneck Avenue School
White Plains, NY

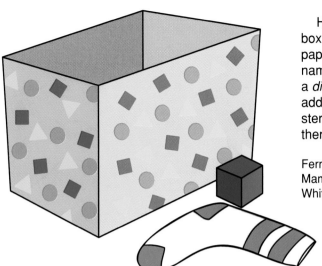

## Back-to-Back ABCs

Excited little giggles will fill the air with this engaging alphabet game. To prepare, tape a different letter of the alphabet to each child's back without revealing the letter to him. At the start signal, direct students to give each other clues about the letters on their backs. For example, a child with the letter *C* might be given the clue "*Cat* begins with this letter." After a few minutes of gathering clues, have the class come back together. Invite each child to recall some of his clues and then guess which letter is on his back.

Joe Montgomery—Gr. K, St. Mary of the Assumption School, Herman, PA

## Plush Reading Buddies

Here's an inviting way to encourage your youngsters to curl up with a good book. Fill a large plastic tub with stuffed animals, and then place it in your reading area. Explain to youngsters that the animals are special reading buddies and should be used only for quiet reading times. Invite each youngster to visit the area, select a stuffed animal, and then share a story with his plush pal. Your little ones will be thrilled to have their own audiences and will want to read again and again and again!

Juli Robinson—Gr. K, Grace Brethren Christian School, Clinton, MD

# Literacy Links

## T-shirt Phonics

Reinforce phonics skills with this "T-riffic" interactive activity! In advance, cut out a class supply of T-shirt shapes from poster board. Print a different lowercase letter on each of the T-shirts. Next, punch two holes at the top of each T-shirt and tie on a length of yarn as shown. To begin the activity, pass out one T-shirt to each student and have him put it on. Then call out a word such as *cat*. Have your students repeat the word slowly, isolating the individual sounds. Then ask the students who are wearing the letter sounds in the word *cat* to come forward and arrange themselves in correct order, so that the rest of the class can read the word. Repeat the activity using other simple words. Your little ones will be sold on these wearable words!

adapted from ideas by:
Michelle S. Morrow—Gr. K, Frances Mack Elementary, Gaston, SC
Becky Johns—Gr. K, South Holt Elementary, Oregon, MO

## Colorful Egg Cartons

Here is a center activity that will give your little ones "egg-stra" color word reinforcement. Prepare by collecting an empty egg carton, 12 plastic eggs of the same color, a bag of jelly beans, and a basket. Print the color word of each jelly bean color in the bottom of a different egg compartment, repeating colors if necessary. Then, in each plastic egg, put a jelly bean to match the printed color word in one of the compartments. Next, place the basket of filled eggs in a center along with the egg carton and extra jelly beans. Instruct each student to open one egg at a time and determine the jelly bean's color. Then have him place the egg in its matching compartment. When the carton is filled, check the student's work and then have him put the eggs back in the basket for the next student. Finish by inviting each spring chick to treat himself to a few jelly beans!

Karen M. Parr, Memphis, TN

## Beginning Sounds of Spring!

This circle game will get your youngsters springing into beginning sounds! Invite a child to pick a beginning sound (such as *b*) and have her announce it to the class. To play the game, the student walks around the circle and taps each child's head while saying a word relating to springtime, such as *flower, rain,* or *grasshopper.* Then she picks a child to tap while calling out a *b* spring word, such as *butterfly* or *bird.* The tapped child gets up and chases the tapper completely around the circle, like in the traditional Duck, Duck, Goose game. Continue playing until everyone has had a turn. Your little b-b-blossoms will want to practice beginning sounds again and again!

Jane Labrie—Gr. K, Rockdale School, Northbridge, MA

## Ending Sound Lotto

This phonetic lotto game will have your youngsters hopping down the bunny trail! In advance, gather a variety of objects that have easily identifiable ending sounds and place them in a bag. Next, make a class supply of game cards from squares of poster board divided into four sections as shown. Inside each section, print a different letter that represents the ending sound of an object in the bag. Add a springlike touch by purchasing seasonal-shaped or pastel-colored marshmallows to use as markers. Pass out a card and four marshmallows to each student. To begin the game, pull an item out of your bag and say its name, emphasizing the ending sound. Then have each student determine if she has that sound on her card. If she does, she places a marshmallow on top of that letter. Continue until everyone's card is covered. Reward your youngsters' efforts instantly by allowing them to munch on the markers. Yum!

Betsy Pottey—Gr. K, Abington, MA

## "Zoo-ming" in on Letters

Practice letter recognition and beginning sounds with this hands-on zoo activity. In advance, collect animal pictures with different beginning sounds. On the bottom of a piece of poster board, draw a zoo entrance gate. Next, print a letter on the poster to go with each animal picture. Laminate the poster and the animals. Place a self-adhesive Velcro® strip underneath each letter on the poster and on the back of each animal. Put the animals in a plastic baggie and store it near the zoo poster. Introduce the activity to your students by demonstrating how to match each animal picture with its beginning sound. Let's see, *h* is for…hippo!

Christy Reichard, Campbell Elementary School, Springfield, MO

## Cap It!

Unbottle some phonics fun with this center idea. Enlist students' help in collecting 26 small clean plastic bottles. Use a permanent marker to print a different lowercase letter on each bottle as shown. On the top of each cap, print the matching uppercase letter. Next, tape a picture to each bottle that begins with the specified letter on that bottle. (If desired, print the name of the picture on the front as well.) Challenge each child to match the caps to the bottles. Clearly "cap-tivating"!

Quazonia J. Quarles—Gr. K, Girls Inc., Newark, DE

293

# Literacy Links

## Fun Fingernail Pointers

Polish up youngsters' reading skills with this idea! At your reading area, place a supply of children's play fingernails (the plastic ones that slide onto the end of a child's finger). Then invite each child to slip on a fingernail and use it to point to words as she reads. For added fun, paint the fingernail pointers in seasonal colors. During Halloween, use the long, black costume fingernails. Word-recognition skills will soar with this well-manicured idea!

Kim Mullis—Gr. K, Pearson Elementary, Pearson, GA

The bear is brown.

The cat is yellow.

## Parting Gifts

Send each student off for the summer with this wonderful parting gift—his own writing kit! To make one kit, use a computer to create a sheet of personalized stationery for each child. Then photocopy a supply. Place the stationery in a personalized bag along with a supply of envelopes and writing utensils such as a marker, a box of crayons, and a fancy pencil. If desired, add a self-addressed, stamped postcard and invite the child to write you a letter. What a super way to motivate little ones to write!

Emily C. Moore—Gr. K, Penny Road Elementary, Raleigh, NC

## Alphabet Action

Use this movement activity to help your little ones learn to write between the lines. To begin, show students the alphabet written on lined paper. Discuss the placement of the letters on the lines. Then teach students the following movements:

1. Hands over heads for letters that rise above the center line, such as *f, h,* or *b.*
2. Hands on hips for letters that stay between the center and lower lines—such as *o, e,* or *r.*
3. Squat for letters that fall below the bottom line, such as *p, g,* or *q.*

After teaching students the movements, show them different letters of the alphabet and encourage them to perform the appropriate actions. For an added challenge, display a word and have students make the movement for each letter in the word.

Jan Messali—Gr. K, Canyon View Elementary, San Diego, CA

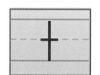

# Busy Bees

Rudolph! Rudolph!
What will you do?
You can't guide Santa
If your nose is blue!

Rudolph! Rudolph!
You're such a silly fellow.
Who will know it's you
If your nose is yellow?

Rudolph! Rudolph!
Your way cannot be seen
Through the wintry winter weather
If your nose is green!

Rudolph! Rudolph!
Santa has his sack.
But you're not ready
If your nose is black!

Rudolph! Rudolph!
Santa gave a wink.
But what will Santa think
If your nose is pink?

Rudolph! Rudolph!
The children are in bed.
And now I know you're ready
'Cause your nose is red!

# Busy Bees

## Fun-filled Learning Activities To Keep Your Happy Hive Buzzing

# Get Ready, Rudolph!

Oh no—what happened to Rudolph's red nose? Use the poem above to reinforce colors, color words, and lots of language skills as your children help Rudolph get ready for his special holiday mission. To prepare, trace the Rudolph pattern (page 298) on tissue paper. Then use a permanent marker to trace Rudolph onto a piece of felt. Remove the tracing paper and fill in the marker lines on the felt. If desired, add details with glued-on felt pieces or fabric paint. Then cut out one 1-inch felt circle (nose) in each of the following colors: blue, yellow, green, black, pink, and red. Finally, write the poem (above) on chart paper. Then display your Rudolph on a flannelboard. As you read each stanza together, invite a different child to select the corresponding nose and place it on Rudolph. You'd better get ready, Rudolph!

Karla Parker—Gr. K
Southern Elementary School
Somerset, KY

## Pop, Pop, Popcorn

Keep those fine-motor skills popped to perfection and feed your schoolyard birds at the same time! In advance, thread a supply of tapestry needles each with a length of dental floss. (This activity is best done with half of your class at a time.) Arrange a large, clean bedsheet on your carpet near an outlet. Have students sit around three edges of the sheet. On the open edge of the sheet, position a hot-air popcorn popper so that the popcorn will pop out onto the sheet. Provide each child with a threaded tapestry needle. As the popcorn pops onto the sheet, encourage each child to string popcorn onto his floss. Do your students see any patterns emerging...such as string one, eat *two?* Or has anyone's popcorn string reached a *foot?* Afterward, invite each child to hang his popcorn string on a tree. They're pretty to look at and "pop-ular" with the birds!

Wilma Droegemueller—Gr. K
Zion Lutheran School
Mt. Pulaski, IL

## Snow Bowling

Strike up some wintry fun with this snowy version of classroom bowling. In advance, collect ten empty, clear plastic 20-ounce soft drink bottles. Remove the label from each bottle. Then transform each bottle into a snowman pin by stuffing it with fiberfill or cotton balls. Tie a fabric scarf around the bottle and tape on construction paper details to complete a snowman look. To do this activity, set up the snowman pins as you would for regular bowling. Using a softball to represent a snowball, have a child roll the snowball toward the snowmen, trying to knock down as many snowmen as possible. Lots of opportunities here for subtraction and—if you're keeping score—addition!

adapted from an idea by Denise Seeley—
Gr. K
St. Bernard's Catholic School
Buffalo, NY

# Heads Down, Hearts Up!

Your little ones will give a thumbs-up for this valentine guessing game! Begin by choosing seven students to stand side by side in front of the class. Hand each of them a heart-shaped lollipop. Have the other students close their eyes and follow your directive, "Heads down, thumbs up!" Once everyone is ready, instruct each of the seven children to place his sucker inside a different fist and return to the front of the classroom. Then cue students with "Heads up, hearts up!" Ask each child holding a lollipop to stand and guess which child gave it to her. If she guesses correctly, have her replace the student standing. Continue in this manner until every child has had a turn to give and receive a lollipop. What a surprise for your sweethearts!

Quazonia J. Quarles—Gr. K
Girls Inc.
Newark, DE

# Busy Bees

## Fun-Filled Learning Activities to Keep Your Happy Hive Buzzing

## The Wind Blows

Here's a breezy way to actively involve students in listening and classification skills. Arrange your students' chairs in a large circle (facing inward) and invite them to sit down. Choose one child to be the leader, remove his chair, and have him stand inside the circle. To play, the leader makes other students move by saying, "The wind blows children [wearing sneakers]!" In this instance, the leader and the children who are wearing sneakers move as though they are in a gusty wind and change seats (the leader will now sit, leaving another student without a chair). The children without sneakers remain seated and produce wind sound effects. The child left standing becomes the new leader and calls out a new direction, such as "The wind blows children [wearing blue]!" Continue in this manner until each child has had a turn to be the leader. What a windy day!

Linda Newman—Gr. K
Washington Hebrew Early
  Childhood Center
Potomac, MD

# Whose Valentine?

All it takes is a little critical thinking from your students to figure it out in this valentine activity. To prepare, obtain a photo of the school principal, secretary, custodian, bus driver, cafeteria manager, media specialist, and any other special staff member. Cut out a large construction paper heart for each person represented. Have small groups of students decorate hearts for the adults, adding pictures of typical items that they use in their work—such as a broom, mop, or trash can for the custodian—to make valentines.

Display the photos in a center and invite students to match each valentine to its corresponding photograph. Once everyone has visited the center, have a different volunteer print the staff person's name and a valentine greeting on each valentine. Then take your children to visit the special staff members and present them with their personalized heartfelt wishes.

297

# Rudolph Pattern

Use with "Get Ready, Rudolph!" on page 296.

# GETTING KIDS INTO BOOKS

# Getting Kids Into Books

## Blizzard Day

Is the weather outside frightful? Then it's delightful for a picnic…a blizzard picnic, that is! To prepare, ask parents to contribute white snack foods, such as white chocolate-covered Oreo® cookies, yogurt pretzels, yogurt raisins, marshmallows, popcorn, and milk. Transform your classroom into a winter wonderland by spreading white sheets on the floor and over stationary furniture to create the illusion of snow. Set up a fan to provide a chilly breeze. When everything is ready, invite youngsters to bundle up in their jackets, hats, and scarves.

Begin the blizzard by reading your favorite winter-weather books, such as *The Snowy Day* by Ezra Jack Keats, *The Mitten: A Ukrainian Folktale* by Jan Brett, and *Katy and the Big Snow* by Virginia Lee Burton. Play some wintry music and let the children pretend to ice-skate around the room. Finally, invite each child to enjoy the white wintry snacks. What a way to spend a snowbound afternoon!

Debbie Musser—Gr. K, Washington-Lee Elementary, Bristol, VA

## Kwanzaa Jewelry

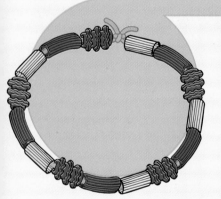

Here's an artistic way to welcome Kwanzaa into your classroom. In advance, dye a large quantity of tube-shaped, uncooked pasta different colors by combining each batch with a small amount of rubbing alcohol mixed with food coloring. Spread the pasta on newspaper to dry. Then cut a class quantity of 30-inch yarn lengths.

Read aloud Deborah M. Newton Chocolate's popular *My First Kwanzaa Book* (Cartwheel Books). After discussing the story, explain to students that beadwork is a traditional African art form. Next invite each child to create his very own beaded necklace for Kwanzaa. Have him string a simple pasta pattern; then help him knot the ends of the yarn to finish the necklace. How stylish!

Kelly A. Wong, Berlyn School, Ontario, CA

## Piñatas for Posadas

Youngsters will enjoy the story of Ceci's first *posada,* or Christmas party, in the classic book *Nine Days to Christmas: A Story of Mexico* by Marie Hall Ets and Aurora Labastida (Puffin Books). This story details her party preparations, including a visit to the Mexican market to choose a beautiful star piñata. Consider paraphrasing this book to showcase the preparation and party. Then have your youngsters make these simple piñatas.

For each piñata, gather two paper party cups, scissors, masking tape, white glue, a paintbrush, a supply of multicolored tissue paper squares, a hole puncher, and a pipe cleaner. To make one, cut out the bottom of one cup; then use masking tape to attach the cups, as shown. Next paint glue on a small area of the piñata; then cover the glue with the tissue paper squares. Continue until the entire piñata is covered in tissue paper. When the glue is dry, make a hanger by punching two holes opposite one another near the open end of the piñata. Then thread the pipe cleaner through the holes and twist the ends to secure it.

Hang these piñatas for a festive, authentic decoration. If desired, fill each child's completed piñata with candies before sending them home. Feliz Navidad!

Kelly A. Wong

# Getting Kids Into Books

## Cloud Formations

Use this enlightening idea to introduce *It Looked Like Spilt Milk* by Charles G. Shaw (HarperTrophy). In advance, choose several simple shapes from the story and draw each one in the center of a different sheet of construction paper. Cut out each shape, leaving the frame intact to create a silhouette. Use an overhead projector to project the silhouetted images onto the ceiling to resemble clouds. Darken your classroom and invite students to lie on their backs and watch the clouds roll by. As you project each cloud, encourage a volunteer to share what object she sees in it. Sometimes it really *does* look like spilt milk!

Cheryl L. Bailey, Indiana, PA

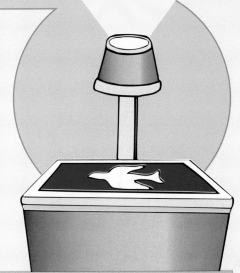

## The Mixed-Up Class

Even your most reluctant readers will eagerly reach for this class-made flip book! Read aloud Eric Carle's *The Mixed-Up Chameleon* (HarperTrophy), and then lead a class discussion about what happens when the chameleon borrows other animals' body parts. To make a book page of each child, take a full-body photo of him. Mount the photo onto a sheet of construction paper. Then cut the paper horizontally into three equal sections (as shown). When all of the pages are complete, laminate them. Sort the pages into body sections; then stack each set of pages. Punch a hole in the edge of each page and then fasten the pages in a three-ring binder. Encourage each child to flip the pages to create mixed-up classmates. Crazy, man!

Margi Saks—Gr. K, Park East Day School, New York, NY

## If I Had a Jar of Money...

What special thing would you buy if you saved a big jar full of money? The family in Vera B. Williams's book *A Chair for My Mother* (Greenwillow Books) bought a rose-covered chair after a house fire destroyed their furniture. After a reading of the book, discuss with youngsters what unique purchases they would save their money to buy. Give each child a copy of a jar pattern that is programmed as shown. Have her write (or dictate) to complete the sentence. Then provide coin stamps and washable ink pads for printing money on the jar. For an eye-catching display, cut out the jars and then mount them with the book's title and the caption "If I had a jar of money..."

Randalyn Larson, Memorial School, Jackson, MI

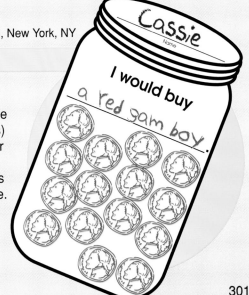

# Getting Kids Into Books

**Space Is Spectacular!**

### Far Out!

Create a sparkling space scene to follow up a reading of a space-related book, such as *Me and My Place in Space* by Joan Sweeney (Dragonfly Books) or *I Wonder Why Stars Twinkle and Other Questions About Space* by Carole Stott (Kingfisher Books). To begin, trace several different sizes of circles onto black paper. Invite youngsters to color the circles with glitter crayons to create planets. Attach the planets to a length of dark blue or purple bulletin board paper. Then have students add sponge-painted yellow stars or shiny star stickers to the background. To *really* show off all the stars in the sky, invite each child to splatter-paint the display with an old toothbrush and white tempera paint. Finish by adding the title "Space Is Spectacular!"

Rhonda Chiles—Gr. K, South Park School, Shawnee Mission, KS

### Ocean Equations

Mix a little math with literature and you'll find a center idea that adds up to fun! After sharing an ocean-related book, such as *Sea Sums* by Joy N. Hulme (Disney Press), set up a center where youngsters can practice simple equations using ocean items as manipulatives. Set out a tub with toy ocean animals, shells, and any other ocean objects you've collected. Print simple equations on index cards and add the cards to the center. After allowing time for little ones to explore the ocean items, ask each child at this center to choose a card and use the objects to create the equation shown on it. Also include some blank cards so youngsters can write their own equations. Let's see, one shark plus one shark equals…

Jo Ann O'Brien, Lilja Elementary, Newton, MA

### Chicka, Chicka, What a Hat!

After reading aloud *Chicka Chicka Boom Boom* by Bill Martin Jr. and John Archambault (Simon & Schuster Books for Young Readers), invite your youngsters to make these eye-catching hats. Provide each child with a green sentence strip (or a 3" x 24" strip of green construction paper), four large palm leaves cut from green construction paper, some scraps of brown paper, and four die-cut letters. Staple each strip to fit the wearer's head. Invite each child to cut coconuts from the brown paper to glue onto her hat along with the palm leaves as shown. Then have her glue one letter onto each leaf. Next, have each child look through old magazines for pictures of items that begin with the letters on her hat. Have her cut out the pictures and add them to the corresponding leaves. Encourage your young hatmakers to wear their creations as you read the story a second time. Chicka, chicka, boom, boom—what a super costume!

Ellen S. Faris, Alberta Smith Elementary, Richmond, VA

# OUR READERS WRITE

# Our Readers Write

## "Bag" to School!

Help ease your little ones' first-day jitters by welcoming each child to school with her own schoolhouse bag. To begin, glue on red construction paper to cover about two-thirds of the front of a paper lunch bag (as shown). Next fold down the top of the bag and glue on a construction paper roof and bell. Use markers and additional construction paper pieces to add details to the schoolhouse. Then use a paint pen to label the roof with a student's name. Place a few school-related items inside the bag, such as an eraser, a pencil, and a bookmark. Position each bag in a child's chair or on her table space. What a wonderful schoolhouse welcome!

Dawn Schollenberger—Gr. K
Mary S. Shoemaker School
Woodstown, NJ

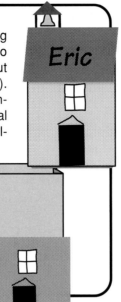

## Bingo Chip Relief

Are you tired of repeatedly counting out bingo chips for each child? Save time and energy with this handy tip! Replace standard bingo chips with Unifix® cubes. In advance, stack the cubes in sets equal to the number of spaces on each bingo card. When your children need bingo markers, simply give each child a stack of cubes. When the game is over, ask each child to restack his cubes and they're ready to go again!

Maenette Hanners—Gr. K
Unity Elementary
LaGrange, GA

## "Stand Up If..."

Use this fun movement activity to help your youngsters get acquainted with one another. Seat students in a circle; then begin the activity with a direction such as, "Stand up if you like pizza." After all the pizza lovers have been acknowledged, have them sit down again. Then give a different direction such as, "Stand up if you have a brother." Continue playing and varying the questions so that your youngsters can easily see their many similarities and differences!

Leslie Bussey
Millbrook Elementary School
Aiken, SC

## Christmas Keepsake

Christmas probably isn't on the minds of most parents as they leave their little ones on the first day of school. However, every parent will treasure a Christmas ornament that displays a picture of her child on that monumental day. On the first day of school, take a photograph of each child in your class. Later, mount the picture on a cute construction paper cutout. Label the cutout similar to the one shown; then laminate it. Finally, punch a hole in the top of the cutout; then thread a length of yarn through it. What a way to light up a tree!

Susan Schneider—Gr. K
Durham Elementary School
Durham, NY

First Day
of
Kindergarten

September 5, 1999

## The Days Keep Bouncin' By!

Give your calendar a three-dimensional, hands-on twist with this unique idea! To prepare, program a set of Ping-Pong® balls each with a different date from 1 to 31. On the back of each ball, attach a strip of Velcro®. Then attach each corresponding Velcro strip in a different square on a calendar. Store all the Ping-Pong balls in a container near the calendar. Each day, invite a different child to add a new date to the calendar. Your students will have a ball!

Marianne Cerra
Kindergarten Enrichment
Family Growth School and
    Day Care
Shillington, PA

| SUNDAY | MONDAY | TUESDAY | WEDNESDAY | THURSDAY |
|--------|--------|---------|-----------|----------|
|        |        |         | 1         | 2        |
| 5      | 6      | 7       | 8         | 9        |
| 12     | 13     | 14      | 15        | 16       |
| 19     | 20     |         |           |          |

## Cash In the Cans!

Here's a great way to help save the earth and earn some class spending money at the same time! Encourage students to bring in empty aluminum cans. Assign different helpers to rinse the cans in the morning and crush the cans in the afternoon (when the cans are dry). When you have a large collection of crushed cans, take them to a recycling center that pays cash for aluminum. Save this money in a large, clear container. If desired, post a chart of your ongoing profits. Continue collecting and cashing in cans throughout the year. Use this stash of cash for field trips, parties, special projects, or classroom supplies. It really does pay to recycle!

Beth-Randall Davis—Gr. K, Lemira Elementary, Sumter, SC

## Meet the Staff

Students will quickly become acquainted with your school staff when you make this class big book. To begin, take a picture of each staff member hard at work; then glue each photograph onto a large, separate sheet of construction paper. Patterned after the text of Eric Carle's *Brown Bear, Brown Bear, What Do You See?*, label each page as shown, changing the name to correspond with the person in the photo. Before binding the pages together into a book, display them in a hallway for all to enjoy.

Kindergarten, Kindergarten, Who do you see?

I see Ms. Lilienthal looking at me!

Linda K. Lilienthal—Gr. K
Hayes Center Elementary
Hayes Center, NE

## Give 'em a Hand

Lend this helping hand to clear up your youngsters' right- and left-hand confusion. Prominently display a large, red right-hand cutout. Encourage your children to practice holding up their right hands (palms facing out) and saying, "Right hand, red." To determine which hand is her right hand, a child simply holds up the hand that matches the cutout. (If desired, also display a large lavender left-hand cutout and use it in a similar manner.) Right on!

Diane Parette—Gr. K
Durham Elementary
Durham, NY

## No-Mess Tempera

Eliminate paint spills forever with this simple solution! Allow a small amount of thick liquid tempera paint to dry completely in the bottom of a small margarine tub or in each cup of a foam egg carton. When a child is ready to paint, have her use the dry tempera paint as she would watercolors. She simply wets her brush with water, dabs the brush on the dry paint, and then paints on her paper.

Anita Comeaux—Gr. K
Smiths Primary School
Smiths, AL

## Quick and Easy Flannelboards

These flannelboards are perfect for little hands or for use in a teacher's lap. Ask your local fabric store for discarded cardboard fabric bolts. Cover the cardboard with felt; then hot-glue it in place. Now let's have some flannelboard fun!

Lori Hamernik—Gr. K
Prairie Farm Elementary
Prairie Farm, WI

## Pitch In!

You're sure to hit a few home runs with this open house display that gets parents involved! Cut out a supply of construction paper baseballs. On each baseball, write a needed classroom item, such as tissues or graham crackers. Next label a construction paper baseball glove as shown; then tape it to the outside of a large, clean, empty coffee can. Put the baseballs in the can and set it near your classroom door. At open house, invite parents to "pitch in" by taking a baseball from the can and donating the item listed on it. Batter up!

Shelly L. Kidd-Hamlett—Gr. K
Helena Elementary
Timberlake, NC

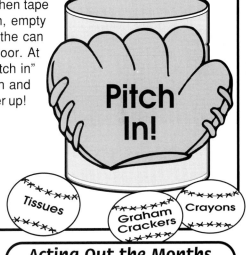

Pitch In!

Tissues

Graham Crackers

Crayons

## Warm Fuzzies

Encourage your little ones to express their feelings by incorporating warm fuzzies in your morning routine. Seat your class in a circle; then have each child, in turn, hold a stuffed animal (warm fuzzy) and share his feelings with the class. For example, a child might say, "I feel sad today because my mom has a cold." After each child shares, conclude the activity with an uplifting song or a light snack. Little ones will appreciate the opportunity to be heard and will concentrate more easily on learning.

Deborah L. Whitaker—Gr. K
Gemini Elementary
Melbourne Beach, FL

## Acting Out the Months

Get your students moving through the months with this fun calendar activity. After discussing the months, help students determine an appropriate action for each one, such as pretending to pick apples for September. Conclude each calendar time by having students recite the months in sequence while performing the corresponding actions. Before long your youngsters will know all of the months and some seasonal events that occur in each one.

Dawn Schollenberger—Gr. K
Mary S. Shoemaker School
Woodstown, NJ

# Our Readers Write

## Our Remembering Bag

Reinforce learning with this fun activity. To prepare, label a canvas tote bag "Our Remembering Bag." Each week, stock the bag with a few items that will trigger specific skills and concepts for your students. For example, you might fill the bag with a book that your class read, a piece of child-made artwork, a letter of the week, a puppet, and objects from your science topic. At the end of each week, display the remembering bag. As you bring out each item, in turn, ask children to share what each object stands for—what they learned. You'll be surprised how much your students can remember when everyone is included in this remembering discussion!

Daphne M. Orenshein—Gr. K
Yavneh Hebrew Academy, Los Angeles, CA

## Memories Are Forever

Here's a touching memento to offer a child who is going to move (and change schools) during the year. Ask each child to illustrate a page for the child who is moving. On that page, have her write or dictate a note to the child. Stack all the student pages behind a letter from you; then bind all the pages between two covers. (If the child who is moving is present during this activity, ask him to draw a picture for the class to display.) Give the completed book to the child on his last day at your school. He'll take these kindergarten memories with him forever!

Michelle Woyshner—Gr. K
Millbridge Elementary School, Delran, NJ

## Recycling Magnets

Have you ever wondered what to do with those great pictures from old nature magazines? Make magnets! Cut out the picture and laminate it. Then attach a magnetic strip to the back of the picture and you're ready to go! These magnets are great for magnetboard use, storytelling, classification activities, and manipulatives.

Sue Lewis Lein—Gr. K
St. Pius X Kindergarten
Wauwatosa, WI

## Thanks, Firefighters!

Since October is fire safety month, wouldn't it be nice to recognize and thank the dedicated firefighters in your area? If you're planning a trip to your local fire department, bring along this special treat. Have each child write about and illustrate why he is thankful for firefighters. Then bake a big batch of cookies. On the day of your visit, present the firefighters with the cards and cookies. Thanks a whole crunchin' bunch!

Marie Iannetti—Gr. K
Clementon, NJ

## Rainmaker

Rain, rain, come today! This easy-to-make prop adds atmosphere and interest to any story about rain. It also makes a great addition to your water table supplies. To make a rainmaker, rinse an empty dishwashing-liquid bottle. Use a pushpin to poke about ten holes in the bottom of it. Fill the bottle with water; then screw the lid on and close the stopper. When you're sharing a rainy story, keep the rainmaker and an aluminum baking pan on hand. When you read a rainy part of the story, pull up the stopper and let it rain!

Jennifer Barton—Gr. K
Elizabeth Green School
Newington, CT

## "Pop-ular" Place Cards

These pop-up place cards help identify special places in a jiffy. To make one, fold one end of a sheet of construction paper down about one inch. Then fold the rest of the sheet into thirds (see the diagram). Draw or trace a character or design so that it overlaps the fold line between sections A and B. Color the picture and write a name or other label in the open part of section B. Next use a craft blade to cut around the part of the character that lies above the fold line. Pop up the picture; then stand the place card as shown.

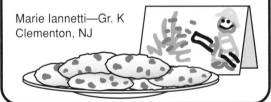

Virginia Chaverri—Gr. K

## Many Manipulatives

Start collecting a variety of those little colorful erasers and before you know it, you'll have a whole supply of manipulatives that are just right for little fingers to handle! The erasers can also be used for patterning activities, as bingo markers, and even as awards. So start collecting them now!

Julie Brown, Wake Forest, NC

## Popping Up to Greet You

Since kindergartners love the novelty of pop-ups, use that concept to motivate children when you're making greeting cards or class book pages. For example, to make a greeting card, cut a folded sheet of construction paper along the dotted lines as shown in the illustration. Open the paper and crease the center section in the opposite direction. Then glue another sheet of construction paper to the back of the first sheet. (Do not glue the center pop-up section!) Have a child write greetings on the front and inside of the card; then have him glue a cut out illustration to the pop-up part of the card. Ready for a popping fresh delivery!

adapted from an idea by Donna O'Malley—Gr. K
Harris Elementary School
Collingdale, PA

## Subs Afloat!

If you're a substitute teacher, this idea will keep your head above water at all times! Label a dishwashing tub "Sub Tub." Stock the tub with a supply of backup activities that can be used at a moment's notice. For example, stock your tub with a whistle, some favorite read-alouds, mints, a sponge-painting activity, stationery, writing supplies, and rewards. Take your sub tub with you wherever you go. Then, just when you need it, it's there for you! And, teachers, you might like to keep a sub tub on hand for substitutes in your classroom.

Laurie Birt—Gr. K
Belinder Elementary School, Overland Park, KS

## Musical Chairs, Part 2!

This adaptation of musical chairs is one where everyone learns and everyone wins! To prepare, program a class supply of cards with the skills of your choice. Then set up a class supply of chairs—musical chairs-style. Use reusable adhesive to attach a different card to the bottom of each chair. Begin play in the traditional manner. Each time the children are seated, ask each child, in turn, to find the card under his chair and tell the class what is on the card. Ask additional questions for each card, as desired. Then resume the music and continue play.

Amy Spence—Gr. K
Harvest Baptist Christian School
Medford, OR

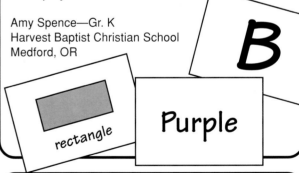

## Native American Vest

If you're studying traditional Native American clothing, here's an idea for you. A week or two before you begin, ask each child to bring in an old pillowcase. Dye the pillowcases brown. When they're dyed and dry, fold each pillowcase in half lengthwise. Cut out a scooped neck hole and two armholes. If abilities permit, have each child fringe-cut the bottom of her vest. Then display pictures of traditional Native American clothing and invite each child to decorate her vest using fabric paints and markers.

Christine Wichser—Gr. K
Langtree School

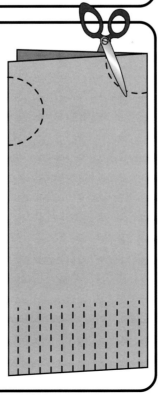

## Twisty Letters

Fine-motor fun paves the way for reinforcing letter and numeral formation. Stock a center with a supply of twist ties and/or pipe cleaners. Each day (or week) program a card with a letter or numeral that you would like children to work on. Then ask each child to bend and twist the ties and pipe cleaners to form the given symbol. Invite children to take these little projects home, encouraging them to try to collect the entire alphabet or all the numerals from 1 to 20.

Marilyn J. Royston, Homeschooling Parent

Dear Santa,
I've been good!
Love,
Mike
Kriste
Keri
Jess
Callie
Toby

## So Be Good for Goodness' Sake!

Use this interactive display to help with classroom management during the holidays. To begin, program a board or sheet of tagboard as shown. Each day that a child's behavior is acceptable, invite her to sign her name on the board. Are *you* on his list?

Angela Van Beveren, Alvin, TX

## Elegant Edgers

Looking for a quick and easy way to decorate for the holidays? Try substituting novelty garland for your traditional borders. Use the garland to trim your bulletin boards, chalkboards, calendar, or door. Simply visit your nearest discount store; then deck the walls!

Heidi Winter—Gr. K, Sam Rosen Elementary, Ft. Worth, TX

## Picture This!

Recycle clear film canisters into keepsakes with this ornament idea. To make a snowman, use a pushpin to poke a hole in the center of the lid. Straighten half of a paper clip, push it through the hole in the lid, and then bend the end, as shown. Paint the canister with craft glue and roll it in iridescent glitter. Snap the lid onto the canister. Make earmuffs by gluing the end of a three-inch pipe cleaner and a small pom-pom to each side. After the glue dries, use fabric paint to create the snowman's face. Voilá—a snowman to hang on your favorite limb!

adapted from an idea
    by Mary E. Maurer
Caddo, OK

## Wreath-Worthy Memories

Create this great conversation piece for the holidays. Decorate a grapevine wreath with ornaments from previous students and hang it on your classroom door. Soon you will hear familiar voices saying, "That's the ornament I gave Mrs. Way when I was in kindergarten!" Each year as you add ornaments, you'll fondly reminisce with your students about past holidays.

Taryn Lynn Way—Gr. K
Los Molinos Elementary
Los Molinos, CA

## A Stocking Stuffed With Love

Give your children a chance to donate a stocking stuffed with pennies to a local food bank or charity. Before the holidays, notify parents and ask them to help their children collect pennies in socks. To prepare the pennies for delivery, have each child count ten pennies from her sock and place them in a stack on a number strip, as shown. Instruct the child to continue counting and stacking until she has five stacks of pennies. Next, have the child place the 50 pennies in a coin wrapper. (Have an adult ready to help with this step.) Each child continues counting and wrapping pennies until her sock is empty. As a group, count the penny rolls and calculate the total amount of money. This stocking stuffer adds up to lots of holiday cheer!

Mary F. Philip—Gr. K
Relay Children's Center
Baltimore, MD

## Roll Out the Snow!

This bulletin board idea will have you singing "Let It Snow..." for seasons to come. Cut one or more large snowpeople from white felt. Then decorate the shapes with fabric scraps, buttons, twigs, or other collage materials. Mount these frosty creations on your bulletin board. If desired, stuff Poly-Fil® behind the snowpeople as you mount them to give a dimensional look. Then, as winter melts away, just roll them up and store until next year.

*Judy Kelley—Gr. K, Lilja School, Natick, MA*

## Fingerpainting Fun

Here's a little twist on the fingerpainting process that makes even the cleanup fun! Before each child paints, instruct her to cover her hands with inexpensive plastic sandwich bags. When she is finished painting, have the child or a friend simply pull the bags off and toss 'em!

*Susan A. DeRiso—Gr. K*
*Barrington, RI*

## "Paintsicles"

These Popsicle® paintbrushes provide a fun experience and promote lots of discovery opportunities about water and ice. To make a "paintsicle," pour six tablespoons of tempera paint into a five-ounce, waxed paper cup. Fill the cup with water; then mix well. Place a large craft stick in the cup. Stabilize the stick by sliding a piece of plastic wrap over the stick and onto the cup. Then freeze the "paintsicle." When you're ready to use it, dip the cup into warm water for a few seconds; then pop out the "paintsicle." Encourage children to explore on art paper with their "paintsicles." What kind of designs can they make right away? What happens as time goes by?

*Nina Tabanian—Gr. K, St. Rita School, Dallas, TX*

## I Can Draw a Star!

Do your little ones love learning how to draw new things? Well, how about stars!
Here's how:

1. First draw a steep mountain.

2. Draw a dot on each side.

3. Start at the bottom and walk up the mountain.

4. Walk straight across the mountain.

5. Walk back down again!

adapted from an idea by
Karen Saner—Grs. K–1
Burns Elementary School
Burns, KS

## Hit the Spot With Dot-to-Dot

Need a numeral sequencing center idea? These large dot-to-dots hit the spot! To make one, use an opaque projector to project a dot-to-dot picture on a large sheet of bulletin board paper. Trace the picture and numerals; then place a sticker dot on each dot in the picture. Laminate the picture. To use this dot-to-dot, post it on a wall or board and keep a supply of dry erase markers and a cloth nearby. After you check a child's work, ask him to erase it so that the picture is ready for the next child who visits that center.

*Tammy Riché—Gr. K, Kaplan Elementary, Kaplan, LA*

## Shimmer and Shine

Recycling concepts shine forth in this creative project. In advance, ask children to bring in shiny scraps of holiday gift wrap, ribbons, and bows. Also suggest that they save and bring in colorful, shiny candy wrappers. When you have a substantial collection, give each child a piece of cardboard or tagboard to use as a base. Then invite each child to mix, match, twist, tie, cut, and glue to make his own original shimmery, shiny collage.

*Elouise Miller—Gr. K*
*Lincoln School, Hays, KS*

## Designer Coloring Pages

Do you have students who just love to color commercial coloring pages? If so, here's a great way to offer some really neat pictures. First select a rubber stamp design that you like; then stamp it on a sheet of paper. Enlarge the design to the desired size; then duplicate it as needed. The result is a collection of new and interesting coloring pages.

*Ann Faris—Pre-K*
*and Gr. K*
*St. Joseph School*
*Keyport, NJ*

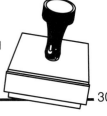

# Our Readers Write

## Me and My Shadow

With this fabulous February idea, the groundhog won't be the only one looking at his shadow! Create a set of silhouette notecards for each child to give as a special gift. Use a copier to make reduced images of the child's silhouette; then glue each one onto the front of a construction paper notecard. Wrap the notecards together with ribbon and have each child take them home to surprise her parents.

Vicki Casso—Gr. K
Islands Elementary
Gilbert, AZ

## Two Centers in One!

Save space in your classroom with this unique storytelling and literacy center. To prepare, cover one side of a cookie sheet with adhesive felt. Place the pan in a designated area along with magnetic letters and flannelboard pieces. Invite each child to use the flannelboard pieces to tell a story on the felt side. Then have her flip the pan over and use the magnetic letters to create words from the story. Ingenious!

Heather Bedel
Highland Heights, KY

## Secret Messages

Here's a unique way to reward students and reinforce literacy. To prepare, cut out a supply of seasonal shapes from white construction paper. Then use a Crayola® Color Changeables™ change wand to write a letter or invisible message on each cutout. Reward small groups of children by giving each child a cutout and a Crayola Color Changeables color change marker. Invite each child to use his marker to color over the cutout. Then watch his eyes grow wide with excitement as the invisible writing begins to appear. Encourage the child to read the message or identify the letter on the cutout. Literacy skills will appear like magic with this idea! (For another idea using Crayola Color Changeables, see page 238.)

Jeanne Nye, C. O. Greenfield, Phoenix, AZ

Good Work!

## Valentines for Veterans

On Valentine's Day, help your little ones spread a little holiday cheer to our nation's veterans. Explain to youngsters that veterans are men and women who have fought in wars. Have each child make a Valentine's Day card; then send the cards to your local Veterans Hospital. What a great way to honor those who have bravely served our country!

Laurel Smith—Gr. K
The Sonshine Place, Fishers, IN

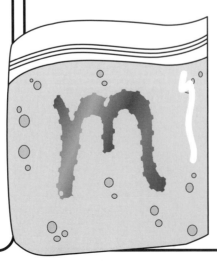

## It's in the Bag!

This squishy gel bag is perfect for little fingers to practice forming letters. To make one, place approximately one-third cup of colored hair gel into a plastic, resealable sandwich bag. Press out the air, seal the bag, and then secure the seal with tape. Spread the gel evenly throughout the bag. Place the bag at a center and invite each youngster to make letters in the gel by "writing" on the bag with his finger. To erase, simply squish, squish, squish the bag!

Carmen Rufa—Gr. K
Samaritan Children's Center
Troy, NY

## Spring Flowers

Sprout spring in your classroom with these 3-D flowers! To make one, fold a sheet of construction paper in half lengthwise. Make cuts along the fold as indicated, leaving about 3/4" intact. Wrap the ends of the folded paper around to form a tube; then staple the intact parts together. Fold the cut strips back to resemble flower petals. Mount these "spring-y" flowers on bulletin boards or invite children to use them in their independent art projects. Spring has sprung!

Elaine Hercenberg—Gr. K
Bet Yeladim School
Columbia, MD

## Precious Moments

How many times have you had a child say something absolutely adorable or hysterically funny—and then you forget it? Try using these notes to keep a record for yourself and also to share the joy with parents. In advance, program a form letter titled "Precious Moments." Write a brief parent note of explanation at the top of the page; then make a supply of the page. When precious moments occur, use whatever you have handy to jot them down—or even just key words to trigger your memory. Later, write about the incident on your programmed form. Photocopy a page for your files and send the original to the proud parents! If desired, use these quotable quips in your weekly newsletters.

Holly S. McCully—Gr. K
West Elementary School
East Rochester, OH

## Recycle and Roll!

Did the cold and flu season leave you with a few empty tissue boxes? Use the empty, cube-shaped ones to make large, sturdy dice. First cover the tissue box opening by gluing a piece of tagboard to that panel. Then cover the whole box with Con-Tact® covering. Program each panel with a different numeral from one to six or dot sets. Use these large dice for group activities. For a variation, make a die in the same manner but program each panel with a different *letter.* Use this die for letter recognition and phonics activities.

Marie Scaglione—Gr. K
Community School Age Day Care
    Services, Inc.
West Chester, PA

## Pizza-O!

Studying pizza? Or just having a classroom party? Here's an opportunity to add a topping of music, a dash of spelling, and a sprinkle of letter recognition! In advance, print each letter in *pizza* on a separate sheet of tagboard; then laminate all the letters. After you teach the song below, give each letter to a different child. Invite the children to line up together to spell *pizza.* As you sing another spicy round of the song, have each child raise his card at the appropriate time. Redistribute the letters and repeat the song until each child has had a chance to hold a letter. That's pizza pizzazz!

**Pizza**
*(sung to the tune of "B-I-N-G-O")*

This tasty pie is round with cheese,
And pizza is its name-o!
P-I-Z-Z-A, P-I-Z-Z-A, P-I-Z-Z-A,
And pizza is its name-o!

Jennifer Corduck, Lincoln Elementary, Melrose, MA

## No-Droop Flowers

Finally! A sturdy-stemmed flower that can stand up to young students! In advance, ask a paint store to donate a wooden paint stirrer for each child in your class. To make one flower, paint a stirrer green and let it dry. Decorate a paper plate to resemble a flower. To make petals, cut out V shapes around the edge of the plate. Glue the paint stick (stem) to the back of the flower. Then add the finishing touches by gluing construction paper leaves to the stem. These no-flop flowers can be used in seasonal plays, as song props, and as classroom decorations.

Nora Flanagan—Gr. K
Pfeiffer Elementary
Akron, OH

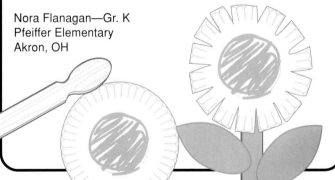

## Fantastic Foam Letters

Titles are sure to pop out with these durable bulletin board letters! Using a die-cutter, cut out letters from craft foam. Decorate each letter with a variety of craft supplies, such as confetti, buttons, and puffy paint. When the letters are dry, pin them to a board or use them as tactile manipulatives.

Pam Szeliga
Riverview Elementary
Baltimore, MD

## Pay and Go

Use the transition time just before lunch to practice a few math skills. Begin by telling children that they're going to pretend to pay to go to lunch. Have a supply of pennies and nickels in a bowl. In turn, have each child roll one or two dice. Then have him count out that many cents from the bowl and hand it to you. If he is correct, have him wash his hands and line up for lunch. By the time the last person has paid, everyone's ready to go!

Maria Meier
Kiddie Academy
East Hanover, NJ

## Vacation Time!

It's vacation time, so you'd better get packing! Begin this activity by sharing *The Bag I'm Taking to Grandma's* by Shirley Neitzel (Mulberry Books). Then extend the story by encouraging students to pretend that they're going on a vacation and they need to pack their bags. Have each child draw a bag on a sheet of paper (or a journal page) and then illustrate the things she would pack in her bag. Invite each child to share her page with the group. If desired, imitate the story's cumulative text by chorally repeating the items after each child shares. Are you all packed?

Linda Solomon—Gr. K
Corlett School
Cleveland, OH

## On the Ball!

Heads up! It's summertime—and that means it's time for parents and children to work together to keep those skills in tip-top shape! So send these cute review booklets home with students for the summer. To make the covers, cut out two identical ball shapes from construction paper. They can be footballs, basketballs, softballs—whatever your kids like! Then cut several sheets of paper sized to fit between the two ball cutouts. On the first page, write a parent letter explaining how to use the booklet. On the remaining pages, write all the skills you'd like your students to practice over the summer and any parent resources that you'd like to recommend. Staple all the pages between the two ball cutouts; then title the book as shown.

Diana Leith—Gr. K
Whitwell Elementary, Ironton, OH

On the Ball!

Jason

Color Words
red        yellow
orange   purple
green     brown
blue      black

## My Song

Teach each child his own version of this song to reinforce personal information skills.

*(adapted to the tune of "The Itsy-Bitsy Spider")*

My name is [Johnny Brown],
And this is my address:
[123 East Apple Lane].
This is my phone number:
[336-555-7371].

adapted from an idea by
Josie Robles—Gr. K
Westminster School
Port Hueneme, CA

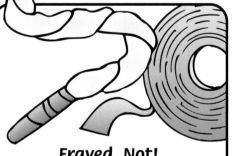

## Frayed, Not!

Frayed yarn ends don't have to be a cause of frustration anymore! When you use yarn for lacing activities, simply wrap the tips in floral tape. This makes a sturdy yet safe point.

Betsy Gignac—Gr. K
St. John the Evangelist
Watertown, CT

## We All Scream for Ice Cream!

Reinforce rhyming skills with this activity that's *almost* too good to be true! In advance, ask volunteers to bring in rhyming flavors of Ben & Jerry's® ice cream, such as Chubby Hubby®, Chunky Monkey®, Wavy Gravy, and Bovinity Divinity™. Encourage children to predict what they think each flavor will taste like and record their predictions. Then, of course, taste them and see! Afterward, have each child illustrate and name her own original rhyming flavor of ice cream—anything goes! Compile all the pages into a class book; then ask each child to share her page. Hmm, will it be Very Berry, Mud Pie Fry, or Chewy Bluey? It's the best-tasting rhyming lesson around!

adapted from an idea by
Catherine Cross—Gr. K
Ranson Elementary
Ranson, WV

**Index**